NOT IN MY GAYBORHOOD!

NOT IN MY GAYBORHOOD!

GAY NEIGHBORHOODS AND THE RISE OF THE VICARIOUS CITIZEN

THEODORE GREENE

Columbia University Press   *New York*

Columbia University Press
Publishers Since 1893
New York   Chichester, West Sussex
cup.columbia.edu

Library of Congress Cataloging-in-Publication Data
Names: Greene, Theodore, author.
Title: Not in my gayborhood! : gay neighborhoods and the rise of the
vicarious citizen / by Theodore Greene.
Description: New York : Columbia University Press, [2024] |
Includes bibliographical references and index.
Identifiers: LCCN 2023053948 | ISBN 9780231189880 (hardback)TW |
ISBN 9780231189897 (trade paperback) | ISBN 9780231548601 (ebook)
Subjects: LCSH: Gay community—Washington (D.C.) |
Gay culture—Washington (D.C.) | Neighborhoods—Washington (D.C.)
Classification: LCC HQ76.3.U52 W184 2024 |
DDC 306.76/609753—dc23/eng/20240223
LC record available at https://lccn.loc.gov/2023053948

Cover design: Elliott S. Cairns

Cover image: The north portico of the White House illuminated in
rainbow lights following the 2015 *Obergefell* decision
legalizing same-sex marriage in the United States.
Photo by David Sunshine / Flickr / CC BY 2.0

CONTENTS

ACKNOWLEDGMENTS

L isting all the remarkable, generous people who have supported this research over the last twelve years would require a section the length of this book. Therefore, I want to apologize in advance if the need for brevity results in the omission of your name. No person can accomplish this alone. However, I wish to recognize several people whose support has proven invaluable to the completion of this project. I am extraordinarily grateful to the many people who shared their stories, offered valuable advice for conducting this research, and supported me when I felt that this project would never see the light of day.

First, I want to thank Amin Ghaziani for supporting this project from the very beginning. We shared our initial projects to study gay neighborhoods nearly fourteen years ago, and throughout our various phases of research and writing, Amin became my first sounding board and champion. I have benefited from his groundbreaking scholarship and his generosity. In addition to offering me opportunities to publish and share my work, Amin introduced me to the amazing Eric Schwartz, editorial director of Columbia University Press. Eric believed in my vision for this book, offering thoughtful feedback for developing its trajectory. Eric possesses not only a keen editorial eye but also the patience of a saint. I cannot thank him enough for guiding me through this process and being in my corner. I am also indebted to Lowell Frye, associate editor at Columbia University Press, for his support.

My work on gay neighborhoods was profoundly shaped by Northwestern University's Department of Sociology and the Gender and Sexuality Studies Program. Mary Pattillo sparked my interest in pursuing sexuality and place scholarship through my work in her Race and Place seminar. I am profoundly grateful for her tough feedback, sage wisdom, and enthusiasm for pursuing this project as an ethnography. Carol Heimer, E. Patrick Johnson, and Gary Alan Fine—my first teachers of ethnography—helped me refine my ethnographic eye. After I received one of the first Dissertation Fellowships from the Sexualities Project at Northwestern, Steven Epstein and Héctor Carrillo encouraged this scholarship. They exposed me to a network of groundbreaking scholars who expanded my imagination about what sexuality scholarship can be. I am also grateful to the Northwestern faculty who continue to captivate me with their brilliance, passion, and vivid sociological imagination, especially Laura Beth Nielsen, Wendy Espeland, Wendy Griswold, Ann Orloff, and Nicola Beisel. I thank the incredible librarians at the Northwestern University Library, especially Susan Lewis of Special Collections, who helped me navigate every version of the *Washington Blade* in print.

At a time when few scholars shared my enthusiasm for studying gay neighborhoods, Lane Fenrich, Celeste Watkins-Hayes, and Héctor Carrillo created the blueprint for what it means to be a good mentor as well as a great scholar. And then there's my mentor and champion, Albert Hunter. I cannot thank him enough for his humor, honesty, and generosity. His love of the city is contagious; his knowledge is encyclopedic. Everything I know and love about urban sociology, I owe to him. I always left Al's office feeling empowered to persevere, even when many questioned the relevance of my work. I appreciate Al's gift to me from the great sociologist Charlie Moskos: "Always remember to give each article a 'memorable concept' for the reader to hang onto." Ironically, Al's memorable concept gave birth to vicarious citizenship. Reading his 1978 chapter "Persistence of Local Sentiments in Mass Society," I stumbled upon *vicarious community*, a concept he developed to convey how residents developed symbolic attachments to community. As I ultimately expanded this idea into nonresidential forms of symbolic community ownership, I witnessed Al's generosity once more, as he offered his blessing to elaborate on his concept and helped me shape my framework. I cannot say enough about Albert Hunter. Nothing makes me prouder than to be part of his legacy.

I am indebted to my Northwestern University peers, whose work continually inspires me. While I was there, I benefited from the unique intellectual culture that many of us refer to as the "NU swagger." To this day, these intellectual powerhouses challenge and uplift me, offering sage advice for navigating this project and my academic career: Jean Beaman, Japonica Brown-Saracino, Corey Fields, Clare Forstie, Marcus Hunter, Nina Johnson, Jeff Kosbie, Armando Lara-Millan, Kevin Loughran, Erin Metz McDonnell, Terence McDonnell, Elizabeth Onasch, Cassidy Puckett, Zandria F. Robinson, Jennifer Rosen, Brian Sargent, Nicole Gonzalez Van Cleave, Lisa-Jo van den Scott, Robert Vargas, Jill Weinberg, and Queen Mecca Zabriskie. Thank you for reading drafts, offering helpful critiques, and providing encouraging words when I needed them.

I have been extraordinarily blessed by being offered a position at Bowdoin College, where I have developed strong relationships with colleagues who have also become great friends. I appreciate the support of Nancy Riley, Ingrid Nelson, Krista van Vleet, Oyman Basaran, and Shruti Devgan. To Lori Brackett and Beth Hoppe, thank you for always being a lifeline, even when I think I do not need one. To my favorite "neighbor" and urban studies enthusiast Brian Purnell, thank you for constantly checking in, having thoughtful and engaging conversations about the city, and setting an example for what a great scholar-teacher should be. I am also profoundly grateful to Matthew Goldmark, Brian Purnell, Judith Casselberry and Dana Byrd, who read various drafts of my book proposal and offered invaluable feedback that improved my work. Kate Stern and Lindsey Lessard gave me the wonderful opportunity to share my work with networks of Bowdoin alumni through speaking tours across the country; thank you for the adventure. And to those in the Bowdoin family who came out and heard me wrestle through ideas, thank you for your kindness and thoughtful feedback. I could not have navigated my life in Portland or at Bowdoin without the support of senior colleagues who became part of my "carpool"—Robert Morrison, Arielle Saiber, Birgit Tautz, and Dharni Vasudevan. Thank you for sharing your experiences and offering your advice about the life of a teacher-scholar. I am also indebted to Bowdoin's Faculty Development Committee, whose generous financial support made this research possible.

While in Washington, DC, I encountered several generous people who directed me to various resources and people who would prove instrumental to my research. A very special thank-you to Vincent Slatt and the Rainbow History Project for offering helpful advice, allowing me access to their extensive Oral History Project, and constantly providing a sounding board when I needed one. My thanks also to Mariam Gillis, Robert Crane, and Alexander Alonso for their long-standing love and support for my research, especially when I encountered roadblocks to that research. During my sabbatical in Washington, DC, the fantastic scholars at American University's Metropolitan Policy Center provided a temporary intellectual home. They helped me think about my research in the context of the many changes in the city. A special thank-you to Derek Hyra for providing a constant source of friendship. To Amanda Elias, the best officemate I ever had, thank you for being a sympathetic ear and a constant source of inspiration—and for introducing me to Marie Kondo. To Jordan Lantz, who revitalized my interest in this research when my life took multiple unexpected turns, your friendship and kindness became one of the best surprises from my research. Thank you for being a bright light in a dark time.

To the beautiful scholars who have read drafts of my work, provided thoughtful feedback, and engaged me in amazing conversations, I thank you. I am profoundly grateful to Jyoti Puri, Vrushali Patil, S. Crawley, Michael Yarborough, Angela Jones, Greggor Mattson, Amy Stone, Ryan Centner, Catherine Connell, Chong-Suk Han, Salvador Vidal-Ortiz, and Leonard Nevarez for their unconditional and inexhaustible support. To Ghassan Moussawi, thank you for always picking up the phone when I needed encouragement. I am blessed to have you for inspiration.

Moving beyond my academic world, I have been blessed by people who gave my life purpose and helped me achieve balance when I became too deeply involved in my research. I am profoundly grateful to my extended family in Chicago, Washington, DC, and Portland: Patricia, Richard, and Bryan Lundgren; Nancy Connor; Charles Moran; Paul Gomez; Yuval Marton; Dina Skrabalak; Tom and Cheryl Hugill; Timothy Diehl; Josh Robinson; Matthew and Evalena Raymer; Kathie and Ira Schey; Rita Djuricich; Paul Djuricich; and Damon Newman. Thank you for welcoming me into your homes and lives; because of you, I have always found a home wherever I go. Thank you Michael Bowser, Emma Vonderhelde, and the incredible staff at Uncharted Tea in downtown Portland for their endless supply of coffee and sympathy. I am also grateful to the wonderful staff as Sagamore Hill Lounge, especially owners Ryan Deskins and Michael Savona, whose support (and boulevardiers) helped me work through my stretches of writer's block. To my ride-or-die, Gregory Hugill, thank you always for being there. You have been a constant source of inspiration and unconditional love, even when I do not always deserve it. Great things lie ahead for us, and I look forward to a lifetime of friendship and adventure.

To my family, thank you for believing in me from the beginning. To my mother, Debra Greene, and my aunt Gloria Wilson, thank you for always allowing me to trust my instincts, even when you might not have understood the method to my madness. Your love, empathy, and compassion have propelled me forward, and none of this would be possible without your support. To my brother and sister, Clayton and Danielle Greene, thank you for believing in me and supporting me. My love for you goes beyond words. To the three greatest gifts of my life—Londyn, Samuel, and Cristian—always know that Uncle Bo-Teddy will be there for you, no matter what. To my godsons—Jacob, William, and Jonathan Raymer—thank you for always finding new ways of making me laugh and think. May this book remind you that nothing is out of your reach if you work hard and dedicate yourself to the people and things you love.

Finally, I want to make a special dedication to my beloved grandmother. Rosie Crump grew up in Mississippi with only a fifth-grade education. Still she devoted her life to ensuring that her children (and later her grandchildren) would have the education denied her as a young Black girl growing up in Mississippi during the Depression. She sacrificed to ensure I had the best education she could provide. And nothing filled me with greater pride than showing her my diploma when I received my PhD. Although my grandmother did not live long enough to see this project to completion, I believe that her guiding hand is always here. Therefore, to my Nana, thank you for filling my life with hope and possibility, teaching me that anything is possible with hard work, and instilling the values of charity, integrity, and grit. I raise your voice so that your name may live in immortality. I will always love you.

NOT IN MY GAYBORHOOD!

INTRODUCTION

Making Dupont Gay Again

"**D**C No Longer Has a Central Gay Neighborhood. Does It Matter?"[1] So begins Andrew Giambrone's elegy to Dupont Circle in the 2016 "Gay Issue" of the *Washington City Paper*. In his article, which features interviews from several local "gay pioneers," Giambrone questions the relevance and future of the iconic gayborhood,[2] as the residential and institutional "fabric of LGBT life" has scattered throughout the city. Once affectionately nicknamed the "Fruit Loop," Dupont Circle became so synonymous with gay life in the city that any man living there faced suspicions about his sexuality. "At least one woman I was friends with said that any man who lived in Dupont Circle was to be considered gay until proven straight," explains Jeff Donahue, a resident and community archivist.[3]

These days, Giambrone argues, many of those who paved the way for Gay Dupont now reflect on its waning days with a mixture of "pride and saudade," as a new generation of LGBTQ citizens has expressed indifference over preserving the neighborhood's queer reputation.[4] Fewer people acknowledge Dupont Circle as "gay central" during Donahue's historical tours through the gayborhood. Gentrification has pushed younger queers east of Dupont Circle, creating new settlements in adjacent Logan Circle, Shaw/U Street, and the now fashionable NoMa (North of Massachusetts Avenue) district. Bars and cultural mainstays like the iconic bookstore Lambda Rising have closed. In their place, gay-friendly establishments mirror the residential diffusion of LGBTQ residents in the city. Geocoded mobile apps like Grindr and Scruff have rendered cruising in gay bars obsolete. And advances in LGBTQ rights have eliminated the imperative for young people to seek protection and community in Dupont Circle as their forbears once did. As local historian Bonnie Morris observes, "Young people gained more rights, more people were accepted in their own families, [and] they didn't have to go to a 'gayborhood' to get that feeling. I miss the sense of a subculture." As "DC [becomes] our Dupont," to quote an online respondent to the article, Giambrone's prognosis for Dupont's gay future looks grim. "Gay Dupont may not be dead," he writes, "but it's slowed down considerably—as have those who vivified it."[5]

Within days of the article's publication, a man carrying two semiautomatic weapons entered a gay nightclub nearly eight hundred miles away. As patrons reveled in the waning minutes of the club's popular Latin Night, the man opened fire, killing forty-nine and injuring fifty-three in what journalists then described as the deadliest mass public shooting in American history.[6]

Within hours of the tragic shooting at the Pulse nightclub in Orlando, Florida, Dupont Circle reemerged as the center of local LGBTQ life. Over the next several days, thousands gathered in Dupont Circle to stand in solidarity with Orlando's LGBTQ community. Groups organized sunset vigils where citizens implored the crowds to protect the community's safe spaces. Mourners transformed the Dupont Circle Fountain into a makeshift memorial, covering the fountain's base with rainbow flags, Pride beads, votive candles, and forty-nine sheets of paper, each displaying the name of a victim. Cardboard posters displaying messages like "Love Is Love" and "Prayers for Orlando" covered the fountain. Youths chalked the surrounding sidewalk with English, Arabic, and Spanish messages, including "Muslims Love Queers" and *"Presente!"* During the day, people lingered in the Circle, admiring the monument while sharing their feelings with others passing through. News cameras encircled the monument as journalists invited people to share their thoughts about the tragedy and its meaning within the local community. Many signed a giant rainbow flag and a banner bearing the words "Washington, DC Is on Your Side. Our Hearts, Thoughts, and Prayers Are with Orlando." Throughout the week, the memorial at the fountain grew, and by Wednesday evening's vigil, commemorative artifacts covered every inch of the fountain and the surrounding walkways (figure 0.1). The final additions to the memorial included hundreds of lighted candles, some arranged in hearts and some spelling out the messages "LGBT" and "Love Is Love."

The following evening, a thunderstorm had washed away most of the memorial. By Friday, people had returned to their daily and nightly routines as if the previous few days had never happened.

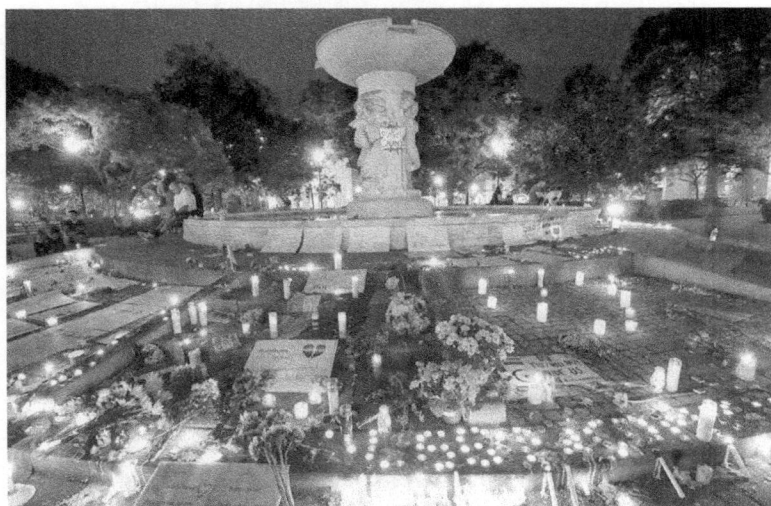

FIGURE 0.1 The Pulse memorial at the Dupont Circle Fountain.

Photo by author.

In the morning, residents sipped their coffee while rushing through the Circle to work. Homeless men sleeping on the park benches around the fountain collected their belongings, storing them away for the day. By afternoon, Black men had filled the park tables in the outer perimeter, playing chess and congregating around a giant boom box blasting Philadelphia soul. Professionals sought refuge from the afternoon heat by eating lunch around the basin while children frolicked in the water. Gray-haired men read newspapers on the benches, tourists reviewed maps and guidebooks, and Black and Brown women chatted on the benches while gently rocking white babies to sleep. As the sun descended, runners jogged through the Circle while dogs pulled their humans from one end to the other. Young white women gossiped while sipping iced lattes, their neatly rolled-up yoga mats nearby. Muscular men in short shorts played on their cell phones while their little dogs explored the area around their feet. The spirit energizing Dupont Circle that week had all but faded. Only splatters of caked-on candlewax along the fountain stairs and basin remained (figure 0.2).

A year later another retrospective, this time in *Washingtonian* magazine, evokes a sense of déjà vu. In "DC's Gayborhoods Are Disappearing. How Should We Feel About That?" Dan Reed also investigates the declining salience of Dupont Circle, echoing many of the themes raised by Giambrone a year earlier. Rising rents have displaced LGBTQ residents from central gay neighborhoods, scattering them throughout the city. LGBTQ bars and other institutional anchors have disappeared with the rise of a digital queer culture embraced by new generations of queer folk who benefit from an increasingly tolerant political and sociocultural climate. Reed even interviews many of the same "gay pioneers," who convey mixed feelings about Gay Dupont's changing complexion. "There's less of a gay community in any particular neighborhood," says Deacon Maccubbin, owner of the iconic bookstore Lambda Rising. "We are everywhere. People feel free to live and party just about anywhere now. Which is great. We've come so far."[7]

FIGURE 0.2 The Pulse memorial at the Dupont Circle Fountain after a thunderstorm.

Photo by author.

Once again, another author predicts a grim future for Gay Dupont, as experts describe the gayborhood as a shadow of its former queer glory.

———

The cognitive dissonance between the two articles and the collective response to the Pulse tragedy reflects the tensions that animate *Not in My Gayborhood!* Giambrone and Reed echo many scholars, journalists, LGBTQ activists, and everyday citizens who have displayed "a curious investment in the purported demise of the gayborhood."[8] None of them are technically wrong; the vibrant cultures that once distinguished these districts as safe havens for LGBTQ people have diminished considerably. Articles and books abound with evidence pointing to the institutional and demographic decline *within* gay-borhoods and the notable diffusion of LGBTQ culture throughout cities. Rainbow flags fly alongside American flags on quiet residential streets and in front of downtown businesses. City halls and other municipal buildings (including the White House) commemorate Pride Month by lighting their facades in rainbow colors. Drag queens fill reading rooms in children's libraries as easily as they do gay nightclubs. And same-sex couples confidently push double-wide strollers down populated sidewalks. These changes also align with shifting attitudes among LGBTQ people about the state of gay neighborhoods. A 2013 Pew Research survey revealed that 73 percent of LGBTQ respondents had never lived in a gay neighborhood. Those who believed that LGBTQ people should achieve equality by maintaining distinctly gay districts equaled those who believed in achieving full equality through complete integration (49 percent).[9] By all observable accounts, the gay urban imagination has expanded to the point that the city itself—especially a progressive city like Washington, DC—has become one giant gay village. "Dupont Circle doesn't seem as central to the gay community anymore because you can be out in virtually every part of the city," Vincent (forty-two, white, gay) explained, evoking a phrase I commonly heard throughout the interviews I conducted while researching this book: "DC is now our Dupont."

Yet when tragedy struck, LGBTQ Washingtonians did not hesitate to return to Dupont Circle to publicly mourn and stand in solidarity with Orlando's LGBTQ community. Within hours of the Pulse shooting, LGBTQ mourners reclaimed control over the fountain, reviving the practices, representations, and traditions that evoked their vision of the local gayborhood. And once the space was no longer needed, these mourners relinquished it, allowing Gay Dupont to recede and the neighborhood to return to its present "postgay" alter ego.[10]

And Washington was not alone. Around the world, mourners temporarily reclaimed and revitalized the very gayborhoods that scholars have relegated to obsolescence. "I didn't realize until that June morning," writes the journalist John Paul Brammer, "when we blinked our eyes awake and were met with the aftermath of Pulse on our TV screens and news feeds, that queers have a built-in homing device. But we do, and mine kicked in."[11] In San Francisco, thousands "wav[ed] banners, brightly lit iPhones, and candles in plastic cups" at Harvey Milk Plaza in the Castro, where locals chalked the victims' names on the sidewalk under the giant rainbow flag.[12] People returned to the plaza days later to stage a kiss-in to protest the homophobia that allegedly sparked the Pulse shooter's rampage.[13] Londoners flooded Old Compton Street in Soho the Monday after the shooting, bowing their heads in momentary silence before erupting in cheers as forty-nine balloons soared overhead.[14] Chicago residents held vigils in Boystown and Andersonville, while Seattle's LGBTQ communities mourned in Cal Anderson Park in Capitol Hill. Gay rights supporters in Rome, Italy, held a vigil on Gay Street hours after their Gay Pride Parade. And in New York, thousands lighted candles and laid flowers outside Greenwich Village's Stonewall Inn, the iconic birthplace of the modern gay rights movement. Across the street, people chalked the victims' names along the brick walkways of Christopher Park.[15] The collective impulse to return to these gayborhoods after the Pulse tragedy reveals their enduring value as anchors of LGBTQ life in the queer public imagination.

Looking beyond the well-documented trends associated with the "decline" of gay neighborhoods, this book explores the various people and practices that preserve iconic gay neighborhoods as areas of the city that privilege public expressions of sexual and gender identity. Regardless of where LGBTQ people live and how the demographic and institutional complexion of the gayborhood is changing, LGBTQ citizens have not necessarily relinquished their sense of ownership over iconic gay neighborhoods. Adapting to these changes, community stakeholders preserve their visions of place and community through a practice I call *place reactivation*, the temporary revival of inactive place cultures within a space, neighborhood, or locality. Like turning a light switch on and off, actors can reactivate places as necessary to mobilize their vision of community and then relinquish them. Place reactivation exposes the fleeting, shifting nature of places despite the locational fixity of space. Places shift from one moment to the next depending on the community that occupies that space at any given moment. At times, multiple conflicting places can exist in the same space simultaneously. Highlighting the diverse communities that converge in a neighborhood, this book also contributes to the urban scholarship that challenges places as fixed, stable, and enduring.[16]

Place reactivation exposes urban neighborhoods as "flexible in the hands of different people or cultures, malleable over time, and inevitably contested."[17] Despite recognizing place as socially constructed, urban scholars often define urban neighborhoods through a single set of practices, narratives, and reputations, privileging the tastes and perspectives of existing residents.[18] However, as neighborhoods transition from one community to another, the place cultures of former communities do not necessarily disappear. Cultural residues often remain in commercial and cultural institutions (e.g., churches, restaurants, and gay bars), historical monuments, and cultural events in public spaces (e.g., parades and festivals), collectively symbolizing the former communities' presence in the area. Whenever needed, former and symbolic communities may draw on these cultural residues to reproduce the traditions, routines, and practices that sustain their ties to the local area.

Consequently, *Not in* My *Gayborhood!* examines how local community ownership is not limited to property owners and existing residents. Without claims of residency, the sine qua non of local community membership, various nonresidential stakeholders use their participation in a neighborhood's sociocultural, economic, and political life to translate their symbolic attachments into expressions of community investment and ownership. I refer to this relationship as *vicarious citizenship*. Vicarious citizens, who represent diverse self-identified community members, including former or displaced residents, draw on various socio-territorial practices to mobilize against perceived threats to their community vision. Whether challenging the increased presence of heterosexual families in a local institution or the declining sexual culture in a gayborhood, vicarious citizens can exert a powerful influence over a local area by appropriating its space and reproducing its meaning. Thus, as gay neighborhoods demographically and institutionally "straighten," vicarious citizens may nevertheless mobilize their spatial practices as a form of self-enfranchisement, protecting their vision of community from threats of heteronormative and homonormative assimilation.[19]

Beyond presenting place reactivation and vicarious citizenship as vital strategies for preserving and protecting iconic gay neighborhoods, *Not in My Gayborhood!* situates gay neighborhoods within a legacy of LGBTQ placemaking within cities. Gay neighborhoods reflect a unique moment in American history. In the aftermath of the 1969 Stonewall riots, gay districts like the Castro increasingly enabled many gay and lesbian communities to consolidate political and economic power within cities and thereby access the promises of the American Dream.[20] However, placemaking also matters for many who are excluded from housing markets within these areas. Many gay neighborhoods depended on vicarious citizens, whose participation in public spaces and local institutions vitally shaped the reputation of these neighborhoods as destinations that celebrated queer political and sexual cultures. Many who found themselves excluded from the economic and cultural life of gay neighborhoods continued to develop complex geographies by refashioning public spaces within and outside their local communities that created and fostered their unique subcultures. And while these geographies may not resemble the residential and institutional formations that we commonly associate with areas like Dupont Circle, they may constitute gay neighborhoods to those who rely on them as safe spaces in which to create and foster communities. Ultimately, despite scholarly concerns over their future, gay neighborhoods will endure in some fashion because, as LGBTQ citizens, we continue mapping queerness onto them. Reviving symbolically significant community spaces and mobilizing queer communities as needed, LGBTQ citizens still value gay neighborhoods as safe spaces where they can publicly enact aspects of their gendered and sexual lives.

REACTIVATING AND RECLAIMING LGBTQ GEOGRAPHIES

LGBTQ communities have always relied on repurposing existing public places within cities. In the late nineteenth and early twentieth centuries, gay people transformed public parks, monuments, and theaters into nighttime cruising areas. YMCAs became bathhouses, and family restaurants transitioned into gay bars.[21] Gay men also refashioned bridges, storefront windows, and doorway entrances into meeting places.[22] In Black enclaves like Harlem and Bronzeville, nightclubs and speakeasies easily hosted elaborate drag balls for Black gay communities.[23] The gay worlds that emerged from these spaces not only presented a stark contrast to their conventional uses but also fostered a "highly sophisticated system of subcultural codes—codes of dress, speech, and style—that enabled [gay men] to recognize one another and carry on intimate conversations whose coded meanings were unintelligible to potentially hostile people around them."[24]

Many gay worlds existed concurrently with a space's more mainstream use. The historians Elizabeth Lapovsky Kennedy and Madeline D. Davis explore how lesbians in Buffalo, New York, developed strategies to meet each other inside straight bars. While these spaces were not exclusively for their use, lesbians referred to them as lesbian bars to reflect their sense of safety in meeting other queer women there.[25] In his controversial study of anonymous sex in public restrooms, sociologist Laud Humphreys reveals an extensive social world governed by unspoken rules and roles that ordered the practices taking place there. Accessing the sexual world of the "tearoom" depended on knowing how to position yourself within the space and interact with the other participants and what to do when an outsider (or a police officer) enters.[26] While "scattered gay spaces," these gay worlds also reflected complex geographies where gay men and women navigated antigay hostility within the dominant culture and mitigated the isolation often associated with the pre-Stonewall era.[27]

Anonymous, brief contact also proved vital in the persistence of certain gay worlds, such as those created in parks, public bathrooms, literary societies, and YMCAs. The anonymous nature of these spaces enables one to imagine community built around their investment in place. Carter Newman Bealer, whose diaries were published under the pseudonym Jeb Alexander, shows how cruising in Washington, DC, parks "was nearly a nightly ritual each spring and summer during the early 1920s."[28] Although often unsuccessful in picking up men, Bealer continued going, fearing "that [he was] missing something if he did not go every night."[29] While cruising areas could facilitate the creation of social networks, gay men also "could recognize that they were not the 'only one' and begin to develop a network of like-minded friends, and perhaps a sense of belonging to the larger community."[30]

Episodic in nature, these gay worlds were both fleeting and lasting. Existing in the shadow of the dominant culture, many gay worlds cultivated communities at that moment, rising and falling as the production of place shifted from "straight" to "gay." Gay men and lesbians fostered restricted relationships that were limited to the places and the times they were together. The anthropologist Esther Newton describes how, between the 1930s and the 1960s, Cherry Grove, New York, became a weekend escape for upper- and upper-middle-class white lesbians who could not live openly in New York City. Many of the platonic, sexual, and romantic relationships that developed among these women were primarily limited to the weekends and summers they could spend in that "magical place."[31] At the same time, the daily and nightly reproduction of queer places facilitated continuity that supported and maintained vibrant gay subcultures over time. Certain commercial establishments earned reputations well beyond the immediate communities they supported. For example, in Washington, DC, during the 1930s and 1940s, "daytime patrons" knew to finish their meals before downtown restaurants transitioned nightly into gay gathering spots. Hotel guests also knew the nights on which to avoid the hotel bars unless they wanted to face being labeled homosexual by association.[32] Therefore, as scholars correctly assume, gay men and lesbians did not always "set the tone" in developing the geographies that iconic gay neighborhoods would become.[33] Nevertheless, they developed the cultural repertoires and traditions that rendered these spaces essential community anchors.

Despite the anonymous and fleeting nature of gay and lesbian geographies in cities, their reputations allowed visitors and newcomers to easily access these gay worlds. In his study of gay life in Chicago during the early twentieth century, the historian David Johnson describes how Harold, a high school student with an "active social life with a bohemian crowd that favored 'smoking, nightclubs, and beer flats,'" easily stumbled upon a gay world during his first encounter.[34] Harold discovered the fairies he was intent on meeting not in some dark alley or obscure tavern but the doorway of the Wrigley building—one of the most central, well-lit, public locations in all of Chicago. In large cities, hidden gathering places had a reputation well beyond the city limits. Johnson recounts how "Jimmy" corresponded with men from Michigan, Indiana, and Maryland who were familiar with Chicago's cruising areas. Describing the reputation of Lafayette Square, just north of the White House, the historian Genny Beemyn writes that "the extent to which Lafayette Square was renowned as a cruising location is shown by the fact that [a white visitor from Philadelphia] had heard about the park while he was in the Virgin Islands."[35] Gay novels also fueled readers' imagination about the city's covert gay gathering spaces. Harold read a series of gay novels that sparked his imagination and fueled his motivation to "meet some of these so-called fairies."[36] Lafayette Square particularly benefited from references in print media. "Gay novels published in the 1930s made reference to the park as a meeting place for homosexuals."[37]

As many U.S. municipalities passed laws banning homosexual acts following the repeal of Prohibition, the few "gay bars" that existed for gays and lesbians depended on the reactivation of these spaces by their patrons. Because these gay bars became prime targets for police raids and harassment, those who owned them circumvented the laws through alternative branding. The Stonewall Inn, famously owned by the Mafia, rebranded itself as a private bottle club, where patrons had to sign their "names" in a book to gain entry (although patrons almost exclusively used pseudonyms).[38] These owners did not have any loyalty to their patrons. However, the availability of spaces for congregating allowed gay men to develop a sense of loyalty through the places they created. "Through the power of music and dance," observes David Carter, "the club fused these elements to create amongst most of its regular customers a sense of gay community and thus a loyalty to the Stonewall Inn."[39] Gay men developed such strong place cultures within these bars that these spaces often developed a supraspatial quality, enabling place continuity across spaces. In her landmark study of gay bars in the 1950s, the sociologist Nancy Achilles observes that, after cities and the police forced the closure of gay establishments, new ones would open in their place where the same customs and traditions would endure: "When a bar closes, its patrons shift their activities elsewhere. In the new bar, the same music comes out of the jukebox, the same bartenders mix drinks, the same faces appear, and the conversation repeats in the same patterns."[40]

Because gays and lesbians did not enjoy the visibility and freedom to live their lives openly in the late nineteenth and early twentieth centuries, scholars easily dismiss these gay worlds as "fragile," lying under the radar of the heteronormative culture. However, these fleeting geographies do not undermine the rich, complex worlds that gays and lesbians developed. Refashioning existing spaces with distinct "values, perceptions, memories, and traditions,"[41] they developed unconventional yet meaningful forms of community attachment and identification. And as police intimidation threatens the peace of these fleeting geographies, LGBTQ people will draw on these attachments to protect the spaces they associate with authentic community.

GAY NEIGHBORHOODS AND VICARIOUS CITIZENSHIP

Once a restaurant that hastily transformed into a gay bar after a fire, the Stonewall Inn stood conspicuously on Christopher Street in Greenwich Village, which was quite unconventional for gay bars during this era. The bar circumvented the New York State Liquor Authority by rebranding itself as a private bottle club. On paper, owners would list the names of patrons and the "bottles" of liquor they purchased to circumvent authorities. In reality, the bar typically served watered-down, overpriced drinks without a license and with alcohol supplied almost exclusively by the Mafia, which owned and operated this bar. It had no fire exits and no running water behind the bar. The unhygienic practices used by its employees to clean glasses were linked to numerous hepatitis outbreaks among its customers.[42] The toilet overran constantly. Yet despite these conditions, the Stonewall Inn attracted a diverse cross-section of gay and lesbian patrons, including the most marginalized contingents of the gay community: male hustlers, drag queens, transsexuals,[43] and homeless street youth, many of whom were nonwhite. Police raids on the Stonewall were common; in fact, they had raided the bar a few nights before the raid that sparked the riots. However, the Mafia paid off the police regularly, so the bar typically reopened the following evening.

The police likely expected a "routine raid" when they headed back to the Stonewall Inn in the early morning hours of June 28, 1969. However, things did not go as planned. As the police moved through the club, customers resisted. Many refused to show identification to the police. Transvestites refused to go into the bathrooms for a police examination. As the cops continued to push patrons outside, a crowd formed on the street, jeering at police officers as they began loading prisoners into the paddy wagon. Those in the crowd outside grew increasingly angry as they began taking stock of the injustices they had routinely endured at the hands of the police. "The gay men who stood outside the Stonewall talked about the destruction of their lovers' lane,[44] and how many of their other clubs had been raided in recent weeks: the Snake Pit, the Checkerboard, and the Sewer. Now not only had the Stonewall Inn been hit twice in one week, but tonight's raid had also come on a Friday night and at the evening's peak."[45]

Two incidents incited the riot. "The first hostile act outside the club occurred when a police officer shoved one of the transvestites, who turned and smacked the officer over the head with her purse. The cop clubbed her, and a wave of anger passed through the crowd, which immediately showered the police with boos and catcalls, followed by a cry to turn the paddy wagon over."[46] The crowd finally erupted after the police threw a lesbian patron who resisted arrest into a police car. "The scene became explosive," Lucian Truscott IV reported in the *Village Voice*. "Limp wrists were forgotten. Beer cans and bottles were heaved at the windows, and a rain of coins descended on the cops. . . . Almost by signal the crowd erupted into cobblestone and bottle heaving. . . . From nowhere came an uprooted parking meter—used as a battering ram on the Stonewall door. I heard several cries of 'Let's get some gas,' but the blaze of flame which soon appeared in the window of the Stonewall was still a shock."[47]

The police retreated into the bar and barricaded themselves "as all kinds of objects continued to crash around the police."[48] Police reinforcements liberated the trapped officers as the violence against the police escalated. Protesters openly mocked the police as they attempted to quell and dissipate the crowd, and the rioting went on into the night. By four A.M. Saturday, the police had finally cleared the streets. Yet "by the time the last cop was off the street Saturday morning, a sign was going up announcing that the Stonewall would reopen that night. It did."[49]

Riots continued around the Stonewall over the next several nights. Throughout the day on Saturday, as people stopped by to inspect the wreckage, slogans appeared in chalk on the walls encouraging support for gay power. That evening many of the rioters returned, along with onlookers and tourists who supported the protests. Speeches and chants intensified: "Liberate Christopher Street!" and "Christopher Street belongs to the queens!"[50] "Hand-holding, kissing, and posing accented each of the cheers with a homosexual liberation that had appeared only fleetingly on the street before."[51] Eventually, the crowd spilled outside onto the street, prompting the decision to block traffic from entering Christopher Street. "When an occasional car did try to bulldoze its way in, the crowd quickly surrounded it, rocking it back and forth so vigorously that the occupants soon proved more than happy to be allowed to retreat."[52] Protesters started fires in trash cans and threw bottles at the approaching police officers who were attempting to quell the demonstration. As protesters overwhelmed the police, the NYPD Tactical Police Force arrived on the scene for the second night to clear the street. The street fights and police chases continued throughout the night and into the early morning as they had the previous night.

A half century later both popular and academic scholars debate the Stonewall riots and their lingering impact. Some consider Stonewall the "spark" that ignited the modern gay rights movement.[53] Others describe it as "a repeated and cherished *movement myth* [that offers] neither an accurate description nor a compelling explanation of the origins of gay liberation."[54] Regardless, the Stonewall riots epitomize vicarious citizenship. The appropriation of Stonewall evinced a spontaneous response among LGBTQ people from across New York City to state-imposed sanctions that denied gays and lesbians the right to visible communities. While the Stonewall Inn did not provide an ideal environment in which gay men could congregate, the bar still "offered its patrons [four] crucial things: space, security, . . . freedom," and a sense of continuity that comes with the bar's longevity in the area. When the police threatened that sense of freedom and safety, Stonewall patrons defended the only sense of community they had— and in doing so, they articulated their legitimate claims of participation as members of a visible gay community. That sense of entitlement extended beyond the bar to Christopher Street and Greenwich Village. John O'Brien recounts to David Carter that "when [the police] tried to clear the streets is when people resented it, 'cause it came down to 'Whose streets are these? They are our streets. And you cops are not from this area; this is our area. It's gay people's streets.'"[55]

As the 1969 Stonewall riots created momentum for gays and lesbians to "come out," gay neighborhoods became essential political and economic strategies for coalescing and fostering community. "When gays are spatially scattered," noted the activist Henry Britt, "they are not gay because they are invisible."[56] Establishing residential and institutional concentration became necessary for early scholars of gay neighborhoods to legitimate these territories as sociologically valid. In the 1970s, through likening gay neighborhoods to Jewish ghettos and ethnic communities, respectively, the sociologists Martin P. Levine and Stephen O. Murray challenged the prevailing assumptions of homosexuality as deviant, "strengthen[ing] the notion that gays and lesbians function like an oppressed minority."[57] Another sociologist, Manuel Castells, connects gay homeownership in the Castro with the emergence of a gay movement in San Francisco, highlighting the gentrification of the Castro as a multi-class affair among gay men, many of whom combined their resources to purchase a home. Conversely, Lawrence Knopp, an urban geographer, attributes the success of the Marigny neighborhood in New Orleans purely to the economic motivations of middle-class white gay men with aspirations of homeownership.[58] Unlike the gay communities in San Francisco, who relied on the Castro for social protection and to centralize political power, the residents of the Marigny held no such aspirations for coalition building.

Long before debating the "de-gaying" of iconic gay neighborhoods, scholars attempted to minimize the differences between gay districts and other cultural enclaves. Despite experiencing gay life and culture throughout much of Washington, DC, the novelist Edmund White distinguishes Dupont Circle as the city's only "gay ghetto" by its "dulcet" conventionality. Without describing a single gay bar in the neighborhood, White evokes a gay version of "Main Street, USA": the clean streets "crowded with strollers and cruisers," the busy bookstores filled with gays and lesbians, the outdoor cafés where "you can sit outside under an umbrella, sip wine and snack on pate and watch the joggers huffing past or women in saris ambling by with their children." "The sidewalks are clean," he writes, "the buildings are low, the shops are fashionable, the overheard bits of conversation are up-to-date (the latest movie, the latest cheese store, the latest play at the Kennedy Center)."[59]

To this day, scholars make much ado about the residential and institutional changes gay neighborhoods are undergoing. Yet this framing overlooks that community belonging in iconic gay neighborhoods never depended on residential propinquity. Housing markets in places like the Castro quickly priced out LGBTQ people, requiring them to find housing in areas where they could easily access iconic gay neighborhoods. By the late 1970s, gentrification in the Castro resulted in gays and lesbians developing cultural archipelagos[60] in "all adjacent areas . . . reach[ing] the Dolores Corridor on the border with the Latino Mission District."[61] In New Orleans, the development of the Marigny resulted when gay men sought affordable housing near the French Quarter, which was "the center of gay social and cultural life in New Orleans."[62]

The attraction of gay nonresidents to gay neighborhoods resulted in shifting placemaking practices throughout the day depending on the specific communities that occupy the area. Despite noting similarities between the gay neighborhood and the Jewish ghetto, Levine observes the peculiar shift of the gayborhood from a quiet residential neighborhood during the day to a crowded, noisy destination on nights and weekends. "Participation in the gay world, for homosexual males, occurs after normal working hours," he writes. "At such times, the areas are flooded with residents as well as with gay men from surrounding neighborhoods who travel in to participate in the local gay scene."[63] To this day, the nightlife that dominates the cultural life of gay neighborhoods contrasts starkly with the daytime routines of the diverse families that live there (e.g., shopping for groceries, eating in local restaurants, and taking children to school or to local parks). Certain practices that once reflected the sexually charged culture of the gayborhood may no longer seem appropriate in the daytime. Businesses and shops must now tone down the sexually graphic window displays to accommodate the gaze of impressionable children.[64] Equally, the "sexy communities" that rely on gayborhoods as sites of sexual exploration and experimentation might seem out of place during the daytime.[65]

As scholars connect the dwindling material culture to the erasure of iconic neighborhoods, various LGBTQ communities rely on strategies of ephemeral placemaking to preserve the area's reputation. Gay bars and nightclubs now accommodate diverse LGBTQ subcultures that temporarily impose their subcultural capital to support their various communities. A gay bar might host a gay country-western dance in the afternoon and have a drag show in the evening. The same bar might host a leather night the following evening, where the crowds and logic governing the place would be entirely different from those found there the night before. The Pulse nightclub reflects this form of placemaking.[66] The tragedy occurred on its monthly Latin Night, which attracted a different population of LGBTQ people than the nightclub might attract on other nights.

As gay neighborhoods residentially "straighten," vicarious citizens develop strategies to exercise what the sociologist Henri Lefebvre calls rights to the city.[67] In the absence of residential or even social ties, vicarious citizens establish legitimate claims to ownership and interest in the affairs of that community through living out their daily routines in the gayborhood. Same-sex couples display affection to one another on the streets without fear of homophobic retribution. Gay and queer-identified men sashay confidently through the streets in high heels and short shorts, their faces "beaten to the gods" with brightly colored eye shadow and bejeweled lips. Trans men and trans women rarely anguish over which bathrooms to use in gayborhood institutions. When problems arise, many feel comfortable mobilizing for change. And restaurants along the "gay strip" bustle with loud groups of brunching companions, recalling their sexual conquests in Dickensian detail. Playing out the routines of their everyday lives in iconic gay neighborhoods, vicarious citizens position themselves as symbolic "old-timers" whose practices enforce cultural norms and protect traditions that align with their imagining of place.

Additionally, as gayborhoods welcome LGBTQ populations unable to participate in the extant culture, these groups write themselves into these areas by imposing traditions and practices associated with their specific subcultures. In Chicago's Northalsted neighborhood (formerly known as Boystown), LGBTQ youths of color draw on street corner practices often associated with the street corner cultures of the South Side and West Side neighborhoods of Chicago where they grew up. These youths travel hours to participate in a community that symbolizes acceptance of nonnormative gender and sexual identities, only to find themselves excluded from the neighborhood's cultural, economic, and institutional life. They often endure racial profiling and discrimination from business owners and the local police and exploitation from residents—many of whom are the same white gay men who publicly lash out against their presence in the community. Undeterred, these youths combine the cultural symbols of the gayborhood with the "codes of the street" to foster communities and make the gayborhood culturally accessible to them. Thus, as residents misrecognize their exercises of vicarious citizenship on street corners as disruptive to the community, these youths nevertheless see themselves as community stakeholders. Challenging their exclusion from mainstream LGBTQ culture, they translate their placemaking practices into a cultural and symbolic investment that preserves the gayborhood as a safe space that fosters the free expression of gender and sexual identities.[68]

Place reactivation and vicarious citizenship do not reverse the well-established trends associated with the decline of iconic gay neighborhoods. However, residency has never mattered in defining gay neighborhoods for many who identify as community members. Place reactivation reveals the resilience of LGBTQ communities in adapting to the demographic, institutional, and cultural changes that threaten their vision of place. Drawing on the remaining symbols associated with their community, they reactivate the cultural representations and spatial practices within various gayborhood spaces to mobilize their communities and maintain their connection to place.[69] Thus, while LGBTQ citizens no longer feel that living in discrete gay neighborhoods is necessary, they nevertheless draw on ephemeral placemaking strategies to preserve them.

LEARNING FROM THE GAYBORHOOD

Not in My Gayborhood! uses gay neighborhoods to advance a deceptively simple premise about urban life: neighborhoods *belong* to the people who inhabit them. Inhabitants of a neighborhood extend well beyond those who establish legal residency there. Instead, I draw on the work of Lefebvre to include a diversity of self-identified members of a community who play out the routines and traditions of their lives in these spaces.[70] This includes former and displaced neighborhood members who return to their "old neighborhood" to attend weekly church services. It includes those who make regular "pilgrimages" to ethnic enclaves to frequent restaurants and participate in cultural festivals to reconnect to their culture. Attending an annual music festival, dancing the night away at the bar in your favorite gayborhood, or blasting soul music out of a boom box on your favorite urban street corner may appear innocuous, albeit disruptive to the existing residents of a neighborhood. Yet as urban revitalization efforts have made housing increasingly unaffordable to working- and middle-class citizens in the last several decades, these fleeting practices reflect part of a broader narrative that fosters and preserves the place-based cultures aligned with a nonresidential community's association with a neighborhood.[71]

Place reactivation reflects a long sociological tradition of ephemeral placemaking in neighborhoods. In 1929, the sociologist Harvey Zorbaugh described the Rialto as a neighborhood of "queer contrasts between the shabbiness of the slum" during the daytime and its "colorful nightlife in which bohemia and the underworld may meet with the curiosity seeker and the slumming parties from the world of fashion."[72] Labeling the neighborhood a "half-world," Zorbaugh draws attention to the instability of place arising from distinctions between the residents and hobos who dominated the neighborhood during the day and the consumers who sought thrills and pleasure at night. Later generations of urban scholars explored how poor urban communities activated places by refashioning the existing ecology of the urban neighborhood. These studies overflow with rich vignettes of children transforming alleys and vacant lots into playgrounds, only for those same spaces to transform into places of "business" that serve a neighborhood's underground economy.[73] Empty warehouses and factories morph from gay clubs one night into straight clubs the next,[74] only to serve as houses of worship on Sunday mornings. Like Zorbaugh in his assessment of the Rialto, scholars assumed a deficit framing to describe these acts of ephemeral placemaking. Ignoring these place cultures' routinized, highly organized nature, scholars viewed these ephemeral forms of placemaking as the results of racial segregation, urban poverty, and the pathologies that arise from these structural inequalities.[75]

Urban scholars have recently explored the varied uses of ephemeral placemaking as strategies for revitalizing contemporary cities. These practices reflect the emergence of moneyed, highly educated urban cosmopolitans whose tastes and spatial practices collectively indicate strong preferences for street-level diversity and experiences of cultural authenticity.[76] "Pop-up" restaurants and events provide spontaneous amenities for these urban consumers. Local governments and place entrepreneurs organize annual music festivals like Coachella to transform otherwise vacant lots into worldwide attractions that boast different subcultural logics than those found among the residents who live in the area year-round.[77] Residential newcomers may transform local spaces into makeshift roundabouts, gardens, and dog parks as exercises of DIY urbanism.[78] Scholars have even given attention to ephemeral practices that disrupt the flow of everyday residents. The sociologist Ryan Centner describes how dot-commers in San Francisco deployed "spatial capital" to appropriate and refashion public parks in poor Black and Latinx communities into temporary places for exclusive networking events.[79] Gregory J. Snyder and Jeffrey Kidder investigate how skateboarders and parkour enthusiasts, respectively, transform the architecture of parks and public buildings into courses on which to perform various tricks and skills.[80]

While scholars have long privileged how residents and place entrepreneurs define the character of a neighborhood, neighborhoods may hold different and sometimes competing meanings for the diverse communities that pass through them. Even as cultural and historic preservation efforts remain strategies for revitalizing urban neighborhoods, different subcultures may conceptualize distinct meanings around a neighborhood's identity. Studying gentrification in the Shaw/U Street corridor in Washington, DC, the sociologist Derek Hyra observes how white gentrifiers transform the historically Black neighborhoods into "cappuccino cities."[81] Newcomers may appropriate elements of Black urban life (i.e., the iconic ghetto)[82] to illustrate their cosmopolitanism. Yet the residential displacement of Black residents from the area has not erased the neighborhood's image as a "chocolate city,"[83] especially among those who return to their former neighborhood and continue the cultural and spatial practices aligned with their vision of community. Thus, while white residents bemoan the worshippers who triple park outside Black churches on Sundays[84] or the Black businesses that blast go-go music through the speakers of their establishments, Black residents may defend these practices as vital to keeping the neighborhood culturally accessible.[85]

Reimagining these ephemeral acts that reactivate place as constitutive acts of urban citizenship, this book offers new ways of thinking about how urban residents live locally and align themselves to neighborhoods in the postindustrial city. As disparities in wealth continue to price middle- and working-class community members out of urban housing and rental markets, this book considers how various strategies for revitalizing cities have abetted the sustained participation of former and displaced residents. The transformation of cities into cultural production and consumption sites for hip, moneyed urban cosmopolitans, anchored by cultural and historic preservation, has yielded cultural residues that remain powerful symbols of identification for vicarious citizens. Being displaced from a neighborhood does not necessarily end a community's participation. As long as the neighborhood's reputation persists in the community's collective memory, vicarious citizens can reclaim these spaces, enacting the cultures and traditions associated with their visions of community.

STUDYING THE NOT-SO-ORDINARY GAY CITY

While lacking the reputation of "gay meccas" like New York, San Francisco, and Los Angeles, Washington, DC, is far from an ordinary city.[86] With an estimated 9.8 percent of its adults identifying as LGBTQ, Washington bears the distinction of being America's "gayest city."[87] Its queer history rivals those of New York and San Francisco, with vibrant and visible communities dating back to the late nineteenth century.[88] Every year DC showcases its diverse LGBTQ communities in myriad events and celebrations. In addition to hosting the country's fourth-largest Pride festival, Washington celebrates Black Pride, Latino Pride, Asian–Pacific Islander Pride, Silver Pride (for LGBTQ people over sixty), Youth Pride, and Trans Pride.[89] Thousands turn out every October to behold drag queens racing along Seventeenth Street in six-inch stilettos. Stonewall Sports fosters community and competition through its six gay sports leagues. And since Marion Barry's first mayoral victory in 1978, no local politician has succeeded without courting the gay vote.[90] Throughout the 2010 mayoral election, both candidates competed for credit for passing DC's Same-Sex Marriage Act in 2009.

Beyond its queer reputation, Washington, DC, offers a fitting case for studying place reactivation and vicarious citizenship. As the nation's capital, Washington evokes the image of a national community where citizens from all over the United States participate in the political process through local placemaking. Nonresidents indirectly influence the city's spatial organization by selecting congressional representatives and senators in federal elections.[91] Disenfranchised groups have protested and marched in Washington's streets and public areas for over a century. Annual celebrations like the Cherry Blossom Festival and the Fourth of July and special events like presidential Inaugurations convene millions whose spatial practices disrupt residents' daily and nightly routines. On January 6, 2021, thousands converged on the Capitol to protest the results and certification of the presidential election. As they stormed the Capitol, many rioters screamed, "Our country! Our house!" indicating the sense of ownership and entitlement many felt in their forced occupation.[92]

Tensions arising from a gay (white) migration into predominately Black neighborhoods offer an additional lens through which to examine these dynamics. Massive investments in development and city services over the last two decades helped reverse a six-decade population decline; between 2000 and 2019, DC's population exploded from a near-record low of 572,059 to 713,244.[93] These gains came at a considerable loss to the city's Black population. In 2010, the city lost its Black majority as white residents purchased homes in predominately Black neighborhoods like Shaw/U Street, Bloomingdale, and Petworth.[94] Yet despite its residential and economic transformation from chocolate city to cappuccino city, Washington preserves its chocolate city reputation by performing long-standing community traditions. Black musicians perform on street corners to the dismay of white gentrifiers in adjacent condominiums. Shaw's streets remain congested with cars displaying Maryland license plates that are triple-parked around Black churches. Black youths "hang out" on museum steps; cheerleaders and bands from local Black high schools practice their formations in nearby neighborhoods. And as newcomers threaten these practices, these vicarious citizens fight back, protecting their tenuous hold on the culture and place they still think of as home.

My project began in 2010 as an ethnographic study of three adjacent gay neighborhoods in Washington, DC, at various stages of development: the "iconic" gay neighborhood (Dupont Circle), the "current" gayborhood (Logan Circle), and the "emerging" gay neighborhood (Shaw/U Street). When I began this research, LGBTQ locals had observed the residential and institutional shift of the LGBTQ community eastward from Dupont Circle to Shaw. In 2006, debates over the opening of a gay bar across the street from a historically Black church in Shaw's Ninth Street corridor amplified those observations on the ground. However, the emergence of queer cultural archipelagos in Northeast and Southwest DC,[95] coupled with LGBTQ events like Pride on the Pier at The Wharf, raised new questions for me about what constitutes a gay neighborhood. Thus, while remaining attentive to the residential dispersion, I maintained my ethnographic attention on these three neighborhoods.

I completed my fieldwork in three stages. In 2010, I moved to Washington and conducted ten months of immersive participant observation as a Shaw resident. After returning to Chicago in the summer of 2011, I revisited Washington over the next six years, collecting data at significant events during summer and winter breaks and holidays. These ethnographic revisits allowed me to witness the evolution of LGBTQ geographies throughout the city, especially the response of local queer communities to the tragedy at the Pulse nightclub and the mobilization of LGBTQ communities of color through #NoJusticeNoPride and #BlackLivesMatter. Finally, in 2018, I relocated to Washington for twelve months for my sabbatical. I conducted more-targeted participant observation, including shadowing the members of the Stonewall Sports kickball teams, who dominated the Seventeenth Street strip on every Sunday game day during their season.

Following the tradition of urban ethnographers, I immersed myself in the quotidian routines of these neighborhoods. I conducted daily and nightly rounds in local gay institutions, such as bars, restaurants, gyms, churches, community centers, and bookstores. I sat in public parks and outdoor cafés while observing street activity. I followed respondents through the neighborhood as they conducted their daily and nightly rounds and took neighborhood tours with bloggers and longtime residents to understand their mapping of the community. I marched in parades and protests, painted streetscapes with the mayor, and participated in walk-a-thons. I observed myriad neighborhood-wide events: local street festivals, church services, community town halls, and block association meetings. The town halls elicited helpful community feedback on multiple local issues: Pride Festival planning, policing and crime prevention, HIV/AIDS advocacy, same-sex marriage, and LGBTQ youth. Typing ethnographic notes directly into my computer while sitting in cafés or public meetings minimized any disruption to others' routines. When using my computer proved challenging, I typed field notes onto my cell phone and transcribed them when I returned home.

My interviews of 105 DC, Maryland, and Virginia (DMV) residents also clarified how participants navigated life in a constantly changing queer landscape. Although respondents included local community and religious leaders, I deliberately compiled a sample in which private citizens who live out their lives in these spaces were overrepresented. Respondents ranged in age from eighteen to eighty, with most respondents between thirty and forty-five. Nearly half identified as a person of color, one-third of which were Black. One-fifth identified as straight or heterosexual, while one-fifth identified as women (including respondents who transitioned from male to female). Interviews focused on the subjects' gender and sexual identities, residential histories, personal and professional goals, and community involvement (recreational and political); on the qualities of the places they most and least value (residential and recreational); and on the changes they have witnessed in the local area. I also posed questions about the local areas where respondents felt the deepest connection to community and about the spaces and activities that fostered those attachments. Interviews varied from thirty minutes to two hours, with most lasting at least an hour.

Finally, consulting local Washington archives enabled me to situate these dynamics in their proper historical context. I collected materials from the Rainbow History Project, the Capital Pride Alliance, the Historical Society of Washington, DC, and the Washingtoniana Collection at the DC Public Library. Oral history interviews conducted by Genny Beemyn and Rainbow History board members supplemented interview data, offering firsthand historical accounts of Washington's LGBTQ communities. In addition to reviewing historical documents and newspapers (including every issue of the *Washington Blade* published during its fifty-plus-year history),

I collected current newspaper clippings, photographs, neighborhood flyers, and other social artifacts. These data proved helpful in identifying the critical issues around which residents of these communities mobilize and the key institutions that have shaped these gay communities over time.

OVERVIEW OF THE BOOK

These pages detail the diverse strategies that everyday citizens employ to keep iconic gay neighborhoods resonant in an age of queer assimilation into the mainstream. This book challenges the narratives about the "disappearing" gay neighborhood by introducing a diversity of community stakeholders whose alternate spatial practices represent powerful forms of community ownership and belonging. Along these lines, it also aligns these practices to different ways of imagining neighborhoods and communities in the contemporary city.

Chapter 1 presents a historical "impression" of Washington's queer landscape. While not intended to capture the totality of that complicated landscape, it offers insight into the complex spatial communities that grew out of appropriating and reimagining space in local neighborhoods. Tracing these multiple community nodes also connects the trends associated with the disappearance of Washington's gay neighborhoods to a long-standing legacy of queer placemaking in cities.

Chapter 2 pivots to explore the subcultural logics and strategies that vicarious citizens use to develop community attachments to iconic gay neighborhoods. The growing visibility of LGBTQ residential clusters in cities has not necessarily supplanted residents' attachments to iconic gay neighborhoods. Instead, residents have developed a spatial division of labor that allows them to develop simultaneous attachments to their residential and vicarious communities. While respondents imagine their gay(er) residential neighborhoods as privileging a *private relational order* where their practices signify sexual identities more subtly, they also consider iconic gay neighborhoods as spaces where they can freely celebrate their sexual and gender identities through a *public relational order*. These distinctions not only represent a conscious understanding of local space but also reflect multiple communities whose spatial expressions reveal different relational orders. In many DC neighborhoods, white LGBTQ residents develop a private relational order because of the public expressions of former and current Black residents who draw on street corner culture to foster Black community in these neighborhoods.

Chapter 3 explores the role of institutional anchors as *place abeyance signifiers*—meaningful spaces imbued with symbolism and collective memory that ground vicarious communities. We often measure the strength of gayborhoods by the concentration of local LGBTQ institutions (i.e., gay bars, bathhouses, and bookstores). Yet their meanings as local community anchors are not inherent; residents and vicarious citizens refashion community and commercial establishments into anchors of community belonging. Local queer communities may embrace an LGBTQ bookstore as a "community center" while rejecting any effort to establish one formally. A gay bar may transition from one place to another throughout an evening as one community leaves and another assumes control over the space. However, thinking beyond anchoring institutions, place abeyance signifiers recognize how various institutions may not always be "active." Place abeyance signifiers ebb and flow as a community requires them. Specific anchors may lie dormant for decades until another group threatens their existence, spurring the indigenous community into action. Varying by culture and community, place abeyance signifiers flourish in the unlikeliest places. Despite their diversity, these community anchors cultivate a sense of ownership among their consumers, transforming brief relationships into lasting, meaningful ties to community.

The following three chapters delve into how community actors mobilize their community anchors and spatial practices into different forms of vicarious citizenship. Chapter 4 describes *normative vicarious claims*—everyday routines and practices that monitor and reinforce norms associated with the area's identity as a gay neighborhood. Holding hands with one's partner or sharing one's "sexcapades" may seem innocuous. However, these remain vital strategies for protecting the culture of gay neighborhoods as safe spaces for the free exploration of gender and sexual identities. Vicarious citizens may also activate normative claims to express their disapproval of behavior that threatens the production of gay space. Confronting amorous straight couples in gay bars and defending themselves against homophobic remarks reflect practices that many LGBTQ people feel are possible only in places where queer public culture is the norm.

The visibility of LGBTQ citizens of color in queer spaces does not negate the persistence of iconic gay neighborhoods as spaces that privilege normative whiteness.[96] Even when LGBTQ persons of color conduct practices that reinforce space production in the gayborhood (e.g., public displays of affection), in specific contexts their public presentation may be illegible to other community members, including white gay men. Chapter 5 discusses *radical vicarious claims*, claims raised by what the sociologist Patricia Hill Collins refers to as "outsiders within."[97] These actors may identify with many aspects of the gayborhood's dominant culture. Yet for many reasons they have been excluded from participation in local community life. Radical claims expand the cultural imagination of place and community in local neighborhoods by appropriating and reimagining public space. As a result, these practices may challenge more traditionally held perceptions of a place's use or meaning. For example, the rise in street corner culture among queer youths of color in iconic gay neighborhoods represents a radical vicarious claim. White LGBTQ residents view their activities as potential threats to public safety. Yet street corner practices offer important ways for queer youths of color to render the gayborhood culturally accessible.

Chapter 6 considers how vicarious citizens mobilize normative and radical vicarious claims into *political vicarious claims*, claims that pursue community interests through local political and institutional channels. Exercising political claims proves more challenging for vicarious citizens. Many local and municipal institutions limit local political decision-making to community members with residential or economic ties to a neighborhood. These challenges do not deter vicarious citizens from political action, however. Many utilize various strategies to draw attention to their concerns—from eliciting residents to support their causes to mobilizing collective protest. By mobilizing cultural claims as a form of self-enfranchisement, vicarious citizens not only expand the political possibilities of who can claim community membership locally but also challenge the notion of citizenship itself.

Reflecting on lessons learned, the conclusion applies this framework beyond Washington's gay neighborhoods. Place reactivation and vicarious citizenship extend well beyond gay neighborhoods. They draw on the unique conditions of the contemporary city, where urban revitalization strategies and new technologies in communication and transportation allow vicarious citizens to maintain connections to local areas regardless of distance. Drawing on a range of actions from the street corner practices of queer youths in Chicago's Boystown, to the tensions around go-go music and gentrification in Washington's Shaw neighborhood, to the efforts to remove Confederate statutes that led to protests like that in Charlottesville, Virginia, the conclusion creates a blueprint for understanding how the symbolic ownership of local space transforms into meaningful forms of local, national, and global political participation.

1

STILL "A VERY GAY CITY"

A Historical Impression of Washington's
LGBTQ Communities

"**F**riday, June 26, 2015, 10:05 A.M." Rishi (forty-five, gay, Asian) rattled off the moment CNN's Wolf Blitzer announced the *Obergefell* decision as quickly as he might recite his birthday. Throughout our interview, the policy consultant narrated with laser-sharp detail the morning the U.S. Supreme Court declared same-sex marriage a constitutional right. He described the "lucky" clothing he wore: "I strutted in the office rocking my rainbow bow tie, rainbow suspender, and the jockstrap I wore the night I first met [my husband] at Town." His husband, Paul (forty-three, gay, white), laughed, shaking his head in disbelief when Rishi pulled out the shadow box containing the policy brief he was drafting when the decision came down. "This was the sentence I was working on when it happened," Rishi explained, pointing to a highlighted sentence on the page. And I could not help noticing the flash of anger across Rishi's face as he explained what prevented him from waiting outside the Supreme Court building with Paul, his fiancé at the time, and their friends. "I should have just taken the morning off," he confessed through clenched teeth before bursting into laughter. "But a looming deadline on a policy brief meant I couldn't be there. Not that I could really concentrate. I typed that brief with CNN in the background on my computer—one earbud hanging out of my ear in case anyone approached my door."

Any pretense of working disappeared the moment Rishi heard the news. He first called Paul. "We didn't talk long," Rishi said. "It was so loud and crazy down there. We could barely hear each other." He tearfully watched President Obama hail the decision as "a victory of America" in the Rose Garden. After a celebratory lunch with office girlfriends, Rishi continued the festivities in his office with two dozen rainbow-frosted cupcakes he purchased from Whole Foods. Once the party subsided, he attempted a half-hearted return to his brief, taking comfort in knowing he would later celebrate in Dupont Circle. "It was a no-brainer," Rishi explained. "That's where we have always gone. Every victory and every tragedy—no matter what happens, we always wound up in the Circle."

Yet much to their disappointment, Rishi and his crew arrived in Dupont Circle that evening to find a quiet, uneventful traffic circle. "No music. No dancing. No crowds. Nothing. It looked just like it did every other night," he recalled. "I couldn't believe it." After a few quick texts with friends, Paul told Rishi to order an Uber to Lafayette Square, the park stretching along the north side of the White House. Within minutes, the four of them had squeezed into a silver Toyota Prius and were driving along P Street toward Sixteenth Street. "We had no idea what was going on," Rishi said. "Our friend just told us to haul our asses over there." Their suspense quickly abated the moment the car turned onto Sixteenth Street. At the end of the street sat the north portico of the White House, saturated in rainbow-colored lights underneath a navy-blue sky. Rishi recalled gripping Paul's hand tightly as they approached, captivated by what he saw. "For a second," Rishi recalled, "you could hear a pin drop in that car. We sat there, just trying to take it all in. I never imagined in my lifetime that we would see something so spectacular."

They arrived at the park and walked toward the crowds standing along the wrought iron fences flanking Pennsylvania Avenue. Flashes flickered as people in front of the White House took photos on their cell phones and compared their handiwork with that of other spectators. Many waved rainbow flags of various sizes. Others draped large rainbow flags around themselves and their partners, kissing one another to rapturous applause. Throughout the evening, the crowd broke out in demonstrations of patriotism. When a woman began singing "America, the Beautiful," people held hands and sang along. Before the song finished, a Black woman shouted, "Free at last! Free at last! Thank God, Almighty! Free at last!" The crowd cheered.

A few minutes later a woman engaged in a call-and-response with the crowd.

"Whose nation?" she began.

"Our nation!" the crowd responded.

"Whose house?"

"Our house!"

Rishi stood there with Paul and his friends, taking selfies while chatting with strangers and occasional friends passing through the crowd. "I just held onto Paul all evening," Rishi remembered. "A couple of times when we kissed each other, the crowd around us began cheering. It was electric. We kept making out just to feel the energy of the crowds supporting us. I don't think I've ever felt so powerful as a gay man."

Paul quickly followed, speaking for the first time in the interview. "It *was* powerful. To have our nation recognize us for the first time as full citizens, with the right to love who we love—I never felt prouder to be an American than I did at that moment."

––––––––

Rishi's experience that evening was far from uncommon. Quite a few Washingtonians, especially older LGBT residents, expected to find "an informal gather of jubilant gays" in Dupont Circle after the *Obergefell* decision, only to find the celebration had moved on.[1] At first glance, many who reflected on that once-in-a-lifetime moment also saw the celebration as another death knell for Gay Dupont. Some queer millennials were surprised when I asked why they did not consider heading to Dupont Circle that evening. "Heading to Dupont never crossed my mind," Dale (twenty-two, white, gay-identified transman) explained. "I don't think any of my friends were planning to [go to Dupont]." Older LGBT citizens like Xavier (sixty-five, white, gay) felt they were celebrating a moment that could not be contained within the "gay ghetto." "[*Obergefell*] wasn't just an LGBT victory," he noted. "It was a victory for all Americans. And that night the proof was displayed in full view across the north portico."

For many, a rainbow-illumined White House was a new symbolic anchor for the LGBTQ community. Although mourners held a silent vigil in Dupont Circle a year later on the Sunday evening following the Pulse shooting, a concurrent vigil in Lafayette Square received more extensive media coverage. Photos of same-sex couples standing in front of the White House, waving rainbow flags while holding one another in tearful embraces, circulated in news stories capturing the worldwide response to the tragedy. In 2017, as the Trump administration expressed open hostility toward LGBTQ rights, protesters marched along that same strip of Pennsylvania Avenue. Shouting through megaphones, the crowds waved rainbow flags and carried signs that read "Fags Hate Trump" (evoking the "God Hates Fags" signs carried by Westboro Baptist Church protesters) and "Remember Pulse" (commemorating the tragedy's first anniversary).

Yet the demonstrations in Lafayette Square also reflected full-circle moments for the LGBTQ community. Few people realized how their actions reinvigorated a landmark once known as the epicenter of Washington's gay life. Famously called the "garden of pansies" in the salacious *Washington Confidential* guidebook, Lafayette Square, a seven-acre park directly north of the White House, anchored an elaborate "gay world" for Black and white gay men in search of sexual and romantic companionship.[2] It has been the site of various political rallies and demonstrations throughout the twentieth and twenty-first centuries, but it also features a monument to an obscure figure in gay American history. A statue of the Revolutionary War drill-master Fredrich Von Steuben stands at the park's northwest corner (figure 1.1). Von Steuben was widely believed to take "familiarities with young boys," and the statue includes several relief scenes that might easily be interpreted as homoerotic nods to his reputation. The rear of the base features a bronze relief of the two men rumored to be his "great loves," Colonel William North and Major Benjamin Walker. Along the northeast side of the sculpture sits a Roman soldier instructing a scantily clad youth on how to hold a sword.[3]

Situating these moments within Lafayette Square's LGBTQ history also highlights a legacy of queer placemaking that continues to shape Washington's queer spatial imagination. This chapter paints a historical impression of these geographies. While not a complete history, it offers four takeaways that expand academic and popular understandings of LGBTQ urban histories.[4] First, expanding existing research on the queer cultural archipelagos,[5] this chapter highlights how LGBTQ spatial plurality has always existed in Washington. Since the mid-nineteenth century, the city has boasted diverse and complex LGBTQ populations that developed distinct geographies to support their subcultures, often refashioning and reactivating gay places out of existing urban spaces. Some geographies grew out of complex public-private relational orders that white gays and lesbians created, while others emerged from the city's residential and institutional segregation.

Second, because of this spatial complexity, accessibility often mattered more than residential propinquity. Fear of discovery required many white gay men to separate their public lives from the places they created in the name of community. Many lived in neighborhoods close enough that they could easily access these communities of interest and yet far enough away that their recreational activities did not generate suspicion.[6] As gentrification later priced many LGBTQ residents out of iconic gay neighborhoods, they moved to neighborhoods that offered easy access to vicarious communities.

FIGURE 1.1 The statue of Colonel Von Steuben in Lafayette Square. Although few likely knew the ironic significance of Von Steuben when the park served as a cruising site, rumors of his homosexuality have become a featured attraction during historical walking tours of Gay Washington.

Photo by author.

Third, this chapter challenges perceptions of Black queer communities as mere casualties of racial segregation and Black homophobia.[7] I draw on "chocolate cities sociology"[8] to illustrate how Black LGBTQ people created vibrant, variably visible worlds in their local communities despite racial discrimination and segregation. While their communities often mirrored the spatial communities of their white gay and lesbian counterparts, Black Washingtonians "in the life" navigated social and political terrain where they could not always hide their sexuality from family and friends.[9] Marshaling their available resources and drawing on their local culture, Black gays and lesbians established communities on their terms, creating places that fostered visibility and leveraged opportunities that mitigated the effects of economic and institutional isolation.[10] Legitimating these placemaking strategies, this chapter exposes Black LGBTQ citizens as active agents in placemaking, intervening not only in the literature on gay neighborhoods but also in the extensive scholarship on Black urban communities.

Finally, extending the call by sociologists to examine queer spatial dynamics outside traditional "gay meccas" like New York, San Francisco, Chicago, and Los Angeles,[11] this chapter reinforces the value of engaging local queer histories when attempting to understand the development of LGBTQ communities in the United States. Popular and scholarly understandings of the evolution of LGBTQ neighborhoods in the United States have been derived primarily from these iconic cities and then generalized across all U.S. LGBTQ communities. As this chapter reveals, Washington's LGBTQ history does not neatly dovetail with this history. For example, LGBTQ Washingtonians were experiencing unprecedented visibility when LGBTQ citizens in larger cities were navigating "the closet."[12] Fitting Washington history (or any local history) into models of gay community and neighborhood formation drawn from more traditional "gay meccas" silences a diversity of people and practices that defines Washington's current queer landscape.

"UNDER THE VERY SHADOW OF THE WHITE HOUSE"

Although gay men socialized and cruised in several downtown Washington parks (including the National Mall) during the early twentieth century, Lafayette Square has anchored much of gay life since at least 1885, when the park began to stay open all night.[13] From spring to early fall, the wooded cover, poor lighting, and lack of regular police presence made the park an ideal location for gay men to initiate a complex social world in which to explore their sexual appetites. "Only those interested in same-sex relationships were likely to linger there at night," the historian Genny Beemyn observes, "nearly eliminating the possibility of hostile encounters with heterosexuals."[14]

Although little documentation exists from this early period, the diaries of Carter Newman Bealer offer valuable insights into Washington's gay worlds in the early twentieth century.[15] For Bealer, an editor for a federal agency, cruising in Lafayette Square became a nightly occurrence. "To hell with the government," he wrote in his diary. "Life begins at 4:30 for me!"[16] Bealer exposes a complex spatial order in his diaries, reflecting the patterns of the men who cruised the park. He named the various benches based on the regulars who often sat there. Although his labels did not extend beyond his writings, his observations suggest various patterns of intragroup segregation among the men who frequented the park. He avoided "Nigger's Bench" on the southwest side of the park, where Black gay men and the white men who loved them sat, and "Sailor's Row" on the park's far northwest end, fearing that sailors attracted too much attention.[17]

The heavily wooded areas provided enough privacy for men to engage in sexual encounters, especially if they lacked private accommodations. Bealer observed men engaged in sexual acts throughout his excursions, including men who mutually masturbated under the Von Steuben statue. However, in many cases, men connected in Lafayette Square and moved their activity elsewhere, especially as police surveillance intensified in the early 1900s. On several occasions, Bealer picked up partners in Lafayette Square and walked with them to the Ellipse or more secluded public spaces in President's Park or to the Lincoln Memorial to engage in sex (oral or anal) or masturbation.

Because federal parks were not racially segregated, Black men "in the life" could also explore their sexual desires there, providing rare opportunities for interracial mixing and the exploration of interracial desire. These spaces did not necessarily insulate Black gay men from racism, however. Bealer did not hide his distaste for Black men, who often sat on the park benches on the southwest side.[18] Black men also became particularly vulnerable to police scrutiny once Metropolitan Police Department officers began routinely surveilling downtown DC parks in the 1890s. In an 1892 journal article, the Georgetown University professor Irving Rosse describes how police officers "have made, under the very shadow of the White House, eighteen arrests in Lafayette Square alone . . . in which the culprits were taken *in flagrante delicto*. Both white and [B]lack were represented among these moral hermaphrodites, but the majority of them were negroes."[19]

Cruising the parks did not come without considerable risks. In the early 1900s, Congress converted Washington's common-law statutes into a criminal code, establishing sodomy as a felony punishable by up to five years in prison. Police records highlighted the challenges of eliciting enough evidence to establish a sodomy charge, which required proof of emission. Charges for consensual oral or anal sex without proof of emission often ranged from indecent exposure to indecent assault. Fearing the publicity of a trial and the sentence associated with a conviction, many defendants pled guilty to the lesser charge of simple assault, which carried a sentence ranging from a few months to two years. Those charged with indecent assault often could not avoid standing trial, and many received several months in the city's workhouse or jail.[20]

Nevertheless, Lafayette Square's reputation grew throughout the early twentieth century, extending well beyond the immediate area. In the 1920s, a man from Philadelphia told Bealer that he "had heard about the park while he was in the Virgin Islands."[21] References to Lafayette Square fueled gay readers' imaginations in queer novels published in the 1920s and 1930s. The characters in Robert Scully's 1932's novel *A Scarlet Pansy* "spent the greater part of a romantic moonlight [*sic*] night in the ever-beautiful Lafayette Park," where the main character, Faye, an androgynous fairy, manages to get picked up on five separate occasions.[22] Yet the square's popularity among gay men forced the government to increase surveillance measures there and in several other city parks. In the 1890s, the chief of engineers for the U.S. Army, who had responsibility for public buildings and grounds, installed lights around the Washington Monument and other park areas and gradually increased surveillance by the U.S. Park Police, which had jurisdiction over most of the city's parks—all in the interest of morality. However, as government officials often found the Park Police presence insufficient, Metropolitan Police Department officers provided additional surveillance, focusing on Lafayette Square.[23]

Plainclothes police officers employed intimidation and harassment to deter cruising in the park. Bealer documented his run-ins with "the Sneak," a plainclothes officer who often followed men around the park. Some officers spread rumors about men suspected of pursuing same-sex relationships in the park. In his diary, Bealer complained that an officer patrolling near Pennsylvania Avenue "set the tongues of all the business neighborhood over there wagging" about him, resulting in many shopkeepers treating him poorly. Although such harassment intimidated Bealer to the point that he relied on the parks less frequently after 1923, many Black and white men endured the risks. Lafayette's reputation only intensified through the 1920s and 1930s as the city underwent a significant population surge in the 1930s.[24]

FROM DOWNTOWN TO BLACK BROADWAY

Outside the federal parks and monuments, the gay worlds of Black and white Washington remained largely separate. By the early twentieth century, segregation prohibited Blacks from patronizing white restaurants, nightclubs, and movie theaters. And unlike white gay men and white slummers in New York City and Chicago who were captivated by the "Negro craze,"[25] white gay men in Washington did not seek out the vibrant cabarets and speakeasies in the city's Black neighborhoods. Instead, these communities developed as parallel worlds that refashioned existing commercial and cultural institutions to foster community. In colder months, white gay men centered much of their activity in downtown Washington, particularly the tenderloin area on Ninth Street north of Pennsylvania Avenue NW. Black gays and lesbians frequented establishments in the Shaw/U Street corridor, popularly known by the 1920s as Black Broadway. Coupled with the Fourteenth Street commercial area, the Shaw/U Street corridor became the center of Washington's Black cultural production in its heyday, offering artistic and commercial amenities rivaling New York's Harlem.[26] Unlike white gay men, who created distinct boundaries around their professional, personal, and sexual lives (provided they did not get arrested), Black gay men often encountered relatives, neighbors, and coworkers during their nightly rounds.[27]

Certain theaters, vaudeville houses, and movie palaces developed a reputation for discreet, anonymous sexual encounters. On Ninth Street, the Strand, a movie palace, became known for same-sex cruising almost as soon as it opened in 1916.[28] Before and during Prohibition, gay men often sought refuge in secluded bohemian restaurants and clubs, such as Krazy Kat near Franklin Park, without attracting too much attention. Like Lafayette Square, Krazy Kat developed a reputation beyond Washington, suggesting that their invisibility from public view did not prevent white gay men from creating gay social worlds that newcomers could easily access.[29] Across town, Black gay men frequented the famous Howard Theater on T Street and the Lincoln Theater on U Street between Twelfth and Thirteenth Streets. Men often sat in the upper galleries in these darkened spaces, hoping to attract other men for mutual masturbation or discreet oral sex with subtle gestures, such as brushing one's arm or leg casually against the man sitting next to him. Cruising indoors came with greater risk. Many targets were heterosexual men who might respond to advances with hostility. Other patrons ignored these subtle overtures, more interested in watching the performance.

White gay men enjoyed the luxury of living throughout the city, often at a distance from the establishments where they socialized. One popular place for men to meet other men in the 1920s was the YMCA's Central Branch, located a few blocks southeast of Lafayette Square. Despite concerns over immoral acts, managers seemed willing to turn a blind eye, provided the sexual activity remained inconspicuous. Rooming houses and apartment buildings near Lafayette Square also proved popular among white gay men. Apartment houses offered greater privacy and anonymity for same-sex sexual encounters than rooming houses and the YMCAs.

Although segregation restricted the residential imagination of Black gay men, residential patterns often mirrored those of their white counterparts. By 1912, a separate YMCA for Blacks opened off Twelfth and T Streets NW, offering additional opportunities for Black gay men to find one another. After World War I, "nearly 100 men were living there, including, for a brief time, the famous Harlem Renaissance poet Langston Hughes."[30] Rooming houses and apartment buildings in the eastern part of Shaw, particularly along North Capitol Street, allowed Black gays and lesbians greater privacy to socialize away from family supervision. Bounded by Seventh and North Capitol Streets NW, Shaw East housed working-class Blacks, who exhibited greater tolerance toward Black gays and lesbians than did the more "respectable citizens" of Shaw West, Ledroit Park, and Strivers' Section, in the northern Dupont Circle area. By the 1920s,

Shaw East had developed an unsavory reputation that created new anxieties among middle- and upper-class Blacks. William Howard Jones, a sociologist at Howard University, observes the popularity of "three or four young men [renting] and [furnishing] an apartment, . . . living a more or less Bohemian life" and of "insurgent women who are seeking ultra-independence and Bohemianism." While not explicitly speaking of homosexuality, Jones suggests that apartment living permitted "much unconventional behavior, since the public eye cannot detect anything 'improper' in the frequent 'coming and going' that characterizes the life of its occupants."[31]

Drag also became a defining feature of Black LGBTQ placemaking in Washington at the turn of the century. In addition to participating in drag balls in Harlem and Baltimore, Black gay men held drag balls and parties in private residences in Washington. These temporary events allowed Black gay men, especially members of Black Washington's middle and professional classes, to explore their gendered and sexual identities. Describing one "drag dance" in 1893, the neurologist Charles H. Hughes expresses outrage over the fact that many of these men, "lasciviously dressed in womanly attire . . . and deport[ing] themselves as women," occupied positions as either domestic employees for some of Washington's elite families or "subordinate" professionals working for the government.[32] These balls and festivals not only centered lavish displays of gender expression but also unapologetically celebrated sex. Rosse depicts one such orgy of "phallic worship," during which a "big buck, with a turgescent penis, decorated with gaily colored ribbons" stood in the center of a room while admirers touched and kissed it.[33]

While Black cross-dressers were often vulnerable to police harassment and arrest, newspaper articles reveal the confidence with which they expressed themselves in public. In 1885, the *Washington Evening Star* reported the arrest of a "Miss Maud" after returning home from a drag ball on New Year's Eve. Miss Maud, dressed in "a pink dress trimmed with white lace, with stockings and undergarments to match," received compliments for her stylish appearance from the judge before he sentenced her to three months in jail for vagrancy. Some cross-dressers even managed to challenge police harassment.[34] The April 13, 1888, edition of the *Washington Post* featured a story about a police raid on a Northwest Washington residence after a lieutenant observed "strange-looking Females" entering the house for "a supper and a dance." Storming the "handsomely furnished room," the officers discovered fifteen Black men dressed as women in "rich material . . . made according to the latest fashions" who were seated for a "luxurious supper." As the men jumped out of windows to evade arrest, one "big negro" named William Dorsey Swann charged at the officers, preventing them from entering. A descendant of enslaved people, Swann, "arrayed in a gorgeous dress of cream-colored satin" and "bursting with rage," brawled with the officers before being arrested and charged with "being a suspicious character."[35]

Despite its visibility, Washington's Black LGBTQ landscape mainly attracted the Black working and middle classes. Fear of ostracism from the area's elite, conservative Black circles often prevented prominent Black gays and lesbians from pursuing same-sex desire locally. As a result, elite Black gays and lesbians had to fashion gay worlds that were "not tied to capital, nor necessarily with any specific location." By exchanging letters and visits with other Black gay and lesbian artists and educators outside the area, they were able to receive "political and professional support without exposing their sexualities to the hostile gaze of other members of the city's Black elite."[36] Certain Black gay elites, like the Howard professor and philosopher Alain Locke, supported Black gay causes discreetly, limiting their pursuit of romantic relationships to cities outside the United States, preferably in Europe.[37] Others suppressed their sexual desire entirely to avoid the possibility of disclosure. Over time, many sought romantic relationships closer to home by fostering closed communities through private relational orders that persist today. Because Black leaders like Adam Clayton Powell labeled homosexuality a white disease that

threatened the aspirations and values associated with Black respect-
ability, the spatial imagination for elite Black gay and lesbian citizens
in Washington during the twentieth century often depended on dis-
cretion within their communities.

"YOU CAN GET LIT ONLY IF YOU SIT"

Both the Great Depression and the repeal of Prohibition reshaped
gay worlds in cities. Local, state, and federal authorities developed
laws and practices in places like New York City that eradicated public
expressions of homosexual life and culture, enabling the production
of "the closet." "Although gay life continued to flourish," writes the
historian George Chauncey, "it became less visible to outsiders and
was increasingly segregated from the broader life of the city. Forcing
the gay world into hiding—or, to the modern idiom, into the closet—
was precisely the intention of the authorities."[38] By contrast, gay and
lesbian Washingtonians enjoyed the visibility that gays and lesbians
had experienced in New York and Chicago a decade earlier. Describing gay Washington in the 1930s, Haviland Ferris writes, "I can honestly say that I never knew what [the closet] was, for there was never a
time when I or my friends were not out of it."[39] Throughout the 1930s,
millions of young singles flocked to Washington to work in one of
President Franklin D. Roosevelt's expansive New Deal agencies. Gays
and lesbians experienced an openness and a visibility that enabled the
creation of vibrant, complex sexual geographies that relied on their
reimagining of semipublic and private relational orders.[40]

Although cruising in Lafayette Square and other federal parks
continued, gays and lesbians transformed several cruising sites into
recreational spaces for socializing. Ladd Forrester, who arrived in
Washington, DC, in the 1930s to work as a file clerk for a federal
agency, described how hundreds of gays and lesbians roller-skated and
picnicked near the Reflecting Pool in front of the Lincoln Memorial

in the warmer months. "There were plenty of park benches underneath the trees for the skaters to rest and talk with one another," Forrester recalled in a 1986 *Washington Blade* retrospective. In contrast to gay cruising in Lafayette Square, public displays of same-sex affection around the National Mall represented a new kind of sexual openness many gays and lesbians enjoyed before World War II. "We would skate holding hands, and the Park Police never interfered," Forrester remembered. "In fact, we used to comment among ourselves how the Park Police seldom came around the reflecting pool." On Sundays, gays and lesbians picnicked in Bartholdi Park, a "secret garden" at the foot of Capitol Hill. "Picnics started out Sunday mornings and would last all day," with the picnickers taking in the seasonal floras in the Botanic Garden and photographing one another in front of the nude sculptures on the nearby General Meade Memorial.[41] Given the integration of public parks, Black gays and lesbians also participated.

Even after the Twenty-First Amendment repealed Prohibition in 1933, bars still did not exist in Washington. Restaurants could serve liquor if they had a liquor license and if at least 50 percent of their revenue came from food sales. Restaurants hoping to function as bars skirted the law by offering limited food items; however, the law required these establishments to have and maintain a full kitchen, which limited available seating for patrons. Additionally, the law required patrons to be seated while consuming alcoholic beverages. "The motto back then became, 'You can get lit only if you sit,'" Forrester wrote in another 1986 article.[42] Only the servers were allowed to carry liquor in an establishment. "If you moved from one seat to another," gay rights leader Frank Kameny explained, "you moved yourself, and the waiter or waitress moved your drink." Because businesses, especially those catering to a gay clientele, feared losing their liquor licenses, staff policed this policy very carefully. "People from out of town who didn't know what was going on would move with their drink, and waitresses would descend from all directions, grabbing the drink out of his hand, plop[ping] it down and go[ing], 'What do you want to do? Lose us our license!'" Kameny remembered. "The poor person didn't know what was going on."[43]

The restrictions did not prevent the opening of several downtown establishments that served white gays and lesbians. "Bars became gay by word of mouth," explained Kameny. "Once they [opened], those of us who went out at all were aware very quickly that they were there."[44] Like the Chicken Hut near Lafayette Square, many restaurants served heterosexual patrons during the day and gay patrons at night. Local straight patrons understood the transitioning communities, ensuring they left these establishments by six or seven P.M. Bars served different clienteles. While the Chicken Hut's campy atmosphere attracted more "openly" gay men, Carroll's on Ninth Street NW favored military personnel and the men who loved them. Professional men looking for more covert cruising could find a significant gay clientele in the Mayflower and Statler Hotels. The "hotel bars" banned women outright during this period; the homosocial environment allowed men to connect for same-sex encounters without raising too much suspicion. In particular, the Mayflower Men's Bar became a "gay bar" on Saturday nights as middle-class white men circulated around the bar searching for someone to take upstairs to one of the rooms.[45]

Throughout this period, social mores discouraged women from going to bars unaccompanied. "Many bars and restaurants which served liquor had a sign in the door which warned 'Unescorted ladies not admitted by order of the Alcohol Control Board.'" During the 1930s, some white gays and lesbians escorted one another in public to give the appearance of being a heterosexual couple during the daytime and at work functions and to minimize the trouble created by an unescorted woman. "The general public in its naivete thought that all [g]ay men were extremely effeminate and wore dresses and that all [l]esbians worked as piano movers," Forrester explained. "So when men and women were seen together, the public took for granted they were heterosexual. As gay men and lesbians, we understood this misconception well and used it to our advantage. We jokingly referred to ourselves as 'Trojan Horses.'"[46] While many drinking establishments banned women outright, some restaurant-bars developed a following. The Showboat, located in the basement of an all-night cafeteria on H Street, provided entertainment for lesbian lovers. After the Showboat closed in 1947, lesbians began frequenting the Maystat, later renamed the Redskin Lounge. In the 1950s, the lounge became famous among women because it featured a butch lesbian performer who sang and told jokes and a band that played contemporary music.[47]

Contrasting the gay scenes in Harlem and Bronzeville, white gay men did not participate in Washington's Black gay scene during the 1920s.[48] However, following Prohibition's repeal, two interracial bars along U Street welcomed gay men of both races. Opened in 1929, Republic Gardens was a large restaurant-bar with a back room that gay men claimed exclusively for their use. Providing a more upscale scene, Crystal Caverns was a straight establishment that welcomed gays. "Its interior had been decorated by a professional and was by far the most elegant of the five bars opened to [g]ays at the time. A handsome head waiter in white tie and tails ushered [g]ays to 'reserved' ringside seats to watch the floor show, which usually included a chorus line."[49]

While not exclusively gay, the alternate social worlds gay men created in these spaces found limited acceptance from bar staff and management. According to Ferris, staff at the Mayflower knew that men were cruising in the bar and did not intervene as long as the interactions remained covert and did not disturb the other patrons. Because the military population in Washington was relatively small, the two waitresses at Carroll's took care to learn the servicemen's names and their backgrounds, anchoring a grapevine that informed gay men of those with "bad reputations." "If they were rough and tough," Ferris explained, "broke furniture or something like that, word got around in the community so that if they came around again, nobody would pick them up."[50] Bars created elaborate codes to warn patrons of police threats. At Republic Gardens, the door to the back room had a small glass window that allowed the entertainer to see the length of the restaurant. If police walked in the front door, the vocalist warned patrons by singing "Alice Blue Gown" from the Broadway musical *Irene*.[51]

Liquor laws required bars to close at 2 A.M. on weeknights and at midnight on weekends. Their early closure did not prevent the party from continuing, however. Gays and lesbians in the 1940s and 1950s had various options for socializing after the bars closed. All-night cafeterias like Britt's in Georgetown and California Kitchen near Dupont Circle allowed gay men to socialize or find a sexual partner if they had been unsuccessful earlier in the evening.[52] Private parties provided another alternative. In the privacy of someone's home, gay men could make new contacts while also dancing—an activity frowned on in places that served liquor. By the time Kameny arrived in Washington in the mid-1950s, Saturday nights had become a well-timed tradition among white gay men. "If you arrived in the bar any time after 10:00 P.M. or so in the evening," he recalled, "the first question you would inquire was 'Where was the party tonight?'" Between eleven P.M. and midnight, men left the bars briefly for a quick trip to the liquor store to purchase alcohol and returned to the various establishments until closing. When the bars closed, they headed to one of the house parties, where liquor was the price of admission. Parties began after closing and went into the morning.[53]

Many of these parties took place in Georgetown, one of Washington's oldest neighborhoods. Georgetown had primarily housed a poor Black community until "highly educated, idealistic newcomers, attracted by [its] low prices and charm and consciously unconcerned about its social status," bought houses there in the 1930s. The neighborhood quickly developed a reputation as "a haven for bohemians, homosexuals, and other nonconformists," displacing many of the area's Black residents throughout the 1940s and 1950s. Describing the effects of Georgetown's protogentrification in 1951, journalists Jack Lait and Lee Mortimer observed that the Blacks "who remain[ed] live[d] in shanties so undesirable that no rich white fairies can be found who want to turn them into something gay. In fact, there's a saying in Georgetown now that you're not 'smart' unless darkies live next door to you."[54]

World War II accelerated the population boom in Washington, bringing nearly five thousand workers each month to work in Washington's war production machine.[55] In cities across the United States, the war became a period of both increased visibility for gays, lesbians, and bisexuals and greater tolerance for sexual experimentation. "The unusual conditions of a mobilized society allowed homosexual desire to be expressed more easily into action," writes the historian John D'Emilio. "For many Americans, World War II became a coming-out experience."[56] The influx of service members and young singles working in civilian posts shaped the production of Washington's same-sex communities in two critical ways. First, the housing shortage resulting from the population boom created new opportunities for same-sex experimentation. Second, the lack of privacy resulting from the shared living conditions increased the reliance on parks for romantic and sexual encounters.[57]

Yet the increased visibility of gays and lesbians in Washington during World War II proved a double-edged sword. "In the nation's capital, the massive influx often had a deleterious impact on the atmosphere within existing gay bars, as shifting clientele and greater visibility made them less safe for cruising."[58] The influx and rotation of service members in and out of Washington made it difficult for Carroll's grapevine to keep track of those entering and leaving the bar. "The war changed everything," Ferris explained. "In the first place, you got everybody from everywhere. They were suddenly thrown, without their consent really, in a situation where they . . . were not here long enough to be absorbed into a community."[59] Consequently, it became more dangerous for men to take a serviceman home. Throughout the war, Carroll's lost many of its gay and bisexual regulars as it evolved into a "rough trade" bar—"a place where a number of the patrons were straight-identified, masculine men who might accept the sexual advances of other men, but who might also violently respond to such overtures."[60]

By the war's end, a national panic over sex crimes led to the purging of known homosexuals from the federal government and increased surveillance in Washington's restaurant-bars and public parks. On October 1, 1947, the U.S. Park Police launched the Sex Perversion Elimination Program, which increased surveillance in the area's public parks. Although police officers apprehended men in parks throughout the city, Lafayette Square became the police's primary target, leading many men to pursue cruising elsewhere.

Efforts to eliminate homosexuals from the federal government forced the expansion of the queer spatial imagination beyond downtown DC. Among the more popular sites for cruising was Dupont Circle: men strolled around the tree-lined traffic circle or along Connecticut Avenue, where they stopped and perused storefront windows hoping to make contact. "The use of subtle questions, gestures, and mannerisms . . . enabled gay and bisexual men to remain largely unnoticed by other pedestrians, as well as helped ensure that they did not approach potentially hostile heterosexual men or an undercover police officer."[61] The commercial areas of Georgetown, which included M Street and Wisconsin Avenue NW, provided similar opportunities for cruising and developed such a reputation that, among gay circles, any man standing in front of a Georgetown storefront was considered to be "on the hunt" until proven otherwise. Across town, Capitol Hill also grew in popularity. Johnnie's, which opened in 1949, attracted a mixed working- and middle-class clientele. Famous for its year-round Christmas lights and décor, Johnnie's gained notoriety for having a postage-stamp-sized dance floor in the bar's back corner when most bar owners feared that same-sex dancing targeted them for police raids. That dance floor became pivotal in reshaping Washington's queer spatial landscape in the next decade.

"IN THE LIFE" IN POSTWAR WASHINGTON

Black gays and lesbians in Washington navigated complicated terrain preceding and following World War II. Acceptance of nonnormative sexuality and gender presentation remained divided along class lines. As the out-migration of middle-class Blacks in the 1950s and 1960s transformed Shaw into an urban "ghetto," attitudes toward homosexuality and gender fluidity also shifted.[62] Nevertheless, Black gays and lesbians experienced unprecedented visibility and acceptance in the war and postwar years, particularly as the Lavender Scare created panic among their white counterparts. Many Black gays and lesbians fraternized in predominately straight bars along the Shaw/U Street corridor. Although few gay patrons openly displayed their sexuality, the lack of anonymity within Washington's Black communities meant their sexuality was no real secret to other patrons. "Because 'everybody knew everybody' in Washington's Black community, they were rarely made to feel unwanted in these places and were generally accepted by other patrons."[63]

Black gays and lesbians often fostered community in private settings during the 1940s and 1950s—mainly through house parties, rent parties, and crab parties. Because restaurant-bars often banned dancing out of fear of police raids, house parties created opportunities for Black gays and lesbians to dance and socialize without harassment. "You could be yourself," remembers Esther Smith, a longtime DC resident. "If I invite you to my house, you can come in and do anything you want to do. You can dance, you can eat, you can talk to who you want to talk to. If you want to talk to a female, you can do that. If you want to talk with a male, you can do that." When attending straight functions, Black gays and lesbians often escorted one another to avoid unwanted attention. "We did that interchangeably," Smith explained. "If [a guy] needed to show up to a family function with a woman, they would call us up." For lesbians, having a male partner mitigated the unwanted attention they received from straight men.

"A lot of times, I didn't want to deal with straight guys. Even though I knew a lot of guys who were fun to be with, you had to deal with a lot of hands and their propositions."[64]

Despite the 1953 Supreme Court decision prohibiting racial segregation in DC restaurants, many gay establishments downtown discouraged Blacks from patronizing them. Some, like the Chicken Hut, placed "reserved" signs on tables, telling Black patrons who entered that no seating was available.[65] Rather than face hostility from their white counterparts, Black gays and lesbians opened their own establishments, developing a small "gay scene" around Howard University. The Cozy Corner opened in 1949, and while it was a straight bar, it became a popular destination for gay Howard students when the second floor became a gay nightspot in the evening. Across from the Howard Theater stood Cecilia's, a restaurant that Black gay men flocked to after a show in search of stars. Nob Hill, in the Columbia Heights neighborhood, first opened in 1953 as a private club for middle-class Black gay and bisexual men. By the time it closed in 2004, it had become one of Washington's longest-operating gay bars. Nob Hill developed a reputation as a place where Howard students sought older men, but sexism, colorism, and class prejudice initially kept Black women and working-class patrons away. "They wanted you to be light," recalled Pat Hamilton, a working-class drag performer. "They wanted you to be a postal worker or something in that area."[66]

Drag also flourished in DC's Black nightlife in the postwar era. Black newspapers celebrated the accomplishments of Black drag queens at out-of-town drag balls, and yet they also fought fervently to prohibit drag balls in Washington. While gay and gay-friendly establishments rarely welcomed male and female cross-dressers out of fear of attracting unwanted police attention, they became fixtures in DC's Black nightlife and were popular attractions in interracial establishments like Crystal Caverns and Republic Gardens. When not performing, they delighted in attracting attention as patrons, enjoying freedom not available to them in gay establishments. "Pansies were the big attraction at the Crystal Caverns Sunday night," Louis R. Lautier reported in his "Capital Spotlight" column in the *Washington Afro-American*. "They occupied seats at ringside tables. They danced with each other, Lindy-hopping all over the floor."[67]

Following the 1953 Supreme Court ruling, Black celebrities abandoned performing in U Street venues in favor of more lucrative engagements in predominately white clubs downtown. Black theaters and nightclubs filled the void by booking "novelty acts whose queer performances would not have been tolerated in white neighborhoods."[68] At the Howard Theater, an interracial drag show known as the Jewel Box Revue appeared over 150 times in weeklong engagements through the 1950s and 1960s. Drag performers earned modest wages doing a variety of tasks in various nightclubs. "You really had to work," Hamilton remembered. "You had to be able to do everything. You had to sing. You had to dance. You had to be able to wait on tables. You had to go back there in the kitchen. You had to do everything." The more glamorous a performer, the more popular they were among audiences. "They wanted to see you made up—nice hairdo and lovely gowns on," Hamilton remembered. "That's what brought the men in, the women. They loved it."[69]

As housing desegregation accelerated in the postwar period, the out-migration of the Black middle class from Shaw significantly affected local Black communities. Economic disinvestment led to a growing "epidemic" of abandoned properties, which were soon occupied by vice industries that catered to what the sociologist Ulf Hannerz referred to as "specialized clienteles: gamblers, 'gorillas,' and homosexuals."[70] By the time of the 1968 riots following the assassination of Martin Luther King Jr., queer sex workers and drug dealers shared space with Black civil rights organizations like the SCLC and the NAACP around the intersection of Fourteenth and U Streets NW.[71] As local police and city government expressed little interest in protecting the "moral health" of Black communities, "abandoned and defective buildings were ideal locales for the establishment of queer social space."[72] Free from unwanted police attention, entrepreneurs could open bars without being shut down for violating municipal ordinances. And as Black gays and lesbians faced discrimination in the various white gay and lesbian establishments, the Black queer spaces that emerged in post-riot Washington offered safety and security in which to explore their sexual lives away from their families and professional communities.

FROM MANY NEIGHBORHOODS . . .

After the Stonewall riots sparked the modern gay rights movement in 1969, gay life percolated throughout the Washington area. Although many gays and lesbians lived secret lives, the Mattachine Society of DC, a homophile organization led by the longtime activist Frank Kameny, publicly protested outside federal buildings to challenge the outing and firing of gay federal employees. Despite strict codes governing behavior, gay bars provided opportunities for socialization. In early 1969, the Hideaway Bar in downtown DC began its subtle revolution, challenging moral laws by allowing same-sex dancing. By May, Bill Bickford and Don Culver had opened the first dance club in Capitol Hill. Their success led other gay establishments throughout Washington to gradually eliminate their self-imposed rules against same-sex dancing. Despite the threat of undercover police officers, cruising in Lafayette Square and Dupont Circle remained popular. Others relocated their sexual activities to the P Street Beach, a wooded area along Rock Creek Park west of Dupont Circle, or to "the block," a one-square-block area in Georgetown where Henry Kissinger famously resided during the Nixon administration.

During the 1970s, several large gay discotheques appeared in Washington's old warehouse district. Located approximately one mile south of the U.S. Capitol, these nightclubs transformed that stretch of Southeast DC into a popular entertainment destination not only for the gay community but also for straight thrill seekers in search of disco music.[73] Club Washington, a gay bathhouse, opened in the early 1970s, and within a few years, two strip clubs and the world-renowned drag bar Ziegfeld's followed. According to Kameny, the warehouse district offered an ideal area for less-mainstream gay venues because many believed the police would ignore gay-oriented businesses if they were removed from the more visible downtown areas. "It became an out-of-sight, out-of-mind kind of thing."[74]

Like the straight bachelorettes seeking refuge in gay bars in the early twenty-first century,[75] "hip" and "trendy" heterosexuals searching for uninhibited sexual experimentation found the gay discos particularly fashionable. "Why do I come to gay discos?" one straight man pondered in Tom Zito's 1974 *Washington Post* article about the popularity of the area's discos. "[My girlfriend and I] come here because we're into bodies. We like sensuality and sexuality. We can do things on the dance floor here or around the bar that would stop the show at any other place. It's relaxed here 'cause everybody figures the next person is just as kinky as you."[76] Disco patrons and bar owners mobilized against the threats presented by the straight appropriation of gay space. Responding to Zito in the *Gay Blade*, Chris DeForrest describes how he and his friends invited a straight friend to accompany them to the discos. "Now there are so many straights pushing their way around the bars . . . and especially going overboard in flaunting their heterosexuality that it makes many [g]ays uncomfortable and more than a few disgruntled." Some bar owners attempted various strategies to discourage straights from coming, including requiring multiple forms of identification from patrons they believed were straight. "I believe that the owners of Washington's gay bars feel their main function is to serve the needs of the [g]ay community," DeForrest writes. "God knows that [g]ays try to be the last to discriminate against others, but gay bars are for gay men and women. Status-seeking straights should look elsewhere for entertainment."[77]

Despite the efforts of several progressive gay organizations to support the interests of Washington's Black gay and lesbian residents, the community remained divided during the 1970s. In 1974, the Gay Liberation Front and the *Gay Blade* protested gay bars like Lost & Found that discriminated against Black gays by requiring multiple forms of identification at the door while allowing many white gays to breeze through without pulling out their wallets. Following these protests, Lost & Found and several other bars pulled their advertisements from the *Gay Blade*, preventing the community newspaper, for the first and only time in its history, from producing an issue that October and threatening its very future.[78] "When you consider that several of these [gay] establishments lie in Black neighborhoods in this predominately Black city," writes Ernie Acosta in *The Blade*, "'carding' goes beyond discrimination against a few individuals. It becomes an affront against the entire community."[79]

However, racial progress during the 1970s happened relatively slowly in Washington's gay community, as political progress in the city often occurred without Black gay participation. "For many [gay] activists," Acosta observes, "pride in these achievements is tempered by the anomaly that in a city where 75 percent of the population is Black, the faces of [g]ay success are predominately, and in some cases exclusively, [w]hite."[80] These divisions took center stage during the 1978 mayoral elections. While many white gay organizations, including the Gertrude Stein Democratic Club, endorsed then City Council member Marion Barry for mayor, the recently formed DC Coalition of Black Gay Women and Men supported another candidate. Justifying their endorsement, the representative of the coalition expressed concerns that Barry had aligned himself too closely with the white gay establishment. "We acknowledged that Barry has closely aligned himself with [w]hite [g]ay establishments," coalition spokesperson Billy Jones explained in 1978. "We question [his] willingness to deal with issues of racism in the gay community."[81]

The perceived exclusion by mainstream gay institutions led Black gays to create their own institutions and organizations. In 1976, Delta Elite opened near Catholic University. The corner storefront bar attracted working-class Black men until it closed in 2014. Between 1975 and 1990, the ClubHouse anchored DC's Black gay and lesbian social life in a segregated queer landscape. The social venue had its origins in the red-light basement parties organized by the Metropolitan Capitolites, a social club for Black gay and lesbian Washingtonians led by John Eddy, Aundrea Scott, and Morell Chasten.[82] Once those parties outgrew their apartments, Scott and his friends sought an abandoned storefront to open a gay bar. That space became the Zodiac, which opened in 1969. "We needed more space," Scott explained, "so we found this little honky-tonk, country and western club at Riggs Road and South Dakota Avenue. We moved into the basement apartment and operated off the owner's liquor license."[83] In 1971, the owners had the opportunity to lease the entire building, which resulted in the Third World. Yet within four short years, the Third World outgrew its space, forcing the owners to relocate to a converted warehouse space at Thirteenth and Upshur Streets, which they would christen the ClubHouse.

The ClubHouse intended to offer a positive, safe space where Black LGBT people could dance and party. As Eddy explains, "It was a place where anyone sixteen and above could go and have the house party that they couldn't have in their house, let their hair down, be themselves, and go home soaking wet."[84] Inspired by the Loft in New York City, the owners established the ClubHouse as a membership club; only members and guests accompanied by a member could party there. While membership was free, prospective members underwent an interview process and signed a code of conduct agreement, promising to abide by the establishment's rules. By the time the doors opened on Mother's Day weekend in 1975, the ClubHouse was already a success, boasting four hundred charter members. At its height, membership swelled to over four thousand. On any given weekend, more than eight hundred people lined up for the chance to party until dawn in the converted warehouse.[85]

In addition to hosting its famous parties, the ClubHouse served as a community center, sponsoring various teams and social groups. "We had our own dance team," Eddy recalls. "We had a football team, we had a basketball team, we had a soccer team, we had a karate group. Meditation groups used the ClubHouse."[86] It also became the headquarters for LGBTQ activism in Washington, hosting political rallies, conferences, and fundraisers for charitable causes. In the early years of the AIDS epidemic, the ClubHouse became an incubator for AIDs-related activism, as city and mainstream LGBTQ organizations were neglecting the Black gay community. In 1985, Scott and ClubHouse manager Rainey Cheeks launched Us Helping Us, using the ClubHouse as its base of operations. Though the ClubHouse closed in 1990, Us Helping Us reflects the legacy of the social venue's mission of advocacy, remaining one of the country's largest HIV/AIDS organizations.[87]

Sadly, as the AIDS epidemic ravaged the Black community, membership dwindled. Financial troubles and increasing competition from other large-scale nightlife venues like Tracks in Southeast Washington also beset the ClubHouse, forcing it to close after its famous Memorial Day party in 1990. Fearing the loss of the annual tradition, Welmore Cook, Theodore Kirkland, and Ernest Hopkins organized the first Black Gay and Lesbian Pride celebration the following year. Over eight hundred people attended that first Black Pride gathering at Banneker Field near Howard University. Carrying on the legacy of the Club-House, organizers developed Black Pride as a call to action, drawing attention to and raising funds for HIV and AIDS organizations serving the Black communities in the greater Washington area.[88] Today the event attracts nearly 35,000 people annually to its various activities. In addition to social events and dance parties, Black Pride includes interfaith services and a weekend conference with seminars and panels centering on the state of the Black LGBTQ community worldwide.

E PLURIBUS DUPONT

Situated approximately ten blocks north of Lafayette Square and easily accessible to popular gay-friendly establishments in Georgetown and downtown DC, Dupont Circle has always attracted a lively and eclectic mix of creative people of all socioeconomic backgrounds. Prior to World War I, it was a haven for high-society celebrities and eccentrics, including Alice Roosevelt Longworth, Alexander Graham Bell, Sinclair Lewis, and President Franklin D. Roosevelt.[89] The area also attracted Washington's Black elite, who settled in the northeast portion of Dupont Circle called Strivers' Section. Its notable residents included Frederick Douglass, the bank founder and entrepreneur James E. Storum, and the architect Calvin Brent.[90] Despite their proximity, Black and white Dupont residents maintained separate social worlds. While Blacks patronized the Fourteenth Street business corridor and the lively commercial and cultural establishments in the Shaw/U Street corridor, white residents patronized the high-end stores and shops along Connecticut Avenue, once known as the "Fifth Avenue of Washington."[91] After World War I ended, the gilded age of Dupont Circle quickly unraveled as the effects of the war, the deaths of longtime residents, and the new zoning laws that transformed Connecticut Avenue into a commercial district eroded the area's "old society belt." As World War II dawned, many of the area's lavish homes were torn down or transformed into affordable rental units for the influx of young professionals.[92]

Although Dupont Circle had attracted gay and lesbian residents since the 1930s, its reputation as a gay haven flourished following World War II. Gay residents living in the area's boarding houses adopted commercial establishments like Paramount's Steak House on Seventeenth Street as their own. Over the next decade, the Dupont Circle Fountain became an increasingly attractive alternative to Lafayette Square as surveillance in and around the downtown parks intensified. Gays found a welcoming community among the bohemians congregating in Dupont Circle, much like those in San Francisco and New York in the 1950s. By the mid-1960s, Dupont Circle anchored the city's growing countercultural movement as newly arrived hippies and transients transformed the traffic circle into an encampment. "Guitar strummers and tambourine shakes amplified the artsy scene on the Circle," writes Phil Lapadula. "Grazing in the grass and outdoor concerts became favorite pastimes."[93]

Despite its growing popularity in the late 1960s and early 1970s, Dupont Circle had initially lacked the institutional and commercial infrastructure to anchor the city's gay life. Property values in Dupont Circle declined precipitously after World War II, and the demolition of many Victorian and Queen Anne mansions during the postwar years left numerous empty lots. These values fell to record lows after the 1968 riots decimated many of the commercial buildings and residences in the area. Residents and business owners fled, making way for those "who endorsed the casual lifestyle of the 1960s [to become] renters [and] even property owners in Dupont Circle."[94] Aside from the shops along Connecticut Avenue, many establishments were "mostly Mom and Pop type shops and what would be called marginal businesses. . . . In the late 1960s and early 1970s, you were hard-pressed to get a decent meal around Dupont Circle," longtime resident and business owner David Tenney recalled in the *Washington Blade*.[95]

Dupont Circle consolidated its reputation as a gayborhood in the mid-1970s, as numerous gay institutions emerged to mobilize and foster a visible and cultural community. Building on the momentum of the 1969 Stonewall riots, political activist groups like Washington's Gay Liberation Front based their operations in Dupont Circle. The *Gay Blade* published its first issue in October 1969 and centralized its operations in a Dupont Circle rowhouse affectionately called the Community Building, which housed several radical, left-wing operations. In 1974, the gay bookstore Lambda Rising opened in the

Community Building. A year later its owner, Deacon Maccubbin, organized the first Pride Festival. Conceived as a block party outside the Community Building, the event drew nearly two thousand people. "It was probably the biggest [g]ay crowd that ever turned up for anything up until that point in the city," Maccubbin told the *Washington Post* in 1984.[96] By 1980, the Pride Festival had quadrupled in size and moved to the P Street Beach, where it stayed for over a decade. Gay commercial life also picked up in Dupont Circle as several gay discos emerged along Connecticut Avenue and P Street just south of the fountain. Mr. P's opened on P Street in March 1976, and the Fraternity House followed six months later. In 1979, Rascals became one of the first gay bars to open along Connecticut Avenue.

By the late 1970s, gentrification had taken hold in Dupont Circle. Gay and straight professionals began moving into the area and reinvesting in its properties. Throughout the 1980s, rents climbed into the four-digit range, pricing out and displacing many LGBTQ residents. Yet as the area transformed into a trendy neighborhood with cafés, bars, and boutiques lining its streets and as straight residents became more visible, Dupont Circle increasingly became a commercial and cultural hub for the city's LGBTQ community in the 1980s. Gay bar owners turned to Dupont Circle for new business opportunities after redevelopment in other DC neighborhoods forced them out. Still, residents attempted to maintain the countercultural quality of their neighborhood. In his exposé on Dupont Circle, Phil Lapadula observes, "Gays have fought on the front lines to save the historic architecture from the invasion of impersonal high-rise office buildings and fast-food restaurants."[97] Wanting to keep out large commercial chains, residents mobilized against efforts to open a McDonald's in Dupont Circle in 1983. However, the community could not fight off big business forever. Within a few years, large chains like Starbucks moved into Dupont Circle, forcing gays and lesbians to question Dupont Circle's survival as a gay enclave.

"DC IS OUR DUPONT NOW"

In a November 26, 1983, article in the *Washington Post*, Linda Wheeler chronicled the efforts of gay "urban pioneers" to transform Ridge Street, a "drug-ridden 'wasteland'" located in the heart of the Shaw/Mount Vernon neighborhood.[98] Wheeler observed that gentrifying poor inner-city neighborhoods is not new. However, the revitalization on Ridge Street reflected "the conscious effort to create an extensively gay community on that one block instead of the unusual pattern of gays within a larger neighborhood such as Dupont Circle."[99] Wheeler's story focused on thirty-two-year-old Tom Garrette, who became so enchanted by the neighborhood's Civil War era frame-and-brick townhomes that he initially overlooked the prevalence of drugs, prostitution, and violent crimes that made the neighborhood one of the most dangerous in the city. "I must have had blinders on," admitted Garrette, who bought a three-story apartment house in the area around 1980. "When I realized what was going on, I was terrified, and I wanted to have some company."[100] Over the next few years, Garrette, the self-described coordinator of Ridge Street, encouraged other gay men to move to the area, highlighting its low property values and proximity to several downtown gay bars.

With the help of gay white residents, Garrette managed to decrease the amount of drugs and crime that plagued the area. "Tom was the lone ranger," Sergeant Allen Marshall explained in the *Post* article. "He was the most persistent person about calling and the only one to call when he first moved in. If we didn't respond, he would call the chief."[101] Although Garrette told the *Post* that he wanted to maintain a "healthy mix of [g]ay, straight, [B]lack, white, and families" in the neighborhood, by 1983 the block had developed a local reputation as a gay ghetto.[102] "[Ridge Street] is a gay ghetto," openly gay resident and Metropolitan Police officer Bob Alstead explained. "I like the idea of a gay street. I have nothing against straights, but you have to depend on your neighbors, and I don't want to have to depend on neighbors who don't like my [lifestyle]. I will be coming and going in my uniform or my leathers, or out with dates, and I don't want my neighbors to think it's unusual."[103]

Wheeler's article generated much controversy, particularly among long-term Black residents who feared displacement by gay residents interested in relocating to Ridge Street. In August 1984, the *Washington Afro-American* published a story highlighting the tensions between long-term Black residents and the new gay pioneers, quoting a variety of long-term residents in such a way that they appeared to say they did not get along with their gay neighbors.[104] In a subsequent article in the September 14, 1984, issue of the *Washington Blade*, Lou Chibbaro attempted to clarify some conflicting information produced by the previous news coverage. His interviews with a combination of long-term residents and gay newcomers revealed the former's complex feelings toward their new neighbors. While most of the longtime residents seemed glad that gay residents were moving in and helping to clean up the neighborhood, many, like sixty-eight-year-old longtime resident Martha Solomon, wished that the newcomers would try "a little harder to understand the concerns of the long-term residents."[105]

The story of Tom Garrette and Ridge Street illuminates complex economic and sociopolitical dynamics that have defined the growth of Washington's gay communities over the last three decades. As soaring housing costs priced gays and lesbians out of Dupont Circle, many sought housing opportunities in adjacent up-and-coming neighborhoods. Gay men found numerous opportunities east of Dupont Circle, primarily in Logan Circle. Officially considered part of Shaw, Logan Circle divided the white residents who resided in the stately Victorian homes of Dupont Circle and Georgetown and the Black residents who lived, worshipped, and played in the Shaw neighborhood. As Black migrants from the South precipitated the expansion of Black DC westward, upper-class white residents began fleeing Logan Circle, and many stately homes in the area were subdivided into apartment buildings. The end of racial segregation saw a period of Black middle-class out-migration from Shaw. Rioting in 1968 devastated the Fourteenth Street corridor and left the area in extreme economic and physical disrepair.

Although white gay men had been moving into various parts of Shaw since the 1980s, the influx of gay residents accelerated at the turn of the millennium.[106] The area around Fourteenth Street and Logan Circle was the city's red-light district in the 1970s and 1980s, with prostitution and drug use growing rampant in the neighborhood.[107] However, the commercial corridor around Fourteenth and P Streets underwent significant revitalization. Anchored by Whole Foods and Halo, the city's first nonsmoking gay bar, the area began attracting young gay professionals who could not afford to buy in Dupont Circle.[108] To attract more residents to the area, real estate entrepreneurs and newly arrived gentrifiers began referring to the area as Dupont East—not only to draw on Dupont Circle's gay reputation but also to distance the area from Logan Circle's (and Shaw's) lingering negative reputation. However, as the area became a fashionable destination, residents began to refer to it as Logan Circle. Consequently, as renewal efforts began in areas east of Shaw around Ninth Street NW, many began using the name Logan East to dissociate the area from Shaw.

Around the same time, the U Street corridor also gained popularity with the area's LGBT community, bolstered by the arrival of popular bars like Local 16 and the gay Results gym. The arrival of the gay discotheque Town and the gay sports bar Nellie's on the corner of U and Ninth Streets NW would cement the eastern section of U Street as a new gay commercial center. Its location became particularly popular among gay residents who had settled in areas north of U Street like Columbia Heights, Mount Pleasant, and Upper Sixteenth Street. Today gay couples feel as comfortable holding hands in the U Street corridor as they do on Seventeenth Street NW. According to a former Capital Pride planning board member interviewed for this book, the area became so popular among gay residents that Capital Pride had once petitioned the city to extend the parade to Ninth and U Streets.

For many, the residential and institution dispersion of gay establishments beyond the Dupont Circle area signals some evidence of political and social progress—that LGBT residents can live openly in areas outside of the iconic gayborhood. The support of local politicians has measured this progress. Since 1992, the District of Columbia has allowed residents to enter into domestic partnerships. In 2009, Washington, DC, became the first jurisdiction in the United States below the Mason-Dixon Line to allow same-sex marriage when Mayor Adrian Fenty signed a bill passed by DC City Council.[109]

Many have also measured this progress through the increased visibility of queer communities of color in neighborhoods throughout the city. For decades, neighborhoods like Shaw, Adams Morgan, and Columbia Heights have been home to a diversity of minority queer communities that carved out spaces in the city that supported their unique needs. In the 1990s, several gay Latinx bars—such as El Faro in Adams Morgan (1991–1995), Escandalo in Dupont Circle along the P Street strip (1994–1997), and Chaos on Seventeenth Street (1998–2008)—emerged to support Washington's growing Latinx population. In recent years, local organizations have also emerged to advance the political interests of the area's LGBTQ Latinx community and preserve the group's history. The Latinx History Project, founded in 2000, archives the area's Latinx history and organizes Latinx Pride every June. Until funding issues forced its closure in 2020, Casa Ruby, a bilingual, multicultural LGBT community center in Columbia Heights, was a central anchor for the Black and Latinx transgender community.

Black gay and lesbian organizations continue to thrive in the area. Black Pride celebrations have occurred in several city neighborhoods, including downtown DC, Columbia Heights, Mount Vernon Square, and Southeast and Northeast Washington. Holding events throughout the city reflects a history of vibrant Black communities outside the iconic gayborhoods. As Everett Hamilton, then president of the DC Coalition of Black Lesbians, Bisexuals, and Gay Men, explained in a 1999 article in the *Washington Blade*, "If you talk to African Americans, you'll find that we are part of all of Washington."[110]

Many bars that once established Dupont Circle's reputation as a gay neighborhood have disappeared. In recent years, many point to the commercial and institutional changes in Dupont Circle, such as the opening of an Ann Taylor Loft on Connecticut Avenue in 2000 and the closing of Lambda Rising in 2010, as indicative of the neighborhood's disappearing salience as an iconic gayborhood. Efforts to open new bars in the area had stalled since the 1990s, when the zoning board established a moratorium on liquor licenses in the neighborhood.[111] Today gay life in Dupont Circle remains concentrated around the Seventeenth Street strip (located between P and R Streets NW), anchored by gay bars like Dupont Italian Kitchen and JR's, alongside restaurants like Annie's Paramount Steak House. Until 2017, liquor license moratorium imposed on Seventeenth Street posed challenges to maintaining the gayborhood's commercial center, as clubs and bars that once supported the local gay neighborhood continue to disappear.[112] When plans to build a baseball stadium in Southeast Washington forced the closure of gay bars on the O Street strip, a proposal surfaced to bring some of the displaced bars to Dupont Circle. However, strong community opposition stalled the proposal.[113]

Dupont Circle remains the cultural, political, and symbolic heart of Washington's LGBT community despite many institutional, demographic, and commercial changes over the last several decades. More than three-fourths of same-sex couples live outside the Dupont Circle area, according to the 2000 and 2010 Censuses, yet it is listed among the neighborhoods with the highest concentrations of same-sex households.[114] Although the popularity of the Capital Pride Festival forced it to relocate from the P Street Beach to Freedom Plaza in downtown DC, the Capital Pride Parade, which takes place the day before, moves through Dupont and Logan Circles.[115] The High Heel Race, which occurs before Halloween on Seventeenth Street, continues to attract crowds of thousands annually. The city has also recognized Dupont Circle's economic and cultural value as a popular LGBT tourist destination. In June 2010, Mayor Adrian Fenty presided over a ceremony renaming a two-block section of Seventeenth Street NW as Frank Kameny Way in honor of the veteran gay activist credited with founding the gay rights movement in Washington.[116] And at the height of the COVID pandemic, residents painted permanent rainbow crosswalks at the corner of P and Seventeenth Streets.

Indeed, like many LGBTQ geographies throughout the city, Dupont Circle has changed. However, many changes have not necessarily diminished its role as a symbolic center for gay community life. As I next show, many residents draw on their vicarious participation in cultural symbols and institutions to help preserve that reputation.

2

"J'AI DEUX AMOURS"

The Promiscuity of Community Attachments in the Postmodern City

To those who know them, William (forty-two, Latino, gay) and Nicholas (forty-two, white, gay) typify the all-American couple. Married for thirteen years, they often prefer quiet evenings playing canasta with friends at their Shaw row house to the bustle of crowded gay bars on Fourteenth. They feel as comfortable debating the Affordable Care Act with William's law associates as they do obsessing over Meghan Markle's wedding plans with Nicholas's girlfriends at Sunday brunch. They hardly exhibit any physical affection in public, yet the frequency with which they call each other "lover" and "husband" leaves no question about their mutual feelings. Their household chores mirror the sexual division of labor in heterosexual marriages: Nicholas prepares (or orders) the meals, does the laundry, and oversees the housecleaning, while William tends to the front lawn, manages the household budget, and tackles minor household repairs. Despite registering as domestic partners in Washington, DC, and obtaining a civil marriage in Connecticut, both insisted on having a "traditional" church wedding, with every detail meticulously arranged according to *Emily Post's Etiquette*. "William and I are two traditional people," Nicholas explained. "We were going to have the most traditional ceremony we possibly could." William quickly chimed in, noting how a church wedding aligned with the values under which they were both raised. "There were some barriers to having a religious ceremony," he explained, "but it was important to me because I believe that being married in the church and having your family there is a very important part of being married."

The couple resides in a charming two-bedroom row house that William purchased several years before meeting Nicholas. When searching for his first home, William had three requirements. "It had to be a house," he recalled, "because I didn't want to have to pay condo fees, it had to be in Northwest DC within a half a mile from the Metro [subway] station, and it had to be under $250,000 to qualify for the city's first-time homeowner tax abatement program." Although William knew little about the Shaw neighborhood, he was immediately attracted to the sense of community evident in its lively street culture: children playing football in the middle of the street, elderly Black women laughing and exchanging gossip on their front stoops, and men blasting go-go music from a boom box while repairing an old car in the alley or standing on the street corner laughing over shared experiences.

While William quickly acclimated to his new community, he initially struggled to make friends among his Black neighbors. "When I first moved here," he remembered, "I think my neighbors were like 'Who was this gentrifier coming in and moving into this house?' And the one on the south side didn't trust me at all, but her daughters thought I was good for the value of the neighborhood, and they convinced her that it was better to have a white boy living next to her than to have an abandoned house. And she eventually turned around. I would always talk to her every day when I came home from work. She would sit on her stoop and teach me about the neighborhood's culture. That's how I found out who used to live [in my house] and what the house was like, what they had done to the house, the year the high school was constructed—learning as much as I could about the neighborhood."

When Nicholas moved in a few years later, both were pleasantly surprised by their neighbors' positive reaction to their cohabitation.

"Our neighbors didn't bat an eye when we moved in together," Nicholas explained. They remained friendly with most of their neighbors, relying on them for gossip. "It was nothing for us to come home and have our neighbors tell us that the cable guy was here or that they signed for our package," Nicholas explained. They kept themselves abreast of significant political and economic developments involving the neighborhood, attending community meetings when they could and carefully considering the feelings of the community "elders" before voting on local issues. As self-proclaimed gentrifiers, they firmly believed in walking a tightrope between encouraging economic development in the area and protecting the interests of their neighbors, many of whom have lived on the block for decades.

Yet despite their active involvement in the neighborhood, both initially hesitated to consider themselves local community members. When I first interviewed them in 2010, both seemed conscious of living in a historically Black community. Many qualities that attracted William to the neighborhood prevented them from developing the sense of community ownership they identified with their Black neighbors. "We don't cohabit in the same way [our neighbors do]," Nicholas explained in 2010. "Like I would never sit out in front of my house, for example. . . . When [street kids] are playing on the street, I feel like this is more their neighborhood, and I feel like I don't belong in the 'street part' of the neighborhood. It makes me want to come in, close the door, and sit behind the blinds. And, please, don't hit my car with the football. But because they have totally taken over the space on the street, I feel like that is not our space." Even as Nicholas found their neighbors accepting of his relationship, he felt anxious about being too open with his sexuality on the street. "Even though [our neighbors] seem to accept us and our relationship, I often find myself tensing up when I get out of my car," he said. "When my neighbors say hello to me, I still find myself lowering my voice, keeping my hand gestures at a minimum, and making a beeline toward my house door."

When asked where they found community, both identified Dupont Circle, where they felt more comfortable participating as openly gay men. They conducted their daily and nightly rounds in Dupont Circle—from going to their favorite "gay" dry cleaners to eating at their favorite restaurants. "I love going to the [Dupont Circle] fountain on Sundays to read the *Washington Blade*," William explained. "It's a way to reconnect with my gay identity—my gay community." In the early days, the availability of Dupont and Logan Circles offered the couple little incentive to explore the available amenities in Shaw. "Perhaps most striking is our lack of dedication to our own neighborhood," Nicholas explained. "We reside in Shaw, but we don't socialize here . . . maybe because there are fewer opportunities here, but also because we are unwilling to search out these opportunities. I'm more apt to get in my car and drive to Dupont Circle to have tea on Seventeenth Street than I am to walk around the corner to have tea at Big Bear [a popular café within a five-minute walk of their house]."

Their neighborhood has changed dramatically in the decade since our initial interview. The vibrant street culture that once distinguished Shaw has largely disappeared as white gentrifiers replaced the Black elders who gave the neighborhood its flavor. Where William and Nicholas were once the only visible gay couple on the block, Nicholas now points to several houses flying rainbow flags over beautifully manicured lawns. Yet while lamenting the loss of their old neighbors, they have taken their time to embrace the new. They acknowledge their neighbors on the street, stopping in their front yards to engage in small talk. New establishments have opened in NoMa (North of Massachusetts Avenue) and along U Street, and Nicholas and William have increasingly explored them with friends. As the neighborhood transitions, both William and Nicholas feel a greater sense of ownership over the neighborhood as they transition into community old-timers. "I certainly feel a greater sense of comfort in my neighborhood than when I first moved here in 2006," Nicholas explained.

And still, despite their growing attachment to their local neighborhood, they identify strongly with Dupont Circle. "While my neighborhood is changing," Nicholas acknowledged, "and I feel more comfortable now than when I first formally moved here in 2006, I still find my urban compass directly squared at Dupont Circle, specifically Seventeenth Street." William agreed. Even as he recognizes the visible gay community in his neighborhood, he feels the most profound connection to the "imagined" LGBTQ communities in Dupont Circle. "The closest thing I could analogize [to Dupont Circle] for me personally is going to Southwest Eighth Street in Miami," William explained. "Being Cuban . . . [the neighborhood] is very Latin in general. When I want to replug into Cuban culture, I can't always head to Cuba! But I can just go to Eighth Street. In DC, you're surrounded by gayness in Dupont Circle. The Gay Pride Parade goes through there every year. The gay restaurants are still there. Although Annie's is not owned by a gay person, it's very gay. It's got a lot of gay history. When you go there, there are obviously straight people there, but they are clearly the visitors. When I go into a bar or a restaurant there—I may not know them like [I know] my friends, but we recognize each other. And I kind of feel like I'm with family."

———

William and Nicholas represent the divided community attachments motivating this chapter. Their growing attachment to Shaw has not diminished their feelings for Dupont Circle. Rather, recognizing that each neighborhood satisfies different aspects of community, William and Nicholas have developed strong attachments to both. Shaw enables them to express their identities in a *private relational order*, which privileges the domestication of their sexual identities. A private relational order neither masks nor hides their identities. Nor does it minimize the differences emanating from being a same-sex couple.[1] Living their lives openly as gay men, their identities align with the production of their neighborhood as a residential area. On the other hand, Dupont Circle allows them to "peacock" their gay identities in a *public relational order*, where they can plug into a visibly gay culture.[2] That visible gay culture affords them opportunities to engage in practices in public that they may hesitate to do in heteronormative spaces, such as publicly displaying affection, discussing sex openly, or dressing in provocative or gender-nonconforming attire.

At the same time, Nicholas's and William's experiences in Shaw illustrate the diversity of relational orders within a single urban neighborhood. Their attraction to Shaw came in part from the lively street culture of their Black neighbors. Wary of disrupting that local culture, they, along with several white LGBTQ residents discussed in this chapter, developed a queer private relational order in response to an existing public relational order, one that has persisted even as the neighborhood residentially transitions. This private relational order also reflects their confidence that they can participate elsewhere (e.g., in Dupont Circle) in a queer public relational order. These distinctions matter. Many of the respondents in this chapter do not base their sense of community in a single neighborhood. Residents may satisfy their sense of neighboring in one neighborhood while deriving their sense of institutional completeness from another. Queer communities of color may associate different elements of their identity with different areas of the city, tapping into their racial/ethnic identities in one enclave while exploring their gender and sexual identities within an iconic gay neighborhood. These practices recall the sociologist Morris Janowitz's "community of limited liability," whereby residents participate in a community provided it satisfies their needs.[3] However, rather than leaving one community to find another that is a better fit, as Janowitz suggests, residents move among several, finding resonance in different neighborhoods for specific reasons.

GAY STREET, USA

Jordan (twenty-six, white, gay) always knew he wanted to live in Washington. Before moving from Chicago in 2017, he did extensive research to find an affordable place within a gayborhood. "I asked around for months where I should move," Jordan recalled. "Everybody told me to move to Shaw. It's the place where all the gay millennials live. Everything was moving east." Although Jordan initially shared a charming townhouse on a tree-lined street near North Capitol Street with several roommates, he quickly realized that the neighborhood lacked the vibrant commercial culture he had long associated with gay neighborhoods. "Don't get me wrong," he immediately countered when I asked for an explanation. "My neighborhood is very, very queer. There are rainbow flags and equality stickers everywhere. And I have no trouble whatsoever inviting my friends over to pregame before heading out for the evening. It's just that my neighborhood is quiet—really, really quiet." Moving between his home and the bars in Dupont Circle and Shaw/U Street with his kickball team members, Jordan rationalizes his sense of attachment to these gayborhoods, noting how each offers something different. "We are beginning to see a difference in what a gay neighborhood actually is," he explains. "There are gay neighborhoods that are residential and those that are commercial."

Like William and Nicholas, Jordan does not derive community satisfaction from a single neighborhood. However, his classification of these areas as gay neighborhoods complicates our understanding of the LGBTQ geographies we associate with gay neighborhoods. Traditionally, scholars have demarcated a gay neighborhood through the presence of both public and private relational orders. The sociologist Amin Ghaziani lays out these criteria in *There Goes the Gayborhood?* For Ghaziani, gay neighborhoods are distinguished by how LGBTQ residents "set the tone" in an area through a distinct geographic focal point, a unique culture, an LGBTQ residential concentration, and a commercial area.[4] While Jordan's definition of a gay neighborhood aligns with how queer people set the tone in an area, he, like many LGBTQ people of his generation, acknowledges that setting the tone can refer to different things. In addition to the iconic gay neighborhoods with their public culture and distinctive commercial areas, there are the neighborhoods where LGBTQ residents set a tone marked by a private relational order.[5]

This expansive definition reflects the shifting realities of LGBTQ geographies in cities. While demographers recognize the diffusion of LGBTQ residents throughout the United States, the patterns they observe reveal that LGBTQ people are relocating to neighborhoods with high concentrations of LGBTQ residents. Referring to these areas as cultural archipelagos, Ghaziani draws attention to how the spatial expressions of queer life have diversified and multiplied in cities.[6] Yet while recognizing the cultural shifts in LGBTQ culture, which have also resulted in the increased diversity of LGBTQ households, our perceptions of LGBTQ neighborhoods have not evolved to accommodate the spatial forms that diverse geographies might assume.

Gayborhoods defined through a private relational order mirror the aesthetic and cultural practices of traditional residential neighborhoods. LGBTQ residents set the tone through subtle yet visible signs of identity: rainbow flags flying in front of homes, rainbow pinwheels planted in tastefully manicured lawns, and, in the politically charged climate of Washington, DC, lawn signs supporting LGBTQ candidates or various political causes. Same-sex couples pull car seats out of minivans with HRC (Human Rights Campaign) stickers on their back bumpers. Local businesses, like coffee shops, churches, and schools, may show their support with rainbow stickers on storefront windows or on school and church signs. These symbols are easily identifiable for new and aspiring residents of a community. What sold Jack (thirty-eight, white, genderqueer) and their wife Carole (thirty-six, white, lesbian) on their home in Shaw was the symbols of queer domesticity they found in the neighborhood. "I loved walking down the street to find a gay couple pushing a stroller or a butch lesbian walking their dog down the street," Jack explained. "That was the environment I grew up in, and that's how I want to raise our children."

Jack highlights the expectations of community within a private relational order. LGBTQ residents engage in the normative, mundane practices of domesticity and neighboring associated with middle-class residential communities. However, in contrast to the white gay suburban men that the sociologist Wayne Brekhus studied, these residents do not necessarily minimize their gay identities to highlight their "ordinariness."[7] On the contrary, LGBTQ community residents cultivate queer identities through successful participation within the private relational order. "These may not be spaces where a bitch can sashay down the block in heels," Viet (twenty-eight, Asian, queer) explained, "but they will invite their friends over to watch *RuPaul's Drag Race.*" Community residents in a private relational order rely on what the sociologist Japonica Brown-Saracino calls "ambient community."[8] Unlike the queer women in Brown-Saracino's Ithaca study, where the wealth of affective ties proliferates in sexually integrated communities, many respondents in my study create more-LGBTQ-specific ambient communities. Forrest (thirty-five, Black, gay) and his husband, Timothy (fifty-one, white, gay), moved to a row house near the U Street area. Within a day of moving in, he found his neighbors at his door with food. "Here come these homos," Forrest said. "These marvelous homos who welcomed us to the neighborhood with fancy casseroles and baked goods wrapped in rainbow cellophane." For Forrest, meeting gay neighbors who expressed their queerness through neighboring set the tone for presenting oneself within the community. "Let's put it this way," he explained facetiously. "I realized I would not invite them over for a sex party in our dungeon."

Nicholas never considered himself a "domestic goddess" by any stretch of the imagination. However, as the neighborhood transitioned and he found himself living between two gay couples, he realized he had to up his game. "We now have gay white men living on either side of us," he explained in a 2018 interview. "The couple to our left is what I would consider the 'A-gays.' Everything they do is perfect. They dress impeccably. Their door is perfect. They even had a perfectly decorated Christmas tree." After one winter storm, Nicholas observed something he had never encountered in all his years living in the neighborhood. "[William] and I were sitting on our couches, drinking hot cocoa, and enjoying the snow day when we began hearing shoveling outside our house. We looked out, and there they were. The A-gays were shoveling our sidewalk and walkway. We were so surprised by that. It inspired us to go out there and be part of that." Yet as Nicholas quickly pointed out, nothing would inspire him enough to pick up a shovel to clear the snow. "We brought them sugar-free cocoa," he said, chuckling. Nicholas describes how LGBTQ residents produce queer space in a private relational order. The A-gays are visible as a gay couple. Their neighbors know their story, and their front-stage presentations center on their ability to maintain an impeccably tasteful home. However, their practices of neighboring, demonstrated by generously shoveling their neighbors' walkways, are congruent with the production of space within a residential community.

Ricardo (thirty-two, Latino, gay) shared a similar experience with getting to know his neighbors when he and his partner, Layton (thirty-six, white, gay), moved into their home in Columbia Heights. When the couple initially moved into their row house, they did not know their neighbors beyond the sociable. "It wasn't like we weren't friendly with them," Ricardo explained. "We would politely acknowledge each other if we were heading off to work or working in the garden. A little small talk here and there. But I wouldn't say that we were initially buddy-buddy." However, after Ricardo and Layton found themselves on the receiving end of an antigay attack, they quickly discovered the strength of their community ties. "After we came home from the hospital," Ricardo explained, "we found our neighbors at our door, asking whether there was anything they could do. They brought us casseroles and lots of wine [Ricardo laughs] and just checked in on us."

Over time, the neighbors became good friends, as the conversations revealed shared interests that led to game nights, barbecues, and *Drag Race* viewing parties. "I hate that it took a tragedy for us to become friends," Layton shared. "But we are grateful for having these people in our lives. They have become our family."

Several respondents prefer living in a private relational order over a traditional gayborhood due to the dominance of quasi-primary ties.[9] They appreciate the closeness that comes with knowing their neighbors without exposing their sexual lives. For some, this contrasts with the experience of living in an iconic gay neighborhood, where several respondents find themselves alienated by everybody knowing something about their sexual lives. While Ethan (twenty-eight, white, gay) enjoyed living in Logan Circle, he detested the pressures of constantly living in a public relational order. "It seems like I was always on stage somehow," he explained. "I could not swing a dick without bumping into someone I slept with or someone who knew someone I slept with. It became too much." Moving to the quieter Eckington neighborhood, he could more easily separate these two worlds. "I love that I get the chance to escape," he said. "Even if I might spend a night or two with my neighbors in Dupont or on U Street, they do not have to be in my business all the time."

In gayborhoods marked by a private relational order, residents minimize explicit expressions of gender or sexuality in public areas. Numerous residents might hesitate to hold hands with their partners while walking down their neighborhood streets or to discuss their sexual practices outside the privacy of their homes. For longtime LGBT residents, that decision reflects a fear of disapproval by their former neighbors, many of whom were older adults of color. Like William and Nicholas, Charles (forty-two, white, gay) moved into his neighborhood when it was predominately Black. Although nobody questioned his sexuality when he moved there, he often worried about being too open about it. "I think there is a difference between people accepting who we are as gay people and thinking about what we do inside our homes," Charles explained. Yet as he further explained, he did not fear homophobic retribution from his neighbors. "I would never kiss another man outside my house," he continued, "not because the neighbors are disgusted about me being gay. I don't see anyone else kissing their partners on the streets. It just wouldn't seem very appropriate." Charles's comments align more with a postgay perspective[10] than with one that draws on stereotypes of Black homophobia. In not showing public affection around his neighborhood, Charles aims to minimize the differences between himself and his neighbors, as this practice did not align with the neighborhood's existing culture.

Respondents emphasize the rarity of public displays of affection (PDA) among straight couples within a private relational order. "I hardly ever notice straight people hanging out or showing a lot of PDA," Graham (thirty-eight, white, gay) explained, "even if it looks like they are on a date. So why would I want to draw attention to myself? That just seems unnecessary." LGBTQ parents also suggest that PDA does not necessarily align with the various spaces they frequent with children. Josephine (forty, Black, lesbian) feels she no longer fears being "outed" as a lesbian—but only because she feels visible as a "queer family." "The jig is up," she stated. "Anybody can look at my wife [with her masculine presentation] and our children and know that we are together." Yet it never crosses her mind to display affection to her wife in public. "I am too busy wrangling my children and my wife to worry about wanting to kiss her at a restaurant or in a park," she explained. Gerard (thirty-two, white, gay) expressed a similar feeling. "I can't think of any parents when they are out with their children, holding hands or kissing in public. That's the least of their concerns."

For some, conspicuous displays of sexuality and gender may also extend to fashion. Renée (twenty-eight, Black, queer) enjoys living in their peaceful Columbia Heights neighborhood. While they like to wear makeup and gender-inclusive fashions, they find themselves uncomfortable walking through the neighborhood in their most provocative outfits. "I am totally at ease around the people I live with,"

Renée explained. "I have no problem wearing a suit with a pair of stilettos or walking around the neighborhood with my face painted. But
I keep it conservative, you know. I don't want to feel like a float in the
parade." Renée does not feel any danger from "femming it up." However, they find more explicit expressions of gender and sexuality to be
out of place there. Instead, they take solace in knowing that they can
express their gender presentation however they want in queer-defined
spaces. "When I go full-glam, rocking a catsuit, or my low-rises and
crop tops, I won't usually walk any [farther in my neighborhood] than
from my door to the Uber." Renée uses her fashion to mark essential
distinctions between the private and public relational orders within
queer geographies. This spatial division of labor between these spaces
enables many to retain strong affective ties to multiple neighborhoods simultaneously.

THE PERSISTENCE OF QUEER PUBLICS

On a typical weekend afternoon during my fieldwork, I grabbed
my usual iced quad espresso with hazelnut from the Starbucks on P
Street NW and headed toward Logan Circle. There I spent an hour
in the sun observing the various activities taking place around the
traffic circle, which provided a contrast to the frenzied happenings at
Dupont Circle. I enjoyed the quiet, ordinary routines of Logan Circle
in springtime: homeless men sunning on park benches next to shopping bags with their worldly possessions, white gay fathers assembling
and flying kites with a phalanx of multiracial children, and groups of
mothers breastfeeding children in circles on the green. Yet of all the
activities I observed in Logan, I was most intrigued by how LGBTQ
couples used hand-holding to distinguish neighborhood boundaries.
Like clockwork, one couple after another approached Logan Circle
on 13th or P Street or Rhode Island Avenue holding hands, only to
pull apart as they crossed east and northeast through the Circle.

By the time they reached the other side of the Circle, continuing onto P Street or Vermont Avenue, they had completely separated, becoming virtually indistinguishable from any two friends sharing the sidewalk. This process seemed almost subconscious, without deliberation or interruption to their current conversations. As these couples crossed Logan Circle into Shaw, they implicitly marked a critical boundary between the public relational order of Logan Circle and Fourteenth Street and the private relational order of Shaw. No monument or physical demarcation distinguished one community from another. Yet these couples seemed to understand the symbolic boundaries that separated a community where their open displays of affection were part of the norm from one where the same behavior might come across as radical—even dangerous.

For many, iconic gay neighborhoods persist as areas that privilege nonnormative sexual and gender identities. As scholars debate the salience of iconic gay neighborhoods, many respondents continue to see these areas as spaces where LGBTQ people can perform a public relational order. In these spaces, queer people can freely display public affection with a partner and walk down the street in heels, passing a straight couple enjoying their brunch. Contrasting the experience of walking through their residential neighborhood, Renée feels empowered sashaying along Seventeenth or Fourteenth Street in gender-ambiguous clothing. "I don't care whether anyone sees me as funny in Dupont or Logan Circle, even on Ninth and U Streets [near Town, Nellie's, and Dirty Goose]. These are *my* streets, and I'm going to feel fabulous!" Respondents highlight a sense of ownership over gay areas, where they feel the freedom to express themselves in the presence of an imagined LGBTQ community. Consider William's comments about straight people in the introductory vignette. When straight people move through Dupont Circle—even if they live there—they seem more like interlopers to the space than do LGBTQ people. "I can kiss my husband on the streets [in Dupont Circle] without fear," William explained, "because I know that this space is ours."

Gay bars and nightclubs offer an important cultural symbol as safe spaces that support public displays of queer identities. Respondents often assign greater significance to the presence of gay bars than a visible LGBTQ residential concentration when defining gay neighborhoods. Samuel (twenty-six, Latino, gay) did not always feel comfortable walking with hookups or dates around Adams Morgan, an entertainment district north of Dupont Circle that privileges drunken heterosexuality. "When you walked around there at night," he explained, "you often felt surrounded by drunken sorority girls and frat boys looking for trouble." However, the opening of the gay bar Pitchers and its lesbian counterpart, A League of Her Own, in Adams Morgan offered Samuel a greater sense of comfort in being surrounded by LGBTQ people. "These days," he stated, "I feel much more comfortable holding hands or kissing someone goodnight, knowing that we won't get our heads bashed in."

Even as gay bars and institutions dwindle due to gentrification, respondents highlight the importance of gay bars in producing a queer public culture. Like Caleb (twenty-nine, Black, gay), some believe that gay neighborhoods cannot survive without gay bars. "I can easily see a gay neighborhood without gay residents. But it would be so odd to have a gay neighborhood without any [gay] bars. . . . The bars would at least bring gay people into the neighborhood." Even those who eschewed the gay bar culture identified the presence of gay bars as a nonnegotiable amenity when selecting a residential neighborhood. Timothy (thirty-one, white, gay) had recently moved into Shaw when I first interviewed him. Proudly declaring that he was "not into the bar scene," he later admitted that the presence of gay bars on U Street convinced him that the neighborhood would be a safe and welcoming environment for LGBTQ people. "You would never likely catch me in any of [the bars]," he explained, "[but] if having them here means that gay men don't have to feel afraid to walk down the street holding hands or kissing on the corner, then I would be the first out there fighting for [the bars'] right to be here."

While expressing no desire to participate in bar culture, Timothy still found personal identification with gay bars in attracting the kind of public gay culture that promotes his vision of community. Moreover, by acknowledging the role of gay bars in fostering that community, he tacitly acknowledged that the LGBTQ presence sustaining gay neighborhoods is not necessarily limited to residential concentration.

Following the Pulse tragedy, residents emphasized the necessity of protecting the spaces that fostered a gay public relational order. For many residents, the shooting signaled a call for the LGBTQ community to invest in iconic gay neighborhoods and rally around the institutions that support that community. At several vigils over the following week, those who lined up to speak at the open mic in Dupont Circle reminded the audience that they could not take their "safe spaces" for granted. "We are still in danger," one Latina speaker shouted through a malfunctioning microphone. "My generation created these spaces to lift each other up," a middle-aged white man told the crowd. "[My generation] is tired, but we are still fighting. We cannot take these spaces for granted. We need to protect the spaces that keep our community strong. And we need them now more than ever. We are still endangered by things that are out of our control." In moments of crisis, preserving the public relational order becomes a shared political project that extends residential propinquity.

DIVIDING LOYALTIES

Many attribute the freedom of living almost anywhere in Washington to the ability of accessing a queer public relational order. Across most respondents, living in or near a gay space like Dupont or Logan Circle did not figure in their residential selection. Access to work mattered more—even for Jordan, whose decision to move into Shaw gave him easy access to a Metro station. However, in many cases where respondents could not live in a gay neighborhood or near a gay public relational order, they often developed attachments to the gayborhood before they developed sentiments toward their residential area. In the twenty years he has lived in the Washington area, Scott (forty-five, white, gay) has never lived inside the city. Due to his job in the government, Scott prefers living in Virginia, which boasts a lower cost of living and allows him to own a car and access the city by the Metro. It took Scott awhile to adjust to living there. Initially, he saw his condo in Crystal City as a place to rest his head and keep his clothes. "There really wasn't much to do here when I first moved to the area," Scott remembered. "A couple of chain restaurants that closed way too early for my tastes." He often found himself hanging around Dupont Circle and the U Street bars, where many of his friends lived and where he could connect to his "gay roots." "My community is there," Scott told me. "Sometimes I love going to the Circle, grabbing a *Blade* or *Metro Weekly*, sitting near the fountain, cruising guys, and taking in the sun. Or I love grabbing a martini with my friends at the Dirty Goose and chatting about work." Scott has no intention of moving into the District. What he appreciated about accessing the gayborhood was that he could stay over at a friend's house if he needed.

Now married, Scott has developed more significant attachments to his community, where he now has a small group of gay friends to entertain at home on various nights and weekends. "I actually have grown to love my little community [in Crystal City]," Scott explained. "I realized I don't want to go to the bars all the time. I can hang out with my friends here—grab brunch or frozen yogurt, hit the gym or the movies, or just throw a barbecue and play board games." Despite his newfound appreciation for where he lives, he still feels the call to drive into DC. "A piece of me still belongs to DC," he said. "I love hanging out at the bars with my friends for happy hour or hanging out in the Circle with a good book or my husband by my side. It is part of my history. I think it will always be a part of me." Scott highlights how residents develop a shared affection for multiple areas at once. At first, Scott saw his residential community as purely functional, deriving much of his sense of community completeness from his time in Dupont Circle. Over time, as he developed a deeper appreciation for his local community, he retained his affective attachment to Dupont Circle.

From my early days conducting this research, respondents expressed a paradox. Influenced by the flurry of reports from scholars highlighting the demise of gay neighborhoods, many associated their freedom to live anywhere in Washington, DC, with the declining significance of iconic gay neighborhoods like Dupont and Logan Circles. However, when I asked how they spent their days and evenings, many of their activities revolved around these two iconic gayborhoods. A typical day for many might include grabbing coffee at their favorite Dupont Circle coffee shop, taking their dry cleaning to the cleaners on Seventeenth Street, going to their favorite gym in Logan Circle or on U Street, and spending happy hour at a favorite bar on Fourteenth Street or eating at Annie's Paramount Steak House. These activities have become so ingrained in their daily and nightly rounds that most overlook how they bifurcate their activities between multiple neighborhoods. After a rundown of what they did in Dupont or Logan Circle, I always followed up with the same statement: "For someone who says they don't need Dupont or Logan Circle, you certainly spend a lot of time there."

The responses tended to go the same way. "Hmm," Garrett (thirty-two, white, gay) said, stroking his beard for a moment. "I guess I do. I never realized how much I depended on Dupont for my sense of community." "Wow," Keegan (twenty-eight, Black, gay) said after I mentioned the time he spent in Dupont and Logan Circles. "I never really thought about it that way before." The answer particularly surprised Keegan, given how often he expressed his frustration over the whiteness of Dupont and Logan Circles during our interview. "As much as I hate to admit it," he said with a chuckle, "I do feel a strong connection to the community there. I can express myself there in a way that I can't in other parts of the city." In some sense, recognizing that "DC is our Dupont now"—to return to a phrase from the book's introduction—reflects how residents rely on multiple gay neighborhoods throughout the city to satisfy their sense of queer community.

The connections respondents developed toward iconic gay neighborhoods typifies the sociologist Albert Hunter's notion of vicarious community.[11] Hunter describes the vicarious community as the epitome of the "consciously created community." Finding themselves excluded from local organized social life, residents "symbolically transform their local world into a meaningful unit of personal identification."[12] In the absence of the local networks that emanate from shared residential ties, residents may develop vicarious attachments to the local area through their participation in local institutions,[13] through symbols tied to the identity of a place, or through the collective memory of an area.[14] Highlighting the value of place communities in the face of rapid technological change, Hunter's iteration primarily focuses on residents, who use vicarious community as a subjective process for developing meaningful ties to their residential communities, which, because of their residential status, may not be recognized by others. This chapter reveals that individuals can develop these attachments outside their residential communities.

Yet respondents do not abandon their ties to their local communities because they develop affective ties to the gayborhood. Residents exhibited attachment to their communities by participating in local politics. When I began conducting fieldwork, LGBTQ newcomers lent their support to political issues that had profound impact on their Black neighbors. "We have a responsibility to take care of our neighborhood," Neda (fifty, white, lesbian) explained about living in Shaw. "We stay updated on local initiatives, and then we discuss the issues with our neighbors to see where they stand." Neda's attachment to Shaw depended on what Brown-Saracino calls social preservation.[15] By supporting the vision of community held by the Black elders, who also felt invested, Neda could protect the culture and diverse community that attracted her and her wife, Robyn (fifties, white, lesbian), to the neighborhood in the first place.

NOT IN THIS NEIGHBORHOOD!

Keith (fifty, Black, gay) has lived in Shaw all his life. As a boy, he attended the area's local churches with his middle-class parents, who served in leadership positions for nearly half a century. When his parents died, leaving their townhouse to Keith and his two siblings, he bought out his siblings so he could stay in Shaw. As white gay residents have begun moving into the neighborhood, he has served as an unofficial middleman, welcoming newcomers and promoting the neighborhood's economic growth while also protecting the interests of the remaining old-timers, many of whom he continues to think of as family. "I ran in and out of these houses with my friends," he recalled, laughing. "Their mothers treated us all the same. If we were hungry, they fed us. If we got into trouble, they would discipline us, then tell our parents so they could have their turn. These people are my family."

Although Keith has been out since college, his sexuality remains what he calls a nonsecret. He will honestly answer questions about his sexuality when asked. He believes his neighbors know (or have some clue) about his perpetual bachelorhood, his long-term "roommates," and the occasional "bachelor" parties he throws that also attract the neighborhood's white lesbian couples. However, despite the increased gay visibility in Shaw, Keith remains reluctant to live as openly as his white gay neighbors do. When not entertaining guests in his home, Keith prefers to spend his time in gay spaces far removed from his community. When asked why he has never chosen to participate in the neighborhood's burgeoning queer culture, he shook his head and answered, "Oh no. You never shit where you eat."

Keith's succinctness reveals the complexity of public and private relational orders in a neighborhood like Shaw. While recognizing a greater sense of acceptance for LGBTQ people, Keith also knows that his long-standing relationship with the area's Black public relational order shapes the performance of his sexuality. In Shaw, for example, many Black gay men believe that the demonstrations of tolerance that many of their white LGBT counterparts enjoyed from old-timers do not apply to them. "There are a lot of old attitudes that think of homosexuality as a 'white thing,'" Trent (forty-five, Black, gay) explained. "Some of the mothers within the community have a live-and-let-live attitude for [our white residents]. However, for many [Black gay men] who grew up around here, we are so close to people here . . . there's just too much to lose to take that kind of chance." Carlos (fifty-five, multiracial, gay) echoed that statement. Although he no longer frequents the church of his youth, he maintains close ties to many "family-friends" who still worship there and remains fearful of their disapproval if his sexuality was discovered. "There are way too many eyes in this hood," he commented. "The last thing I need is somebody to step up to me and tell me my business." When he is not socializing in the privacy of his own home, he also "gay[s] it up" in a different neighborhood.

Keith, Trent, and Carlos each speak about how, as gay men, they relegate their sexual activities to different parts of the city when they are outside the privacy of their homes. These men find a sense of "home" in the Shaw community, which grew from connections made through the Black church. Scholars have thoroughly documented the paradox of being LGBT in the Black church: while Black gay men are often visible as part of the leadership within the church (as choir directors, deacons, and organists) and their sexuality might be no secret to the parishioners and the church leadership, their sexuality is rarely acknowledged or discussed in the open.[16] The centrality of the Black church to the lives of Black residents of Shaw makes it difficult for many Black gay men to completely break away from the local community, even if they no longer affiliate with a local church. However, they each maintain that the ties they have cultivated and maintained among old-timers are significant enough to protect at any cost, even if that means concealing their sexual lives from those they value and respect as extended family.

The alliances they have cultivated within their local communities often shape their local political participation. Few felt any real investment in political issues that protected or promoted a queer public community in their neighborhoods. In 2006, plans emerged for a gay bar to open in Shaw across the street from a historically Black church. As newcomers championed the bar to bring much-needed economic investment into the neighborhood, Black church leaders and their parishioners mobilized a campaign to prevent the bar from gaining the liquor license needed to open its doors.[17] In a letter to the District's Alcoholic Beverage Regulation Administration, one church leader argued that a gay bar would "undermine the moral character of the Shaw community, stain its tradition and send the wrong message to children and families." Allowing the bar to open, the letter continued, would "only promote an alternative lifestyle that runs counter to the values" of the neighborhood.[18] While the bar's opening generated passionate debate among white gay newcomers and Black old-timers, many local Black gay residents actively abstained from the discussion. Like Deirdre (forty-eight, Black, lesbian), some believed that the bar's presence undermined the Black culture that defined the community. "You won't find people with a problem about your sexuality," she warned me. "But there is a difference between living your personal life and throwing it in other people's faces." For Dierdre, the bar symbolized the neighborhood's revitalization; to many Black residents, it also signaled their displacement. Others who discussed the bar in interviews reasoned that since they would likely never patronize it anyway due to its proximity to the neighborhood, they saw no reason to, as Keith said, "put their neck out for no good reason." "Many of us just didn't see how it mattered," Julian (thirty-seven, Black, gay) explained.

Those without social and affective ties to their local communities often spoke of keeping their sexual lives private to protect their property. When I interviewed Barry (fifty-five, Black, gay), he had only recently moved to the Washington area and purchased a home in the up-and-coming NoMa neighborhood. Although he was on friendly terms with his neighbors, he kept his neighborhood footprint small due to his conservative presentation. "I get a little nervous sometimes when I get out of my car. These kids are hanging out on the street corner, and when I walk to my porch, they give me the funniest looks. I don't know whether they are looking at my car, the [professional] way I dress, or if they have figured me out, but I try not to draw attention to myself, especially—this is my home, man. The one place where a person should feel safe. And I can't have anything happening to give me pause about that, you know?" Barry viewed his home as an investment and a safe space that he did not wish to see disturbed.

While Black LBQ women did not express the same fears as their male counterparts, white queer women expressed similar anxieties over minimizing their public displays of sexuality to protect their safe space. Neda and Robyn, her partner of nearly twenty years, have never encountered any hostility from neighbors in Shaw on account of their sexuality. They never expected that their neighbors—especially the Black "mothers" who sit on their front porches and informally monitor the street during the day—would so readily accept them as a lesbian couple. In her initial encounter with a neighbor, an elderly Black woman she referred to as Miss Ella, Neda attempted to dodge questions that would reveal Robyn as her partner. "She kept asking me questions," she explained, "and I kept dancing around the fact that Robyn was my girlfriend. . . . Finally, Miss Ella just stops me. 'Baby,' she says, 'who you think you foolin'? It doesn't matter that you two's lady-friends.' [She and Robyn laugh.] Lady friends! My mouth hit the floor."

Over the years, Neda and Robyn have felt increasingly comfortable among their Black neighbors in Shaw, participating in community events and local area politics. Neither expresses affection openly to the other around their home or neighborhood, fearing they might be targeted by those who do not approve of their lifestyle. "I'm a little conscious of walking down the street and holding hands and kissing [my partner]," Robyn stated. "I don't imagine that anything would happen, but . . . I just tread lightly in this neighborhood." Part of Robyn's reticence has centered on an incident that she witnessed when they first moved in and that has since raised her suspicion about their house being a target for antiqueer violence. "I remember one time, there was—you know, on the street, our bedrooms overlook the street, and we hear everything on the street, and I remember some young people—I don't even remember who they were, but they were walking by and go "Oh, dykes." And luckily, we have not had that happen to us very often, but it was curious to me that we were like the dyke house. Like, whoever it was walking down the street knew that it was the dyke house. And so, it was like, oh, we're not fooling anybody—not that we are trying to fool anybody, but this is my home. It's not like being out in Dupont Circle or even H Street. I'm not going to risk putting my home or my family in danger."

SAME NEIGHBORHOOD, COMPETING RELATIONAL ORDERS

One crisp fall afternoon I prepared to interview Josiah (thirty-four, white, gay) in his row house along a quiet, tree-lined street in Shaw. Within seconds of pressing Play on my cell phone to record the interview, the staccato of a marching band whistle pierced the silence. A drumline soon followed, and before I could cross the living room to peek through the closed wooden blinds covering Josiah's front window, a marching band turned the corner, playing Flo Rida's "Low." Surprised by the afternoon concert, I turned back to Josiah to make sense of what was happening.

"That's just the high school marching band," Josiah shouted over the din. "They usually come through the neighborhood every afternoon rehearsing their formations."

It suddenly hit me why he chose a weekday afternoon for our interview. "Is this the reason why you wanted me here now?" I asked, peering through the window.

"Indeed, it is," he replied with a sheepish grin. "I thought you might appreciate a little slice of life from the neighborhood." I opened the blinds to watch the students practice their formations while Josiah brought over two full glasses of wine. For the next hour, we sat on the long couch in front of his window, taking in the impressive performance of the marching band. Between numbers, we managed to squeeze in bits of conversation.

"I don't know if I could take this every day," I said during one of the band's breaks.

"Well, it bothered us at first, too," Josiah answered. "Some of the new residents find it annoying, especially those with small children. But there's really nothing they can do about it. After all, the school was here first."

Josiah's answer surprised me. Throughout my observations of transitioning neighborhoods, I discovered that various newcomers openly expressed dissatisfaction with practices that seemed incongruent with their neighborhood vision. Yet his acknowledging the presence of the band and its entitlement to rehearse in the street indicates Josiah also recognized the sense of ownership former or displaced residents can express in the neighborhood. While scholars have defined a neighborhood's character through the tastes of its current residents or of the place entrepreneurs eager to shape its institutional identity, displaced or former communities also enact practices aligned with their vision of the community. Newcomers may find these practices odd, inappropriate, or illegal, and yet they are vital if members of the originating community are to preserve the place-based cultures that align with their community vision.

Even as many Black residents have found themselves priced out of the Shaw/U Street area, the neighborhood remains dominated by a Black public relational order, accomplished through the reproduction of spatial practices associated with the neighborhood's reputation as a historic Black neighborhood. Black men continue hanging out on neighborhood street corners in front of condominium buildings, gossiping around a boom box playing classical R&B music. Full bands play impromptu reggae concerts on warm summer nights, attracting pedestrians of all backgrounds who obstruct the sidewalks with lively dancing. Residents have learned to navigate the obstacle course of cars with Maryland and Virginia license plates that are triple-parked around Black churches. Residential newcomers, many of whom are white, may grumble over the impediments to their daily and nightly rounds through the neighborhood. However, many quickly discover how these practices reflect a long-standing neighborhood tradition, now preserved through the efforts of a former community. Sometimes the biggest pushback against those who challenge the practices comes from their white neighbors, many of whom reflect what Brown-Saracino refers to as social preservationists—gentrifiers who align these practices with the authentic culture of the historically Black neighborhood.[19]

Ironically, many white LGBTQ gentrifiers in Shaw view the Black public relational order as one of the neighborhood's main attractions. Several noted that the lively street culture—children playing football or jumping rope in the street—displayed the values of neighboring and community attachment that harkened back to their childhoods. "Sometimes you can't walk around the street without bumping into some kids tossing a football around," Ronan (forty-five, white, gay) revealed. "And in some way, that's comforting . . . it's such a throwback, you know. Sometimes I find myself fighting the temptation to join them [laughs]."

Yet while many LGBT respondents claimed to know the longtime Black residents quite well and found many benefits in the elderly Black women who sat on their front porches, they expressed anxiety over groups of Black men hanging out on front lawns and street corners. While they acknowledged that these men were likely doing nothing wrong, they still associated the groups of Black men with the potential of danger or violence if provoked. "I hate admitting this," Frank (thirty-eight, white, gay) confessed, "but I do find myself tensing up whenever I'm passing by . . . a lot of Black men hanging out on the street. I'm sure they are doing nothing wrong, but I don't want to draw attention to myself when I'm in that situation." "I don't see why they choose to hang out on the street," Shaw resident Christine (thirty-eight, white, lesbian) declared. "It's not something I would see myself doing; hang out in your house or backyard." By expressing concern that they are being watched and even potentially targeted by their neighbors, Frank and Christine expose their anxieties over being community outsiders in Shaw.

These anxieties around the public relational order of Black vicarious citizens reinforce the importance of white residents maintaining a private relational order. Similarly, Nicholas acknowledged that the visibility of his Black neighbors on the street makes him more hesitant to openly display flamboyant gestures that would draw attention to his sexuality. He described the terror he often experienced when groups of Black men used his parked car as a makeshift table. "So I would come home from work," Nicholas began, "and there would be a group of men, and one of them seems to live in the neighborhood. But he has a lot of friends. And it seems like whenever I was coming home from work, they would be congregating together. And if I just park my car and go out of the house to go somewhere else, sometimes they would be hanging out around my car, and they put their cups and cans down on my trunk. If they have a cookout, they will sometimes put their plates on my trunk or the roof of my car. And so, for me to get to my car, I would have to approach them, and, of course, my socialization pattern is not to speak but just to assume that people are going to read the same social cues and disperse. And I would almost not talk to them and try to get to my car. And they would get off the car, but that was very intimidating. I didn't know how to negotiate that particular circumstance, which made me uncomfortable."

Nicholas did not explain why residents might appropriate his car for this use. He has never experienced any antigay sentiments from his neighbors. However, his fears were not wholly unfounded. Nicholas has found his car windows smashed on multiple occasions. While he does not believe these incidents reflected deliberate acts of retaliation or homophobic violence against himself or his husband, he approaches these groups cautiously. Despite his disapproval, Nicholas would rather allow them to appropriate his property for their uses than ignite the kind of retribution that could jeopardize his property or his own life.

———

This chapter explores how LGBTQ Washingtonians make sense of their attachments to iconic gay neighborhoods like Dupont Circle. Community scholars often describe how residents develop attachments to a single neighborhood. When they feel their community no longer satisfies their needs, they transfer those affective attachments elsewhere. However, many respondents patch together multiple, complementary attachments to different neighborhoods to satisfy their sense of community. The notion that LGBTQ residents would substitute attachments to their local communities with those to iconic gay neighborhoods is not new. As gentrification within iconic gay neighborhoods priced out community participants, they often located in neighborhoods where they could access the institutions and culture aligned with their visions of community.[20] However, the growing spatial plurality of LGBTQ geographies results in residents satisfying their community needs through different relational orders. While LGBTQ citizens may seek community by playing out the routines and cultures of a residential community, they also rely on the public cultures of the iconic gay neighborhood. Even as iconic gay neighborhoods evolve and the material cultures that once distinguished these areas diminish, LGBTQ citizens will nevertheless draw on the memory of space and the remaining institutions to protect the areas that anchor their sense of community.

However, neighborhoods do not possess a singular character or reputation. While neighborhoods might once have distinguished themselves through both their private (residential) and their public relational orders, the revitalization of urban neighborhoods and the residential displacement of their indigenous communities have complicated that relationship. The residential transition of a neighborhood does not necessarily end its significance for former or displaced communities. As a result, while one community may define a neighborhood's character through a private relational order, another community may define that neighborhood through those who appropriate and produce meanings in public spaces. In fact, as cultural and historical preservation efforts reflect strategies for revitalizing urban neighborhoods, residues remain that allow former, displaced, and priced-out residents to continue the sociocultural practices aligned with their vision of community. These cultural residues, which I discuss in the next chapter, not only provide former or displaced communities with the continuity necessary to sustain their place within an area but also entitle them to defend the values and traditions that make that area socioculturally accessible to them.

3

PLACES IN ABEYANCE

Placemaking and the Construction of Community
in Institutional Anchors

eacon Maccubbin started Lambda Rising with several bookshelves of gay- and lesbian-themed reading material in Earthworks, his paraphernalia shop in Dupont Circle. Maccubbin,
a native of Norfolk, Virginia, and one-time Goldwater Republican,
opened Earthworks in 1971 after purchasing a failing consignment
shop with one hundred dollars he earned selling underground comix
on the streets of Georgetown.[1] "It wasn't much at the time," he remembered in a 1998 interview. "Everything in it belonged to someone else.
So I didn't own any real property."[2] Earthworks, DC's first openly gay
nonbar business, was located in a dilapidated Dupont Circle townhouse, colloquially referred to as the Community Building that housed
a diversity of leftist and antiwar political organizations in the 1970s,
including the Gay Switchboard and the *Gay Blade*, the precursor to
the *Washington Blade*.[3] Maccubbin recalled, "We used to joke that the
building was so old it would fall in if it weren't for the wiretaps holding
it together." Although he began selling *The Advocate* and a few books
of gay interest, Maccubbin never thought that he would translate his
interest into a gay and lesbian bookstore. However, visiting the Oscar
Wilde Memorial Bookstore in Greenwich Village, the world's first
gay bookstore, piqued his interest. "It had a hundred or so books, and
I thought *this was neat*. Maybe someday, somebody might be doing it
in Washington, never realizing that I would be the one to do it."[4]

Eventually, his book inventory outgrew the corner shelves in Earthworks. When a leather shop vacated its retail space across the hall in 1974, Maccubbin decided to take a chance. "I thought, *what the heck, let's try it and see what will happen*, never dreaming that you could make money off of gay books because there weren't that many of them out there."[5] Scraping together $3,000 and borrowing an additional $1,000 from Craig Howell, a local activist, Maccubbin opened Lambda Rising on June 8, 1974.[6] The 300-square-foot store initially had an inventory of 250 books. Much to the surprise of Maccubbin, the store did rather well financially, often exceeding his daily goal of $25 in sales. However, he marked the success of his store in a different way. "A couple of weeks into it, I was in the store on a Saturday afternoon. And this guy walked into the store, and he stood in the middle of the store, looked around at all the books on the shelf, and he gave a sigh that said 'Home at last.' And soon as he did that, I got this really warm feeling. It really didn't dawn on me until that moment that this was really going to touch people in a special way."[7]

Within three years, Lambda outgrew its tiny space. Maccubbin moved its operation around the corner to a storefront on S Street, with a large window that initially made patrons nervous. "In the old place," Maccubbin remembered, "they could walk up the steps into the building, and nobody knew whether they were going to one of the two stores or one of the offices upstairs. Now they are going to be coming off the sidewalk into a storefront, and everybody would know that they were going into a gay bookstore." Maccubbin refused to cover the storefront window with curtains. Within a month of reopening, many patrons who expressed concerns over the store's visibility returned. History repeated in 1984 when Maccubbin moved the store to its final location on Connecticut Avenue. "We were going from a side street to the middle of one of the busiest blocks in Washington," Maccubbin explained.[8] Although he marveled that his store would land in such a prominent location, Lambda Rising cemented its reputation as a cultural and commercial anchor for the city's gay community. When the 4,000-square-foot store reopened on November 17, 1984, Mayor Marion Barry declared it Lambda Rising Day.[9] Its new location boasted an inventory of 15,000 titles with approximately $750,000 in sales annually.[10]

Maccubbin used his businesses as outlets to support his considerable activism in leftist and LGBT-related causes. When the Gay Activist Alliance's community center closed in 1973, Earthworks and Lambda Rising became a social and civic engagement hub, offering space for organizational meetings and notice boards that posted community events, protests, and announcements from new organizations.[11] In 1975, Maccubbin drew on his fledgling business to provide financial support for Washington's first city-recognized Gay Pride Day—a block party held outside the Community Building on S Street NW.[12] In addition to creating the first gay youth support group in DC and starting the Washington Area Gay Community Council, Maccubbin remained a guiding force behind the Community Building, "turning the building into an incubator and haven for many new and struggling community groups."[13]

By the time Maccubbin and his husband/business partner, Jim Bennett, closed Lambda Rising in 2010, it had become synonymous with Dupont Circle as the center of gay life in Washington. Area residents considered going to Lambda Rising as an initiation into Washington's LGBT community. "Going to Lambda Rising was one of my rites of passage as a young gay man in Washington, DC," the local author Louis Bayard told *Metro Weekly* in 2009. "It was one of those places you could go where you felt safe to explore the gay world."[14] Tourists made the pilgrimage to Lambda Rising regardless of the nature of their Washington visit. During the 1993 LGBT March on Washington, people waited in long lines that "wrapped around the corner" to purchase something from the famous bookstore.[15] Therefore, when Maccubbin and Bennett announced their retirement in 2009, they decided to close Lambda Rising instead of selling it to someone with a potentially different vision. "We had people that wanted to buy the business and continue to run it," Maccubbin stated in a radio interview, "but they were mostly investors. They didn't share the same community connection that we had always had. And I just decided that I couldn't stomach walking down the street and seeing my store in the hands of somebody else running it a different way."[16] Lambda had such a powerful impact on the city's LGBTQ community that Maccubbin even delayed his announcement after the *Washington Blade* abruptly ceased operation in 2009. "I thought, 'We just can't do this today,'" Maccubbin explained in an interview with *Metro Weekly*. "'The double whammy would just be too much for me and everybody.' And so we postponed it for a couple of weeks to let things shake down."[17]

When he announced his retirement in a December 4 press release, Maccubbin celebrated the bookstore's closing as "mission accomplished," highlighting the availability of LGBT-themed books in mainstream bookstores. "When we set out to establish Lambda Rising in 1974, it was intended as a demonstration of the demand of gay and lesbian literature," the release read. "We thought we would encourage the writing and publishing of LGBT books, and sooner or later, other bookstores would put those books on their own shelves, and there would be less need for a specifically gay and lesbian bookstore. Today, 35 years later, nearly every bookstore carries LGBT books."[18] While many understood Maccubbin's rationale, not all agreed with his "mission accomplished" declaration. "My feeling is that that's premature," Frank Kameny, a DC activist who often incorporated Lambda in his weekly round, told *Metro Weekly*. "His mission is well advanced, but not accomplished yet. A huge amount of material that you find at Lambda Rising simply is not available anywhere else I know of. . . . I hold Deacon with a great deal of respect. He's a longtime friend. I hope maybe he'll change his mind."[19]

PLACES IN ABEYANCE

Lambda Rising closed for good in January 2010. When I arrived in Washington the following September to begin my fieldwork,

I quickly discovered that many had yet to adjust to its absence from Connecticut Avenue. Occasionally, I caught couples and small groups of men and women stopping in front of the darkened store and chatting briefly with one another before moving along to their next destination. I overheard conversations ranging from predictions of what would take Lambda's place to self-deprecating comments for forgetting that the store had been closed for a while. Craig (thirty-five, white, gay) recalled a time when his friends were looking for something to do after dinner in Dupont Circle. "We were walking toward the Circle when I suggested to them that we go into Lambda Rising for a bit and putz around the store," he explained. "Everybody was like 'Yeah, let's go,' and so we walked down there like we would any other Friday evening—only by the time we got there, we were standing in front of an empty storefront. Then it hit us: 'Shit! Lambda's gone.' And what was so funny was that at that moment, nobody remembered that it had been closed for a while then. We just looked at each other and laughed."

Virtually every respondent shared a personal "Lambda experience," where the bookstore provided the backdrop for diverse experiences— coming out, starting relationships, finding roommates, and even buying condoms on your way to a hookup. "If you wanted to know what was going on," Mark (forty-eight, white, gay) reflected, "you'd stop into Lambda on your way home from work. If you were going on a first date, you'd rendezvous in front of the bookstore. If that date didn't work out or you were feeling a little horny, you'd head to the back of Lambda to check out guys checking out porn rags." Regardless of one's relationship to the store, support for Maccubbin's retirement, or intellectual opinions about the state of brick-and-mortar LGBT bookstores, many longtime DC residents expressed sadness over the bookstore's closing. "Oh, my God!" Nicholas (introduced in chapter 2) explained. "It was like my heart being ripped out and stomped upon because I used to love browsing the bookshelves before going to dinner. You felt a sense of community with the people browsing in the bookstore with you, even as some were cruising you, which was not always welcomed. However, you felt, you felt connected."

As a gay bookstore, Lambda Rising epitomized the qualities of an *institutional anchor*—a neighborhood institution with official and unofficial amenities that satisfy many of the functions associated with a community.[20] Institutional anchors are enduring settings imbued with symbolism and collective memory where significant life events exist in space. They vary by the culture and community in question, ranging from commercial and cultural places that once operated or are currently operating within the area,[21] to public monuments and street iconography (e.g., Boystown's neighborhood streetscapes),[22] to social institutions (rituals and celebrations) that cement solidarity.[23] Specific organizations play a crucial role in grounding the material culture of a community to a particular locale, "seal[ing] the area's character and collective identity into the local imagination."[24]

These days, as cultural and historic preservation efforts have become strategies for revitalizing postindustrial cities, institutional anchors also reflect "indicators of cosmopolitanism,"[25] evoking the "authentic culture" of an ethnic or cultural enclave for the hip, moneyed urban cosmopolitans who consume them.[26] Washington's Gallery Place–Chinatown neighborhood yields very little evidence of the Asian communities that once lived there. The neighborhood has transformed into a commercial and entertainment hub that now includes the Capital One Arena, the home of the Washington Wizards, the Washington Capitals, and the Georgetown University men's basketball team. Yet the *paifang* stretching across H Street near Seventh Street and the names of businesses written in Chinese reflect institutional anchors that symbolically mark the neighborhood's history as a Chinatown. In many cases, residential newcomers may also appropriate and reinterpret these institutional anchors in ways that reflect their visions of community. In *There Goes the Gayborhood?*, the sociologist Amin Ghaziani describes how some straight newcomers develop "cultural amnesia" over the rainbow streetscapes flanking Halsted Street in Northalsted (formerly known as Boystown). Instead of seeing the rainbow pylons as commemorative markers of the city's LGBTQ communities, many reinvent these symbols as markers of the neighborhood's growing diversity.[27]

Yet former communities may also draw on these cultural residues of their community to maintain their connection to the neighborhood. Whenever needed, they reactivate these residues to align with practices and traditions aligned with their collective memory of the neighborhood. As the material culture distinguishing Connecticut Avenue as a gay neighborhood disappeared, Lambda Rising "absorbed" many of the functions associated with those lost institutions. While certain patrons viewed Lambda Rising as a traditional bookstore, those with deeper ties to the space activated alternative practices within the bookstore to align with their visions of place and community. Through traditional and insurgent forms of placemaking, Lambda became a space where LGBTQ people could temporarily reimagine their vision of Gay Dupont in its heyday. I refer to these spaces as *place abeyance signifiers*—institutional anchors that provide a sense of continuity for vicarious communities. Vicarious citizens generalize these spaces, which are emblematic of a community's values, culture, and ambiance, to the local neighborhood. Further, they ground the sense of ownership and investment they claim over a neighborhood by frequenting and participating in these spaces. Place abeyance signifiers may remain inactive until a community reclaims and recreates the spaces aligned with their collective memory of the area.

Place abeyance signifiers draw from the sociologist Verta Taylor's concept of abeyance in social movements.[28] Examining the women's movements, Taylor argues that a social movement does not disappear when its activity declines. "Rather, pockets of movement activity may continue to exist and can serve as a starting point of a new cycle of the same or a new movement at a later point in time."[29] These abeyance structures, including social movement organizations and activist networks, exist as holding patterns to be sustained until the next mobilization wave occurs. Ultimately, instead of thinking of social movements in terms of life-and-death cycles, Taylor applies her theory of abeyance to highlight how movements ebb and flow depending on available political opportunities.

Similarly, place abeyance signifiers exist as holdovers of the former community. Popular and academic scholars have generalized institutions like gay bookstores as ersatz community centers, highlighting the role of business and community leaders in elaborating their organizations into formal and informal meeting places, resource centers, and information hubs. While instructive, these arguments elide the extent to which these institutional anchors reflect consciously claimed *spaces* arising from the various socio-spatial practices initiated and reproduced by patrons as a substitute for essential community functions. As the LGBTQ institutions in Dupont Circle disappeared, Lambda Rising absorbed many placemaking functions from those institutions. It assumed the role of a gay community center, offering a bulletin board for people to learn about various events, rooms for rent, and political initiatives impacting the LGBTQ community.

As other gay-friendly establishments closed on Connecticut Avenue, bookstore patrons compensated for these losses by infusing the bookstore with the practices and traditions of places no longer available in the area. The front of the store, illuminated by the light radiating through its large, flamboyantly decorated display windows, provided a convenient rendezvous point. While waiting for friends or dates, individuals made themselves visible by perusing the tables stacked with the latest gay biographies and best-selling gay-themed novels. Some amused themselves with the random collection of souvenirs and campy gay-themed games lining the display windows. They admired shirtless men plastered on calendars sitting on the short bookshelves.

The bookstore even functioned as an alternative to cruising in bars and public places. Those who wanted to stay visible without appearing too eager could admire the collection of academic and relationship books on the floor-to-ceiling bookshelves lining the side and back walls of the front section. Others could make their way to the middle of the store to check out the bookshelves containing the rare first editions and used books or the queer-themed movies stored behind locked glass. The back of the bookstore, where a rack of erotic and pornographic magazines lined the back wall, gained a reputation for being a safe cruising location. Obscured by tall rows of bookshelves, men stood in front of the rack, perusing the magazines while checking out the men who assembled nearby. Neither sexual activity nor open sexual overtures would occur there. Men would express interest through nonverbal contact and initiate innocuous conversation. Interactions blended so seamlessly into the bookstore's normal activities that they would often go unnoticed by uninitiated visitors.

These structures exist merely as commemorative symbols of a community's history when not in use. In New York, the Stonewall Inn commemorates Greenwich Village as an iconic gay neighborhood. Throughout most of the year, the bar sits quietly on Christopher Street in a wealthy residential neighborhood, attracting patrons and tourists making their pilgrimage to what many consider the birthplace of the modern gay rights movement. Yet the Stonewall, as a place abeyance signifier, symbolizes queer ownership of the neighborhood when the LGBTQ community needs it. The streets around the Stonewall come alive during New York's annual Pride Parade as millions converge to celebrate queer history and culture publicly. In 2011, after New York passed the Marriage Equality Act, people celebrated at a public rally outside the Stonewall. Following the tragedy at the Pulse nightclub, LGBTQ citizens reclaimed the neighborhood again to mourn collectively. Between these moments of reclamation, the Stonewall offers continuity—a holding pattern that allows LGBTQ people to sustain their presence within the neighborhood. Some place abeyance signifiers are accessed by their communities regularly, while others can lie dormant for decades before their communities reclaim the space for their use.

Certain abeyance signifiers may serve as a starting point for new generations to commit themselves to the area. Even as the subcultural practices that once defined an area may fall out of vogue, new generations may reclaim these institutions by infusing new practices that could continue their presence in the area. Lafayette Square may no longer exist as a cruising area, yet it remains an enduring symbol of the LGBTQ community's relationship to the area. However, the lighting of the White House in rainbow colors back in 2015 (see chapter 1) enabled LGBTQ community members to develop a new relationship with the park, one that allowed them to appropriate the space in 2016 to mourn the tragedy at Pulse and again in 2017 to protest the new presidential administration.

In some cases, vicarious citizens may create new place abeyance signifiers to protect the production of a neighborhood's street culture. Along Dupont Circle's Seventeenth Street, one of the most popular place abeyance signifiers for the gay community was the neighborhood McDonald's. During the day, it functioned as a regular fast-food restaurant. However, in the evening it became an extension of the Seventeenth Street bar scene, especially on Friday and Saturday nights, when it was open around the clock. After the bars closed at one A.M., LGBTQ patrons reactivated the space as a makeshift after-hours nightclub, infusing the restaurant's functions with those of their nightly rounds. Patrons danced to Britney's and Lady Gaga's music while waiting to order. As couples made out in booths while sharing french fries, single men sat at tables lining the center of the restaurant, searching for a last-chance hookup on Grindr. Groups of men scarfed down McFlurries while describing sexual conquests in graphic detail. On a given evening, you could find drunken couples breaking up and reconciling in the short time it took them to finish their cheeseburgers. Drag performers, reveling in a postshow afterglow, devoured Big Macs while removing their lashes and wigs. As the street transitions into a quiet residential area after the bars close, this restaurant provides another safe space for patrons to express a queer public relational order.

Place abeyance signifiers provide continuity for former communities in the area, which, through acts of ephemeral placemaking, build the base that attracts and sustains former and displaced communities. As neighborhoods transition, the cultures and traditions of the previous communities do not necessarily disappear. Instead, these former communities may invest the functions of absent places in the remaining vestiges of that community. Some place abeyance signifiers have long existed in the area, while others have arisen through the appropriation of new institutions. As a result, place abeyance signifiers can achieve a measure of influence, especially when confronted by hostile forces. The remainder of the chapter focuses on three distinct place abeyance signifiers that shape Washington's queer landscape. Each one reflects different strategies of placemaking for gay vicarious citizens. However, they all have persisted over time due to the substantial investment LGBTQ subcultures have made in them.

CLAIMING ANNIE'S AS
A GAY ESTABLISHMENT

When George Katinas opened Paramount Steak House on Seventeenth Street NW in 1948, he had no set customer in mind. His sister Annie Kaylor, who became the bar's namesake in the early 1960s, explained in a 2006 interview that "my brother . . . wanted everyone to be treated equally." Paramount Steak House, known primarily as a beerhouse, attracted a cross section of locals who lived in the rooming houses on Seventeenth Street. "Most of the people would come into the restaurant at night to eat and have a beer. You had the Irishmen, the Greeks, Italians—all different types of nationalities around the neighborhood. And you had a lot of construction workers in the rooming houses." When Kaylor started working at Paramount Steak House in 1952, she did not realize that gay men also frequented the restaurant. "When the gays would come in," she remembered, "we wouldn't know they were gay. We just noticed that every time you turned around, we'd be filling up with guys and filling up with guys. It was a gradual thing without us even being aware of it."[30]

What initially attracted the gay men to Annie's Steak House was the treatment they received. Many of the waitresses were mothers and likely projected the kind of empathy and acceptance that many gay men did not find in their own families, given the hostile climate for homosexuals at the time.[31] "Back in the '50s, [when] the gays started coming in," recalled Kaylor, "I had these waitresses that were all mothers, and they used to treat them very nice. We didn't even know they were gay. They would just pass the word about how nice we were and how you got a good steak."[32] Neither the authenticity nor the sincerity of these performances mattered significantly. Whether sincere or cynical performances,[33] these maternal displays created a safe and tolerant environment where gay men felt they could express themselves openly. The restaurant's popularity grew as gay men realized that they could interact openly without judgment from the staff. One longtime Annie's customer recounted what he heard from other customers: "In the late '60s or early '70s, two men were sitting at a table, and [Kaylor] saw that they were holding hands under the table. . . . And she walked up to them and startled them. She said, 'You guys don't have to hold hands under the table.' She said, 'No, no—you hold those hands right up here on top of that table.'"[34]

Following the 1968 riots, many Washingtonians fled, but the gay community rallied around Annie's. "Along the [Seventeenth Street] strip, businesses had their windows broken out. . . . The gay community, they still came here," remembered Leigh Ann Hendricks, a former employee and a longtime member of Annie's community. "They continued to come here because this is where they felt comfortable. This is where they could be themselves. They said, 'Riots aren't going to keep us out. This is our place.'"[35] Insulating Annie's from the violence and subsequent economic downturn that would decimate the local economy, gays claimed Annie's as their own, anchoring the gay revitalization of Seventeenth Street around the popular restaurant.[36]

Annie's Paramount Steak House has undergone a variety of changes since the riots in 1968: the "controversial" decision to hire gay male waiters in 1974,[37] the move one block north to its permanent location at Seventeenth and Church Streets in 1985, the renovation of the restaurant and addition of an upscale bar on the second floor in 2008,[38] and the death of Annie Kaylor in 2013. The AIDS crisis also presented financial and personal challenges for the restaurant, and Kaylor expressed the personal sense of loss. "We lost a lot of customers," she remembered. "It got kind of jittery. We did lose a lot of waiters, a lot of friends . . . a lot of nice boys. It was very difficult."[39] The devastating losses sparked the restaurant to contribute to numerous causes supporting the LGBTQ community, including the Whitman-Walker Clinic, the NAMES Project, and Food and Friends.

Despite the various changes that have impacted the restaurant, its reputation as a gay institution has never wavered. The community has demonstrated loyalty to Annie's as an LGBTQ space on many occasions, including in times of unspeakable tragedy. While walking home after the Sunday night shift in August 2004, Adrien Alstad, a gay waiter at Annie's for over fifteen years, was shot and killed in a failed robbery attempt. Alstad's murder rocked the community, many of whom fondly remembered him as a brilliant yet eccentric waiter who occasionally broke into song while serving customers.[40] "He was funny, and he was brilliantly funny," a coworker remembered. "He would make his customers laugh. If you were having a bad night, he would say something to lift you up."[41] Celebrating his life, members of the community came together for a public town hall to discuss the area's rising crime and a Saturday night vigil at a local church that concluded with a candlelight march to Annie's. The memorial celebration filled the second floor of the restaurant with customers and well-wishers who capped an evening of sharing memories of Alstad by joining hands and singing along to ABBA's "Dancing Queen," his favorite song. While many who mourned Alstad knew him only in his capacity as a server, his death nevertheless engendered a profound sense of loss for the community.[42]

Most of Annie's patrons, who comprise a multigenerational, multiracial, multiethnic clientele of LGBTQ and straight regulars, eat there at least once a week. On any given night, you might find a drag queen holding pre- or postperformance court at the bar or two young gay men engaging in the awkward small talk that immediately marks their first date. A group of Black middle-aged gay men might sit in a booth laughing loudly and clinking cocktail glasses over bad dates and funny sex stories. A retiree might quietly read his paper in a front corner booth while the server brings his steak dinner and offers another Manhattan. At times, you might find yourself in a conversation with the group seated at the table next to you. Former residents of Washington make regular pilgrimages to Annie's when they come to town. Wilson (forty-five, white, gay) moved from Washington to Chicago about fifteen years ago. Whenever he returns, he always stops at Annie's to be seen. "You will always bump into someone you know there," he told me. "And some of the bartenders and waiters still recognize me from my time there, so it's great to stop in at the bar, throw back a few vodka sodas, and catch up."

Today most of Annie's servers are gay men, many of whom have worked in the restaurant for more than ten years. At a time when the foot traffic on Seventeenth Street reflects the changing demographic makeup of Dupont Circle, these servers balance creating the welcoming and inclusive environment that has served as the restaurant's ethos for the past sixty years with maintaining one of the remaining anchors of the LGBTQ community on the strip. Several servers distinguish themselves through loud and flamboyant behavior, reminiscent of—and perhaps a throwback to—the maternal, no-nonsense diner waitresses who helped shape Annie's gay reputation in its early years. It is not uncommon for the servers to call you "honey" or "Mary" while taking your order.

While the servers often refer to their most loyal customers by name, they promote camaraderie through face recognition. When dining there with my friend Vincent, I often found that any delay in acquiring a table occurred because Vincent was engaging in friendly banter with one of the waiters, many of whom knew him by name. On one occasion, a server came up almost immediately when we were seated, kissing Vincent on the cheeks as a welcome. After another brief and entertaining exchange, the server asked Vincent whether he would have his usual Long Island iced tea, which the servers replaced the second Vincent slurped the last drop. At times, Vincent introduced me as his out-of-town friend conducting research on gay neighborhoods in DC If Annie's was not too crowded, the server would engage me in small talk, asking a few questions and making a couple of jokes before taking our order. After a few visits, servers might not remember my name, but they knew my regular order: a grilled chicken and avocado sandwich, french fries, and a side of ranch dressing. Sometimes they brought over my favorite drink—a lime-rimmed glass filled with Tito's vodka accompanied by an unopened bottle of soda water—before they even said hello. Once, upon returning to DC for a visit years after finishing my initial research, I found myself surprised when a server asked me whether I would have my usual order. I dared him to remember, and without hesitation, he blurted it out.

Giggling in surprise at his extraordinary memory, I nodded my head. "I'm impressed," I told him. "With all the people who come here, I would never think you'd remember me."

Pursing his lips, the server rolled his neck and snapped his fingers. "Honey," he said, "this ain't my first time at the rodeo." The men at the table next to me joined in as we all laughed at his *Mommy Dearest* reference.

Nearly eighty years after it first opened, Annie's Paramount Steak House remains a place abeyance structure, anchoring the area's LGBTQ community. Before gay bars opened on Seventeenth Street, the restaurant provided a safe space for gay men to meet and find each other. Bars and residents have come and gone, and tables now fill with parents feeding their small children in high chairs. However, many LGBTQ people feel a strong ownership of Annie's. New generations of servers sling steaks and burgers with the campy sensibility of their forebears, and gay friends still regale each other with stories of their sexual conquests and disappointments. For many who patronize the restaurant, Annie's defines Seventeenth Street as the heart of Dupont Circle and Queer Washington. "I can't think of anything gayer than Annie's on a Saturday night or a Sunday brunch," Johnny (thirty-two, white, gay) explained. "I don't even want to think about what we would do if it disappeared tomorrow." Waving his hands and shaking his head in disbelief, he quickly followed, "Nope. I can't even."

GAY NIGHTLIFE IN ABEYANCE

Before closing in 2018, Town Discoboutique held a weekly Bear Happy Hour every Friday. Hosted by the local small business DC Bëar Crüe, the free event attracted a racially mixed crowd of gay "bears," "cubs," and chasers" of all ages.[43] However, the U Street megaclub did not hold the popular event first. Previously, Bear Happy Hour took place at Be Bar across town in the Ninth Street corridor. After Be Bar became EFN Lounge under new management, the event continued until the club closed unexpectedly in 2010 and then moved to Town. From 6 to 10 P.M., Town's main dance floor (and later the outdoor deck) was filled with as many as two hundred guests, standing in groups while splitting pitchers of beer, wolfing down free pizza, and gossiping over the events of the week. Loners leaned against walls and railings, busying themselves on their cell phones while cruising the crowd. The music, an assortment of Top 40, disco, and eighties pop hits, played in the background. Often a song's lyrics were barely audible over the conversation. Next to the table of pizzas, the stage displayed colorful t-shirts, caps, and paraphernalia bearing the DC Bëar Crüe logo for purchase.

However, by 8:30 P.M., like clockwork, the bright lights began to dim. Strobe lights radiated blue and purple beams from one end of the room to the other. The music, now predominately dance remixes of Top 40 hits, intensified, overwhelming conversations. The pizza boxes and sales items disappeared. Within minutes, the gay bears made their way out of the club, and a crowd of young, sinewy gay men entered, some arm-in-arm with impeccably dressed twenty-something women. Some sported colorful wristbands indicating their ability to purchase a drink. Others bore the black X on the back of their hands, outing them as under the legal drinking age. The new crowd began spreading throughout the club, dancing and gossiping while holding clear plastic cups containing Vodka Red Bulls and bright red Cape Cods. The remaining bears moved from the periphery into the center of the room for some dancing. Bar staff shuffled around them, setting up chairs near the stage for a drag show—a magnet for bachelorette parties. By 10 P.M., almost all the happy hour guests had departed. Entry now carried a cover charge, and the line of those waiting to get in extended halfway down the block. As I walked away from the club's pulsating beats, the purple light of the building's moniker colored the lean, athletic bodies waiting below. Town had transitioned entirely from a laid-back happy hour to a dazzling gay nightclub.

Over the last two decades, scholars worldwide have sounded the alarm over the disappearance of gay nightlife in cities, connecting the closure of gay bars and nightclubs with the decline of gayborhoods.[44] While the data justify these scholars' concerns about the future of gay nightlife,[45] their observations reveal little about the nature of LGBTQ nightlife. Yet the moment that I have jokingly referred to as "The Great Bear Exodus" reveals how gay bars and clubs have evolved as place abeyance signifiers. As the number of gay nightlife venues has decreased, many nightlife czars have welcomed displaced LGBTQ subcultures into their spaces, hosting nightly or weekly events that accommodate diverse cross sections of the LGBTQ community. As these subcultures reactivate their traditions and practices in these spaces, a gay bar or nightclub becomes a container for multiple, sometimes conflicting places that accommodate diverse participants. Different LGBTQ subgroups may activate different cultural representations and spatial practices within the same space so as to mobilize and support specific communities and subcultures, resulting in multiple place reputations arising out of a single place or space.

I refer to these as *episodic places*. Resembling what the sociologists Ryan Stillwagon and Amin Ghaziani call "queer pop-up geographies," given their temporary and transient nature,[46] episodic places differ by their regularity. Events like Show Tunes Night, Hip-Hop Thursdays, and Ladies Night attract different crowds with minimal overlap. However, the fact that these events occur weekly gives these subcultural groups a sense of ownership over the space at that moment. Over time, as a result of these attachments, gay nightlife venues developed multiple, sometimes competing places with different place reputations depending on the patrons occupying the space at any given moment.

While gay bar and nightclub spaces might be symbolic indicators of gay neighborhoods during the day, many functions as episodic places. Rising property costs within cities have forced bar and nightclub owners to develop innovative placemaking practices. Some bars and nightclubs share a building with other nightclubs, dividing a given week or day among them. Velvet Nation, one of DC's most popular LGBT nightspots in the early 2000s, usually operated on Saturday nights. Then, branded only as Nation, it hosted various concerts and parties for straight patrons during the rest of the week. In the same period, many gay respondents used to refer to 1223 Connecticut Avenue as Lizard Lounge, but that name referred only to the Sunday night party the space hosted. Throughout the week, the venue operated as a chic straight bar that patrons identified by the address of the building. Also, many nightclub owners rent the space their clubs occupy, thus owning the place and not the space. Both Town and Cobalt closed their doors after the developers that owned their respective buildings converted the properties into luxury housing.[47]

As nightlife venues develop a repertoire of episodic events, patrons become aware of the point when one form of placemaking ends and another begins. In the case of Bear Happy Hour, the changes in lighting and music signaled to patrons a transition from one form of placemaking to another. Once that transition took place, patrons did not expect to see Bear Happy Hour again until the following Friday. Whether they occur weekly or annually, episodic places develop reputations that allow participants to fall back into practices aligned with that event. Additionally, episodic places possess a supraspatial quality. If an event develops a distinct cultural repertoire, it can move from one space to another with minimal interruption. Bear Happy Hour had developed a reputation that allowed it to relocate rather seamlessly from EFN to Town despite efforts to create an alternate event once EFN closed. After Town closed, Bear Happy Hour relocated down the street to Uproar, where, on beautiful days, patrons could enjoy pizza and beer on the bar's rooftop deck overlooking U Street.

Episodic placemaking can shape one's perception of a specific venue. When interviewing respondents about their favorite bars or establishments, many qualified their answers by identifying specific nights rather than particular venues. Henry (twenty-five, Asian, gay) frequents Trade, a popular gay bar along the Fourteenth Street corridor, several times a week; however, he stopped short of naming it his favorite spot. Instead, he spoke primarily of the various parties he attends there: *RuPaul Drag Race* watch parties on Friday nights; Glam Box competitions, where competitors dress in drag using supplies from a large box; and Mass, a dance party occurring late on Saturday nights. "[These nights] feel different from the other nights [at Trade]," he commented. "Sure, I see some of the same people, but their attitude is different . . . the vibe is different. It's not the same bar I would hang out at during a happy hour or some random night."

Queer women and queer people of color also preferred a party on a particular night. For example, Mo (twenty-six, Black, lesbian) loved Ladies Night at Cobalt on Seventeenth Street, which happened every third Saturday before the club closed in 2019. "I can't [mess] with those white boys and their lame music most other nights," she explained. "But I can fuck with Ladies Night." In a town where few opportunities exist for queer women to assemble publicly, the promise of a sexual field was not the only appeal to Mo. Hip-hop music predominated on Ladies Night, which ensured a largely Black clientele. "For one night, we get to take that shit over," Mo explained, laughing. "We get sweaty on the dance floor, grinding and drinking. Most [white people] can't get down with what we're getting into."

While some respondents exhibited a distaste for certain establishments, they often made exceptions for moments when the bar enacted a place or places that aligned with their values and preferences. Regarding JR's Bar & Grill in Dupont Circle, Raoul (forty-three, Latinx, gay) had few positive things to say. "Have you ever been there on Sunday?" he asks. "It sucks. It gets so crowded. You must push your way through guys that don't care they are standing in your way, and unless you know the bartender, it can take forever to get a drink. I can only stand there for one drink unless I'm there with friends." However, when asked about his favorite gay bars in which to hang out, Raoul did not hesitate to identify JR's on Monday nights, popularly known as Showtune Nights. Raoul did not go to the bar to meet new people. What kept him returning every Monday was the energy of the crowd and the sense of camaraderie that he did not experience on other nights. "Everybody's singing and reciting lines," he explained, "and it's infectious. . . . No matter what mood I'm in when I'm there, I somehow always find myself with an arm wrapped around a stranger singing 'Oklahoma' by the end of the night [laughs]."

For those who might not otherwise frequent a bar or nightclub because of its reputation, episodic places can change one's negative perception of a space. Alim (thirty-six, Asian, gay) usually did not attend Town outside of Bear Happy Hours. "Too cliquey and judg-mental," he explained. "I always felt judged by the muscle queens and twinks who stood around in their designer clothes and expen-sive cocktails, ignoring me. I always felt invisible, like I didn't belong." However, attending Bear Happy Hour challenged his specific preju-dices about Town. "I love Bear Happy Hours because I can go there and just be me," he explained. "I don't have to worry about impressing people. I feel like everyone there is comfortable in their own skin. And if Town can create spaces that welcome regular guys like me, I realized that [Town] couldn't really be all that bad."

Some episodic places occur without changing the production of a bar's or nightclub's space. In these cases, a shift in a sexual field might transform certain nights into spontaneous episodic places. Tristan (forty, multiracial, gay) usually avoided Dirty Goose on U Street until he discovered that the space transformed into a makeshift Black bar on Sunday afternoons. The bar does not advertise itself as a "choco-late bar" on Sundays; the upstairs bar and dance floor do not open. The shift resulted from the overflow from a popular Black gay event next door. "Some of the brothers didn't like standing in line to get into the Brixton," Tristan said. "And so they began exploring U Street for places to drink and party. Some went to Nellie's (the gay sports bar across the street), while others entered Dirty Goose." Although the men stand around, drink, and enjoy some loud conversations, their practices do not deviate from what takes place there every happy hour. However, a critical mass of Black gay men shifted the sexual field enough to shape Dirty Goose's reputation on Sundays.

Gay bars have always served as place abeyance signifiers, as they require activation by the communities participating. It does not always follow that a place disappears because its space does. Places can endure the loss of space. However, places cannot exist absent the people and subcultures that breathe life into them. While scholars have rightly raised the alarm over the disappearance of LGBTQ nightlife, many LGBTQ subcultures have developed new ways to reimagine meaningful places that mobilize and foster a sense of community. By claiming ownership over the designated spaces through queer episodic placemaking, LGBTQ subcultures draw on the resilience and endurance of nightlife as an important anchor in community making. Further, the diversity of subcultures carving out places within the same space has redefined gay bars and nightclubs as collections of places that shift depending on the people who participate in the appropriation of space and the production of meaning at any given moment.

REACTIVATING THE CHILDREN'S HOUR

Of course, not all place abeyance signifiers exist through physical spaces or material culture. Certain events or rituals can also conjure up what the geographer Emma Spruce refers to as situated memory or "site-specific narratives about the individual or collective past."[48] Communities associated with these memories may draw on these narratives to reactivate places that no longer exist. Every Memorial Day, DC Black Pride transforms Washington into a Black gay mecca as thousands of Black LGBTQ people gather to celebrate Black queer culture and community. Yet for a particular generation, DC Black Pride evokes memories of the Children's Hour, an all-night party held every Memorial Day weekend at the legendary ClubHouse (chapter 1). Fondly remembered by one respondent as "the biggest, Blackest, gayest, pageantry of faggotry" in the country, the Children's Hour, so named because the Saturday night patrons called themselves the children, debuted in 1976 as a small gathering for ClubHouse staff and members. Organizers planned the event around a theme that established the attire for the event. Over time, word of mouth resulted in the annual party becoming an international affair. Black gays and lesbians from across the United States and Europe clamored to receive one of the one thousand invitations distributed each year. At its height, 1,300 guests squeezed into the converted ware-house, dancing the night away.[49] Even as AIDS took the lives of many ClubHouse patrons, the Children's Hour, according to the Club-House manager Bishop Randy Cheeks, "established Memorial Day Weekend as the most significant time on queer African-Americans' celebratory calendars."[50]

The ClubHouse closed in 1990 after hosting its final Children's Hour. The following year the first Black Pride event took place at Banneker Field. And while the Children's Hour and the ClubHouse are not often remembered, they live on in the spirit of DC Black Pride, from the lavish weekend parties to the various dialogues on issues pertinent to the Black queer community. "Though today's celebrants of [DC Black Pride] may not realize it," writes the historian John P. Olinger, "they keep the glow of Children's Hour alive."[51] More importantly, the Children's Hour challenges the deficit-based origin story that casts Black Pride as a response to white racial discrimination.[52] Although commonly viewed as a commemoration of the Stonewall riots or as a by-product of racial discrimination within the mainstream LGBT community, the country's first official Black Pride celebration emanates from its own distinct cultural and political traditions.

In 2018, twenty-eight years after the ClubHouse closed, two of its original DJs organized a ClubHouse reunion that Memorial Day weekend at the Latin club Bravo in downtown Washington. While not an official Black Pride event, the one-night-only reunion became a featured attraction. Organizers sold tickets in advance and warned people to buy early because they would not sell any tickets at the event. The event sold out three weeks after tickets went on sale. As Rayceen Pendarvis would later explain in her speech to the audience, the reunion was the only event that weekend that sold out completely. On a hot, overcast Sunday afternoon, hundreds of original ClubHouse members, along with a healthy representation of younger Black Pride participants, arrived to dance and relive the

memories of the ClubHouse and its famous Memorial Day weekend extravaganza. Organizers hoped the reunion would recapture the
magic of the original nightclub, infusing the space with elements that
transported people back to the place "that would not only rock the
body with musical vibrations but soothe the soul with spiritual vibrations as well."[53] Several original DJs returned to spin the hits of the
ClubHouse era on vinyl. Bouquets of red balloons hovered around
the dance floor—a trademark of the nightclub's festive yet simple
décor. Next to the dance floor, a makeshift store offered ClubHouse
apparel and CDs of the music from the ClubHouse era. Even a signature drink was created, reminiscent of what the coorganizer DJ
Jay Jay Tate jokingly referred to as "the Mythical ClubHouse Acid
Punch," a potent concoction that many believed contained the powerful drug, as it helped the partyers dance throughout the night. (Tate
later revealed to the audience that the secret ingredient was "pounds
and pounds of sugar.")

Yet for the organizers, the ClubHouse reunion meant a celebration of family—of the people, past and present, whose energy infused
the venue with life. "This is not just a party," Tate explained in a press
release for the 2019 reunion, "but a party with a purpose. To salute
those who have passed on, those who are still with us, and to pay
honor to the ClubHouse."[54] Above the DJ's booth, a large screen displayed photos from the ClubHouse era. As I stood by the dance floor
throughout the evening, I overheard groups of members identify various faces as they appeared. At certain moments, the party evoked the
feeling of a family reunion, where long-distant relatives reunite as if
little time has passed. While I stood in line for a drink, a short Black
woman in front of me was grooving to the pulsating house rhythms.
As she approached the bar, someone to the left of us shrieked, "Alma."
As the woman turned her head, she shrieked at a round Black woman
dancing in her direction with her arms outstretched. They danced
toward one another, and when they finally embraced, they laughed
joyously. As the women walked back to the line, their arms over each

other's shoulders, they tried to figure out the last time they were together. I must admit I found the reunion so touching that it took me a minute to realize both women had cut in line in front of me!

Throughout the evening, members demonstrated their deep feelings for the ClubHouse. During a brief presentation, Tate asked the crowd, "How many people still have their membership cards?" The crowd on the dance floor cheered as many raised their hands. A few raised their old membership cards, brandishing them like badges of honor. While loitering by the dance floor (or taking a respite), several enthusiastically shared favorite memories from their days at the ClubHouse. A tall, bald, dark-skinned gentleman wearing an African-print tank top and cargo shorts approached and stood next to me for a few minutes before he leaned in and shouted in my ear, "You don't look like you could have been at the ClubHouse." I turned around, smiled, and shook my head. He smiled back, his head glistening with sweat from being on the dance floor.

The man introduced himself as Dwayne. He was a lawyer in his early sixties, although he looked much younger. He explained that he had been a ClubHouse member since the early 1980s when he lived in Washington. Now living in Atlanta, he explained that the moment he heard about the reunion, he had to return to relive the experience. We chatted for a few minutes before a photo of a familiar face flashed on the screen. Pointing at the photo, Dwayne identified the man as Andre, an ex-boyfriend; they had partied at the ClubHouse for years before the latter succumbed to AIDS in the late 1980s. "Andre would have loved this," he said, his eyes watering with tears. "We would come on Saturday nights at about eleven P.M. and stay on the dance floor until they kicked us out." When the photo changed over, Dwayne shook it off the memory and, flashing a smile, invited me to dance. We danced to a couple of songs when a remix of Diana Ross's "The Boss" began to play. Seemingly transported back in time, Dwayne closed his eyes, threw his head back, and pumped his hands in the air. "Oh, God! This takes me back!" he shouted through the music. "I haven't danced this much in a long time. Y'all young people have no idea what it's like to dance to really great music."

Sharing site-specific memories reflects an essential strategy for reactivating the ClubHouse. Exploring dyke bar commemoration, the sociologist Japonica Brown-Saracino describes how commemorators mourned their lost bars by discursively situating them geographically and temporally, highlighting aesthetic and demographic attributes. Drawing on public memories of a "situated bar" not only commemorates the past but also works to build present communities by sharing testimony and bearing witness while "jumpstart[ing the] future through . . . future events"[55] that bind old-timers and newcomers together through new experiences. Part of the presentation at the ClubHouse reunion included testimony of the "typical experience" of being a ClubHouse member. Before introducing Rayceen Pendarvis, a local legend, DJ Jay Jay acknowledged to the crowd the difficulties of sharing just one experience. "I know everybody has a memory about the ClubHouse. But I had to pick one person to represent all y'all." Still, when he announced Pendarvis, the crowd cheered wildly. Although Pendarvis's recollections may not reflect *every* experience, the enthusiastic reception from the audience revealed that at least part of her portrait would resonate with audience members.

Rocking a black turban and holding a hand fan, Pendarvis painted a vivid image that brought the diverse generations together. After throwing around a few Shady Pines jokes, referring to the TV show *Golden Girls*, she testified like a Black preacher on a Sunday morning. She recalled how she managed to get into the club without getting a membership, which the audience warmly received. "One, before I became a member, I had to stand outside and whisper, 'Do you have a membership? Can I get with you?' And they would ask, 'How many are with you?' And I would say, 'Six.'" The audience responded with laughter and applause. "And we would get in, and we would break them down in either two by twos or three by threes." She then described how she paid that kindness forward once she finally became a member. "Then once I got my membership, *baby*," she continued. The audience members howled, almost as if they knew what was coming next. "I was running in and out every thirty minutes, bringing in a group of girls." The crowd went wild, snapping their fingers in the air in agreement while yelling back phrases like "Right on!"

Pendarvis continued, describing how older people warned newcomers against drinking the club's famous punch. "They would say, 'Bitch! Don't drink this punch. Cuz if you drink this punch, you will jump over the balcony.'" Then, pointing to her hip, she joked about getting a new one and explaining to the doctor what she did to merit one. Responding to her doctor's inquiry, she joked about how she used to jump off the balcony, onto the speaker, and into a split. "That's why I got a new hip today," she screamed to the thrill of the audience. Pendarvis explained the resourcefulness of the patrons when infrastructure problems arose. "Sometimes when the toilets would overflow," she said to more audience approval, "and the water would run out, the girls would stomp and kick and sometimes *sliiiide* across the floor in water." By this point, the crowd went wild with laughter and applause. "And then, at a certain time, here come the Cha Cha Girls and the Hustlettes. When they would hear 'The Hustle' record or 'Cherchez La Femme,' the girls would hit the floor, with their twirl skirts and their cha cha heels, and we would hustle across the floor."

Calling on the participants to join hands, Pendarvis explained the blessing of making it through moments of adversity to celebrate that afternoon. "We made it through," she explained as the audience shouted, "Yes!" in response. "We made it through the marches and the riots and the epidemic of AIDS, and we are still here."

"Yes!" the audience shouted back.

"Some of us didn't make it over," Pendarvis continued. "So we think about it and lift their hands high while we think about our friends." As she listed the names of ClubHouse members and staff, the audience shouted, "Yes!" in affirmation. Drawing on these experiences, she urged the audience not to let the losses of so many within the community be in vain. Concluding her speech by stating that the ClubHouse reunion should take place every year, she incorporated newcomers who, by their presence, would be able to carry the history of the ClubHouse into the next generation.

As speakers remembered their time at the ClubHouse, they provided a road map for reliving the experience that evening. In his brief comments, Bishop Randy Cheeks reminded the crowd that the Club-House was always first and foremost about music and dancing. "I will be out on the dance floor," he stated. "I hope I will meet some of you *on* the dance floor. And as we used to say at the club, if you can't dance, get on up off the floor." Many of the audience members finished the motto alongside Cheeks and cheered wildly. Indirectly, Cheeks also explained a critical rule of the ClubHouse that distinguished it from most LGBTQ nightlife venues. Loitering on a dance floor might be expected in many spaces but not at the ClubHouse. Similarly, John Eddy, one of the founders, indirectly described how ClubHouse patrons conducted themselves. "One of the most important things for me," he explained, "was that in the fifteen years that it was open, we entertained thousands of guests from around the world, and we never, *never* had to call the police." The audience cheered. "Fifteen years! Because the ClubHouse members knew that I would snatch that *damned* membership card if any of them started any problems." As in a call-and-response, the audience cheered, shouting "Amen!" Once again, Eddy reminded people that misbehaving compromises the reactivation of the ClubHouse as a place.

Many people, including Eddy, believed that the ClubHouse reunion should occur every year. In 2019, organizers planned a second reunion during Memorial Day weekend. It proved more successful than the one held the previous year, with tickets selling out immediately. While the COVID pandemic prevented a three-peat, many who participated hope that the tradition will continue once the pandemic lifts. Even respondents who never experienced the original Club-House hoped the event would return. When DeVante (thirty-eight,

Black, gay) was researching events for Black Pride Festival in 2023, he hoped the event would continue. He hoped that Black Pride would pick up the mantel and incorporate it somehow into their programming. "That shit would be so cool," he explained. "Black queer people need to know about how this all started. We have such an awesome history that nobody ever tells us about. And that's really fucked up."

———

Neighborhoods accumulate the cultures of the communities that once occupied them.[56] As these neighborhoods transition, newcomers may incorporate the cultural residues of a former community into the collective representations of the new. This process of incorporation has become more apparent in recent years as the evolution of cities from sites of cultural production to sites of cultural consumption results in the preservation of a neighborhood's history and culture as a strategy of neighborhood revitalization. Yet the very same institutions that place entrepreneurs conserve in order to rebrand urban neighborhoods may also anchor community among former, displaced, or priced-out residents. When needed, these communities may reactivate previous neighborhood representations by appropriating community anchors and reproducing their meaning through ephemeral placemaking. These acts of placemaking, from eating dinner at a local restaurant to experiencing community through gay nightlife, reflect meaningful ways by which vicarious citizens can locate themselves within a community and make meaningful connections to the places and cultures that satisfy their sense of self.

These representations do not always exist every day, and they are not necessarily apparent to or desired by residents. Instead, they lie in abeyance or in a holding pattern, available for indigenous populations to mobilize as necessary to foster and maintain their connection to the community. Like with social movements, these representations exist within abeyance structures—specific spaces or places within a neighborhood—that provide a sense of continuity for vicarious citizens who retain their relationship to the neighborhood without residential ties. Place abeyance signifiers operate as institutional anchors for nonresidential communities; they are enduring settings imbued with symbolism and collective memory that ground the material culture within a particular locale. As newcomers adopt these symbols for their use, place abeyance signifiers can often contain multiple contradictory meanings. Yet they also represent the territorial bases that enable vicarious citizens to pursue community interests and exercise their rights as local stakeholders. These place abeyance signifiers can emerge from the unlikeliest places, and yet they operate as important reminders of a community's presence within the local area.

4

HETEROS, BEWARE!

Monitoring and Preserving Queer Culture
Through Normative Vicarious Claims

On the last Tuesday of October, thousands of people crowd the sidewalks of Seventeenth Street to cheer a crowd of drag queens running two blocks in six-inch stilettos. The annual High Heel Race lasts only a few short minutes, but patrons arrive up to two hours in advance to enjoy the makeshift fashion show. In that brief time, the street is transformed into a catwalk as the drag racers showed off their elaborate costumes to adoring fans, posing for photos and exchanging barbs "in character" with audience members. Sometimes the racers treat the audience to an elaborately choreographed skit, often replaying famous scenes from movies and television. One year two racers recreated the famous catfight scene between Joan Collins and Linda Evans from the hit 1980s soap *Dynasty*. Another year several participants dressed as "sexy" fruit warmed up for the race by running away from Miss Pac-Man. In 2018, a group processed solemnly up and down the street in ankle-length red dresses, white caps, and heavy boots in homage to *The Handmaid's Tale*.

One year, during the ersatz fashion show, I was standing next to a white gay couple in their early twenties who were holding hands and playfully kissing each other on the lips. A tall, scruffy white man in his late thirties approached them with a little girl on his shoulders. Tapping one of the men on his shoulder, he asked the couple if they "wouldn't mind" refraining from kissing each other on the street. "There are children present," the man said.

The gay couple looked at each other in surprise. "So what?" one of the gay men replied. "What's the big deal if she sees us making out? This is, after all, a gay neighborhood."

"Well," the father replied, "this is our neighborhood, too. And there is a time and a place for you to do that. Certain things are better kept off our streets and away from our children."

"You've got to be fucking kidding me!" the other gay man yelled back. "You know where you are, right? If you're so worried about your daughter, then why the hell are you at a drag race?"

As the exchange escalated, a tall, slender blonde who appeared to be the man's wife jumped in. "We're here to support this community and expose our daughter to a little diversity. You should be lucky that we're here to support you, that this event has the support of so many of us in Dupont."

Her statement caught the attention of others in the vicinity. "Nobody gives a shit whether you support us or not," the second gay man spat back. "This is our space, honey, and if you don't like what we're doing, you shouldn't be here."

A second straight couple jumped into the argument, supporting the parents' position. A few gay men jumped in to defend the gay couple, and before long, the back-and-forth intensified into a full-on screaming match.

"Nobody says that you don't have the right to be here!" the second woman yelled at the group of gay men. "But this space belongs to all of us."

"We're just asking you to show some consideration," the father replied.

"You breeders think you can take over everything!" one of the gay men shouted.

The exchange intensified. The original gay couple began making out more aggressively, and the crowd cheered. Another gay couple also started kissing. Then two women followed, which elicited more cheers from the crowd. Before long, queer kissers had surrounded the two straight couples. Exasperated and defeated, the straight couples looked at each other before pushing their way through the crowd. Their departure intensified the cheers from the spectators.

In this example, all parties exercised rights to space based on competing visions of Dupont Circle as a gay neighborhood. As residents of Dupont Circle, the straight couple's participation in the High Heel Race epitomizes the diversity consumption that has become commonplace in gay neighborhoods as straight residents select into them. Their presence in the neighborhood reflects the successful assimilation of gay neighborhoods and gay culture into the mainstream, which has shifted practices of gay sexuality often found in iconic gay neighborhoods to a private relational order. However, their acceptance of gay culture reflects the limits of what the sociologists Adriana Brodyn and Amin Ghaziani refer to as performative progressiveness, the cooccurrence of progressive attitudes and homonegative behavior.[1] While both straight couples reveled in drag performances, which always existed within the LGBTQ community as subversive and countercultural before the success of *RuPaul's Drag Race*, the public displays of affection exhibited by the gay men went too far. Policing behavior antithetical to their perception of gay neighborhoods, both straight couples relied on their residential ties to monitor and prevent behavior antithetical to their vision of local community while underscoring the importance of their support as straight residents of gay cultural traditions like Pride and the High Heel Race.

Conversely, the gay couple drew on symbolic ownership of space to make a *normative vicarious claim*, predicated not on residential ties (past or present) but on shared identity and beliefs shaping their ownership over Dupont Circle and the High Heel Race as LGBTQ places. Normative vicarious claims draw on the routines and practices of everyday life to monitor and reinforce norms consistent with an area's perceived local character. While often fleeting, these everyday practices collectively represent vital strategies for protecting the culture and practices that attract vicarious citizens to and sustain LGBTQ communities in these areas. Regardless of the demographic and cultural changes, LGBTQ citizens still imagine iconic gay neighborhoods as spaces that privilege public expressions of queer life. Consequently, they defend their right to publicly express affection, which for many LGBTQ citizens represents the primary reason for gay neighborhoods in the first place. This chapter explores how vicarious citizens engage in place reactivation to enact normative claims to community.

"WHO ARE YOU CALLING A FAGGOT?"

In his landmark study on the creation of the Castro, Manuel Castells argues how creating a gay community in the area was indistinguishable from creating a gay movement in San Francisco.[2] Gay settlers deliberately constructed gay neighborhoods to facilitate political mobilization, to provide physical protection, and to create a distinct culture that would enable them to live openly gay lives.[3] While scholars have since challenged those claims,[4] many LGBTQ citizens maintain that gay neighborhoods represent the culmination of queer political and spatial capital resulting from a history of queer occupation in the area. At minimum, that includes an understanding of gay neighborhoods as safe spaces where LGBTQ citizens can openly express their sexuality without fear of homophobic retribution. This expectation of safety has become so closely associated with the definition of gay neighborhoods that many LGBTQ residents and vicarious citizens tend to take their sexuality for granted in gay areas. In his study of the changing composition of contemporary gayborhoods in American cities, Ghaziani finds that many of his respondents believed their sexuality mattered less after living or having lived in gay neighborhoods. "I have no consciousness of even being gay when I'm here," one of

Ghaziani's subjects said about living in a gay neighborhood. "It's just so easy and normal that I never really have to worry about it."[5]

Unfortunately, the sense of confidence that allows LGBTQ residents to take their sexuality for granted in gay neighborhoods often does not apply to the rest of the city. The opening of a gay bar or the influx of gay residents in a neighborhood can quickly establish a neighborhood's reputation as a queer-friendly space, while a violent incident can just as quickly shatter perceptions about the relative safety of LGBTQ citizens. While I was collecting data in Washington, DC, many residents expressed concerns about the rise in anti-LGBT violence in the city. In November 2010, a former videographer for the *Washington Blade* was attacked after hugging a male friend goodbye near the Walter E. Washington Convention Center, located in Mount Vernon Square a few blocks south of the Shaw neighborhood.[6] "That incident totally shocked me," Julian (introduced in chapter 2) recalled during our interview. "I thought that Mount Vernon was a decent, safe area. When I walk[ed] home from the bars [on Seventeenth Street] or Nellie's, I never had problems [if] I was walking [through Mount Vernon Square] with some guy. Since that [beating] happened, I now take a taxi."

These incidents become particularly acute when they occur near gay institutional anchors, as these anchors often signify the changing cultural landscape when they appear outside iconic gay areas. Recalling an incident when a gay man was shot near Nellie's, a gay sports bar on U Street NW, Raoul (introduced in chapter 3) reflected on how the shooting shook his confidence. "So there was a shooting," he began. "It was just a gay guy who was seen kissing someone, and I think it was right there near Vermont Avenue, like near Nellie's and all that . . . the [area] between Nellie's and Logan Circle . . . it's that neighborhood that sort of looks gay, but it's not quite there yet. So, all of a sudden, I was like 'Oh! I'm in this place where I can frolic and skip and sing 'Somewhere Over the Rainbow.' Not really. So there have been these little wake-up calls." This incident made Raoul more careful about drawing too much attention to himself as a gay man when walking home from the bars near this area.

As gay bars have become increasingly popular destinations for straight patrons, some LGBTQ respondents have identified feeling discomfort in self-described gay venues, especially outside of iconic gay neighborhoods. When I began my research in 2010, I encountered Larry (24, white, gay) and his husband Peter (27, white, gay), who both recalled an experience when they patronized a gay bar that had recently opened in Adams Morgan, a popular entertainment area that attracts young straight crowds on the weekends. They were initially reluctant to go to the bar; however, they felt pressure from various gay friends to give it a chance. "Our friends kept asking us, 'Are we going to this place?'" Peter explained. "We were very reluctant to go. It was in Adams Morgan! That doesn't make any sense! We don't go to Adams Morgan! It's just a bunch of frat guys and sorority girls!" Within minutes of being there, Larry and Peter realized that the bar did not match their expectations of a gay bar. "We barely finished one drink before we realized that we had to leave," Larry recalled. "It was lousy—a lousy gay bar that was filled with lousy straight people." When prompted why they left so quickly after arriving at the bar, the couple stated that, despite the bar's self-identification as a gay bar, the critical mass of straight people made them feel less comfortable being open in the space as a gay couple. "I was worried that we would be putting a target on our backs," Peter explained. "I didn't want to do anything that would get us followed out into the street and attacked by some drunken frat boys trying to prove some point."

Larry and Peter's experience illuminates how institutions cannot always be disconnected from a neighborhood's (or area's) reputation. Although gay bars and establishments have traditionally distinguished an area as a safe space for LGBTQ denizens, this gay bar could not necessarily overcome the area's reputation as being inhospitable and even dangerous—at least not enough to convince Peter and Larry that being open with their sexuality would be accepted as

the norm there. Respondents are also cautious about being too conspicuously queer in areas that attract many tourists. In these spaces,
the threats to one's safety arise out of a fear of the unknown. The
National Mall, for example, has a mixed reputation among LGBTQ
residents in Washington. Sometimes LGBTQ communities claim
the National Mall to mobilize the community. During the Capital
Pride Festival on Pennsylvania Avenue, LGBTQ participants confidently walk around the Mall during the day, holding hands with their
partners and wearing outfits that conspicuously mark them as queer.
Capital Pride participants can enact normative claims aligned with
queer placemaking in these moments.

The need to reactivate Pennsylvania Avenue into a queer space
was on full display the day after the Pulse nightclub tragedy. As news
trickled in about the shooting, many worried whether celebrating at
the Pride Festival would be appropriate. Others worried that being
in such a large gathering of LGBTQ citizens in a prominent public space—within a mile of the Capitol—would put their safety at
risk. "For a moment," Carter (thirty, white, gay) explained, "I felt that
I had a target on my back. If you weren't safe in one of the few places
where you are supposed to be safe, where can you be?" Despite the
anxiety many felt about participating, others realized the importance
of going. "I thought going to the [Capital Pride Festival] was the only
way to go," Joya (twenty-six, white, queer) said. "It didn't seem right
that we would celebrate after such a tragic event. But I realized that,
at moments like this, I wanted to be with my community." For Mason
(thirty-five, Black, gay), celebrating constituted a political act that
had to continue. "All I wanted to do was dance," he explained, "and
show the haters that they will not push me into the shadows."

That Capital Pride Festival became the most attended in Capital
Pride history. Although tinged with sadness, anger, and confusion, the
festival did not lose its celebratory tone. When I arrived at one P.M.,
people flooded Pennsylvania Avenue, waiting to enter the festival.
People drank and played games at the various booths. They danced

and cheered the performers taking the main stage while sharing their excitement for the festival's major attractions: Meghan Trainor and Bob the Drag Queen, the season eight winner on *RuPaul's Drag Race*. Yet throughout the day, people also checked their phones for updates, sharing any information they received with those around them. Queer youths with rainbow-tinted hair and gender-bending costumes walked along the hot, humid streets wearing signs that offered "free hugs" to anyone who approached them. As performers took the main stage throughout the day, organizers called for moments of silence for the victims. Headliners offered encouragement, reminding the community that refusal to hide in the face of tragedy was the greatest revenge. "We know you were all scared and shit," Bob the Drag Queen teased. "But you are here today, and we are winning. . . . Don't let anybody scare you because if you don't fucking go out, they won." For the thousands of attendees, continuing the tradition represented a normative claim. When the celebration took place, their presence offered a clear reminder of the power and resilience of the city's LGBTQ community.

The association of the Mall with Capital Pride has empowered some to make claims to space, elaborating those expressions of safety and queerness ascribed to that time to other times of the year. For example, Ravi (thirty-three, Asian, gay) found the city's monuments a fun romantic destination, especially at night. "I love taking a date to see the monuments at night," he explained. "You must know where to go and how to steal moments—like kissing a guy behind the Jefferson Memorial or finding a secluded bench where you can see the monuments from afar. It can be fun if you do it right." Others, like Brian (thirty-eight, white, gay), felt too conspicuous when they expressed affection openly in these areas, vulnerable to the judgment of conservative tourists. "You never know how they are going to react if you are holding hands with somebody there . . . and when it's dark? Forget about it." Brian remembered the unwanted attention he and his partner received from disapproving tourists when he "unconsciously" grabbed a boyfriend's hand while walking along the Reflecting Pool at the Lincoln Memorial one afternoon. "We got so many looks that day. People were turning heads, pointing, and muttering to each other. I even thought I heard someone mutter 'faggots' under his breath when he passed us." Although Brian admitted he wasn't sure about hearing the slur and nobody specifically confronted them, his perception of the National Mall as a conservative place made him feel conspicuously out of place as part of a gay couple.

The comfort of being openly affectionate in gay neighborhoods gives queer vicarious citizens a particular claim to the space that they are willing to protect. One night while walking arm-in-arm with a date, Stanley (thirty-three, white, gay) was approached by a man who shoulder checked him as he walked past, mumbling a homophobic epithet at the couple. While Stanley usually ignored these homophobic slights in other areas, he refused to let this happen to him on Seventeenth Street. "I walked up to the man's face," he explained, "and I yelled, 'Who are you calling a faggot?'" Surprised by Stanley's aggressive response, the man initially snapped back at Stanley and his date. However, realizing Stanley was attracting attention from the crowds in nearby bars and restaurants, the man slowly began backing down. "I yelled loud enough where people around us knew what was going on," Stanley recalled. "If we got ourselves into a situation that we couldn't handle, I felt—at least I hoped—that somebody would've had our backs." At this moment, Stanley articulated a normative claim to space, believing that he could activate an imagined community that would understand and come to his defense against a homophobic threat.

Those protective feelings can also apply to gay neighborhoods that have lost their institutional cachet. In an article in the *Huffington Post*, Michelangelo Signorile, an author and LGBT activist, described an incident in New York's Chelsea neighborhood when a man called him and his partner "disgusting" for kissing on the street. After his partner pointed at the man, Signorile and his partner started chasing him down the street, calling him a homophobe so everyone could hear them. "As I approached the man," he writes, "he darted into the street, swerving around taxis while screaming 'faggots,' then scampered back onto the sidewalk, then into the street again, trying to get away from us." Eventually, Signorile and his partner caught up with the man, pointing at him and calling him a homophobe for others to see. "He was cornered, and I got into his face and asked him why he was running away like a pathetic coward and who he was calling a 'faggot.' Clearly stunned, he stammered a bit and then mumbled, 'Um, I, um . . . I meant me . . . I was calling myself a faggot.'"[7]

Challenging acts of homophobia seems almost natural to many in iconic gay neighborhoods. "I don't even think about it, really," Carey (thirty-six, white, gay) explained. "Seventeenth Street belongs to [LGBTQ people], so when I see a problem, I have no problem saying something." This sense of fearlessness extends to moments when important anchors face external threats. As Dupont Circle became the epicenter of collective mourning after Pulse, news of anti-LGBTQ vandalism circulated on social media. Vandals set fire to the rainbow flag flying outside Bourbon, a restaurant in nearby Adams Morgan. And at Thaiphoon, a popular restaurant in Dupont Circle, vandals left a spray-painted message—"Down with the Gay Agenda"—on the concrete outside the entrance. The next evening a new LGBTQ flag flew over Bourbon's sign, and within hours after the graffiti appeared in Dupont Circle, someone had spray-painted "Gun" over "Gay," pivoting attention to the country's gun control laws (figure 4.1). Although these acts raised residents' concerns about safety in both areas, those fears did not last for long.

Correcting the message outside Thaiphoon highlights the importance of creating place abeyance signifiers that center on LGBTQ history and culture. In the absence of permanent symbols, newcomers whose values do not align with the gayborhood's normative culture can quickly appropriate space and create alternate meanings. Many respond to these attacks through various practices that reinforce local culture; however, creating permanent symbols that act as place abeyance signifiers is equally important for many others. While LGBTQ

FIGURE 4.1 Acts of LGBTQ vandalism following the Pulse tragedy.
Here the message "Down with the Gay Agenda" spray-painted outside the
popular Dupont Circle restaurant Thaiphoon was quickly corrected to reflect the
normative culture in Dupont Circle. In addition, a rainbow flag outside
Bourbon Restaurant in Adams Morgan was burned.

Photo by author.

cultural and commercial institutions serve as symbols of queer space,
many within the community hope to provide more conspicuous displays of LGBTQ history and culture, which can also empower others
to protect the spaces vital to open sexual and gender expressions.

STREAKING RAINBOWS ALONG
FRANK KAMENY WAY

Frank Kameny Way is a two-block stretch of Seventeenth Street
between Q and R Streets NW.[8] Mayor Adrian Fenty dedicated the

corridor on June 10, 2010, after the Dupont Circle Advisory Neighborhood Commission (ANC) unanimously voted to honor the gay rights activist. Marked by green street signs under the "official" street signs, Frank Kameny Way represents the city's first official monument to the iconic gay neighborhood. And while celebrated, in the years since then, as other gayborhoods have commemorated their LGBTQ history with streetscapes and rainbow crosswalks, residents and vicarious citizens have found the inconspicuous street signs a relatively muted tribute. "Yes, I know that a few of the blocks on 17th Street are designated as Frank Kameny Way," reflects writer Brock Thompson in his plea for more colorful streetscapes. "Sadly, though, not a lot of people are familiar with who Frank Kameny was or what he did."[9] Some expressed frustration that the signs did not reflect the "real" boundaries of the gayborhood. Most LGBTQ-related events, including the High Heel Race, begin in front of JR's Bar & Grill, a gay bar a block south of where the signs end. "It doesn't even reach JR's!" Connor (forty-five, white, gay) screeched while taking me on a walking tour through the neighborhood shortly after their installation. "Why would anyone think it a good idea to stop the street signs there!" Others have naturally assumed that the signs extended to P Street. When covering the dedication, several media outlets, including the *Washington Blade*, incorrectly assumed that the street signs flanked the intersection of Seventeenth and P Streets NW. When the Department of Transportation refreshed Frank Kameny Way with new brown commemorative street signs in 2021 (figure 4.2), locals blasted the agency for not "replacing" the signs along P Street.[10]

In 2017, Randy Downs, the advisory neighborhood commissioner for the area, launched a Change.org petition to install rainbow crosswalks along the Seventeenth Street strip. In an interview with the *Washington Blade*, Downs said he hoped the rainbow crosswalks would "instill a sense of community and advance the awareness of the diversity and equality through public art and community outreach."[11] A second petition, initiated by the transgender activist Kelly Wright, soon followed, requesting that the city install crosswalks

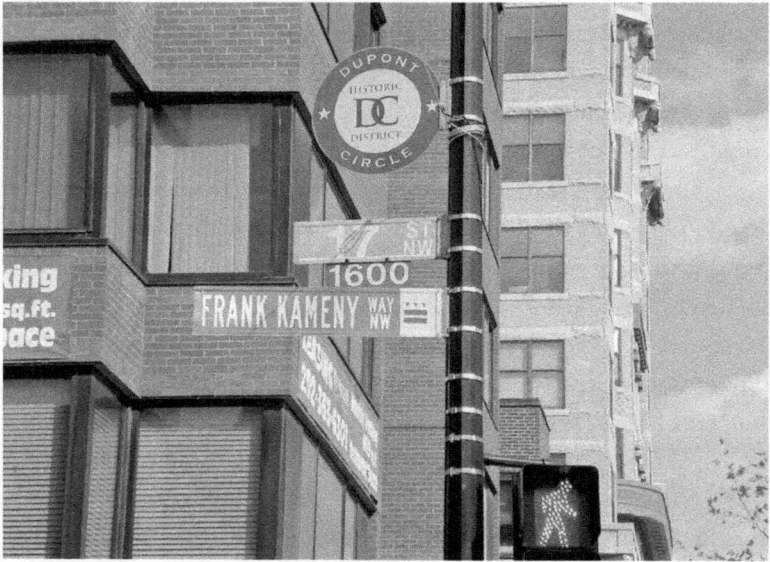

FIGURE 4.2 The original street sign for Frank Kameny Way, a portion of Seventeenth Street named in honor of the famed gay civil rights hero.

Photo by author.

painted in the colors of the Transgender Pride flag for Pride Month. Within days, both petitions garnered thousands of signatures from supportive residents. The desired rainbow crosswalks not only were modeled after those found in other cities but also found precedent in the Barnes Dance—an intersection where all traffic lights turn red simultaneously so pedestrians can walk in all directions—recently installed at Seventh and H Streets in Gallery Place–Chinatown. The crosswalks there featured a permanent installation with dragons and decorative lamps along the diagonal crosswalks to honor the neighborhood's history of Chinese New Year Parades and with the twelve animals of the Chinese zodiac on the four outer crosswalks.[12]

Combining Downs's and Wright's proposals, the DC Department of Transportation permitted the installation of temporary rainbow crosswalks along Seventeenth Street. Thus, eight crosswalks along Frank Kameny Way were allowed to feature rainbow flags before the 2017 Capital Pride Parade. Seven crosswalks were to resemble the colors of the rainbow flag, while the eighth was to bear the colors of the trans flag. Despite the permanent installation of the crosswalks in Gallery Place–Chinatown, the city's crosswalks remain under the purview of the U.S. Department of Transportation, which traditionally forbids permanent changes. As an alternative, the city allowed a permanent installation of rainbow banner flags on lampposts along Frank Kameny Way and four storm drain murals, which aimed to draw attention to the storm drains' significance to the city's waterways. The city's Department of Energy and Environment, partnering with the Anacostia Watershed Society, was to solicit designs from the community for a permanent installation. However, in the meantime, in honor of Pride Week, storm drains along Seventeenth Street featured sample murals, including a glittered rainbow flag design surrounding the words "Love Is Love" in the center (figure 4.3).

FIGURE 4.3 A sample mural painted over one of the storm drains outside JR's Bar on Seventeenth Street.

Photo by author.

FIGURE 4.4 A sample mural painted over one of the storm drains outside JR's Bar on Seventeenth Street.

Photo by author.

The day before the Pride Parade, I joined Downs and Wright and a number of volunteers outside JR's to paint a sample crosswalk for a news conference with Mayor Muriel Bowser that afternoon. Representatives of the city arrived, and after a brief discussion with Downs about the plan for the day, police blocked off the intersection where we would paint the sample. We sprayed chalk paint on the pavement between the existing crosswalk lines. To ensure the chalk paint would not bleed onto the white lines of the crosswalk, we first taped white butcher paper over the lines. Several volunteers grabbed canisters of chalk paint and began spraying their chosen colors in an even coat over the pavement. Other volunteers grabbed sidewalk chalk and walked toward the end of the street to block out the hashtag #dcrainbowcrosswalks to encourage community members to take photos and post them on social media.

Using chalk paint presented several challenges. Due to the limited supply, we could not apply multiple coats to ensure complete coverage of the pavement. The warm breeze did not help; as volunteers spray-painted, the wind blew paint in all directions, covering volunteers and the white butcher paper protecting the permanent crosswalk lines. Adding the topcoat also did not help, as the force of the spray dissipated the chalk paint, resulting in a spotty finish in some areas. Despite the challenges, we persisted in painting the crosswalk, leaving about a foot of pavement for the mayor to finish off after the news conference. By the time news crews and representatives from the DC Council and the local ANC began congregating outside JR's, volunteers were touching up blotchy crosswalk areas and removing the butcher paper.

The mayor arrived shortly before eleven A.M. Downs offered a few introductory words about the crosswalks, highlighting his hope that they would endure as a symbol of acceptance for LGBTQ people. "Missouri was a hard place to live as a gay man," he told the crowd, "so when I moved to the city six years ago, I instantly felt welcomed and valued. And so I wanted to make sure that others who might be questioning their identity, their acceptance, or their worth saw a symbol of that celebration. It's really important that we have these symbols and show that queer folks are part of the community and [are] valued."

Concluding his remarks, Downs turned the microphone over to Mayor Bowser. She hailed the rainbow crosswalks as a symbol of the city's inclusive values in the face of a hostile presidential administration. "We know a lot changed on Election Day last year, didn't it?" Bowser began her speech to applause. "But I know what didn't change, and that's us. And that is our commitment to the values that make us an inclusive and diverse city." Highlighting the grassroots efforts to make the rainbow crosswalks possible, Bowser invited DC residents to participate in the Capital Pride festivities, including painting the other crosswalks. "We couldn't be more proud of what we stand for in Washington, DC, and to kick off the celebration of Capital Pride." After the mayor finished her address, a volunteer handed her a can of green spray paint. I grabbed a can of yellow spray paint and took the spot next to her. She asked for some advice on using the spray paint, and I warned her about the wind and the blowback on her black slacks and open-toed shoes. After a countdown, we began spray-painting the remaining area to the sounds of applause and the clicks of cameras from the media. After we completed the painting, volunteers added the sealant on top of the newly painted area while the mayor took photos with the members of the council and residents who attended the news conference.

The mayor and her staff exchanged small talk with Downs and several volunteers for several minutes before departing. Among the residents posing for photos in front of the crosswalks were several groups of schoolchildren who skipped along the rainbow-colored crosswalks during their daily walk along Seventeenth Street. About half an hour later, the police removed the barricades. While several volunteers lingered with Downs to discuss a game plan for the following day, a truck drove over the freshly painted crosswalk, tracking the rainbow colors across the intersection of Seventeenth and Church Streets. My friend Vincent and I stared at the intersection for several minutes as car after car continued to track the colors through the intersection and down the street. At first, we felt some disappointment and shock as the work that took us hours to complete seemed so easily ruined. However, as I shot photos of the rainbow-streaked intersection, Vincent made a statement that resonated with the group standing around. "I guess you can't keep a good gay inside the lines," he said. The crowd laughed as we walked over to Annie's for lunch.

The next day hundreds of volunteers came to Seventeenth Street to participate in spray-painting the remaining crosswalks. Although the paint ran out, leaving several crosswalks with just the essence of a rainbow, many viewed the effort as a success. In 2018, the tradition continued as volunteers spray-painted the crosswalks. Although the COVID pandemic resulted in the cancelation of Pride events in 2020, the community received some good news that June when Mayor Bowser announced the DC Department of Transportation would install a permanent rainbow crosswalk at the intersection of Seventeenth and P Streets in time for the fiftieth anniversary of Pride Month. On the morning of June 25, 2020, a small crowd gathered to witness the installation, which included the bands of the rainbow and trans flags and brown and black bands representing LGBTQ communities of color. "While we wish we could have celebrated this month at our annual Capital Pride Parade," Mayor Bowser said in a prepared statement, "we hope this artwork will serve as a reminder of our DC values in promoting inclusivity and equality for all our residents."[13]

These forms of commemoration do not necessarily function as normative vicarious claims. Often they symbolize the geographies where communities feel entitled to enact and police behaviors aligned with the production of space. The installation of a permanent crosswalk came with the promise of more rainbow crosswalks along Seventeenth Street. However, its placement at Seventeenth and P reflected a different normative claim to the area. Neither the Frank Kameny Way signs nor the temporary rainbow crosswalks extended as far south as P Street, even though, for many, the intersection of Seventeenth and P Streets represents a key marker of the gayborhood. Thus, they believed the permanent installation finally mapped the boundaries of LGBTQ space within the popular imagination. These normative behaviors are not exhibited solely by official place entrepreneurs. As I describe next, sometimes protecting the normative culture of the gayborhood falls into the purview of everyday citizens who feel empowered to engage in DIY urbanism to protect LGBTQ spaces.[14]

"SISSIFYING THE FOUNTAIN"

The sound of Vincent pounding on my bedroom door jolted me from a sound sleep.

"Theo!" he yelled in his famously high-pitched voice.

"What is it?" I slurred, turning over. I reached for my cell phone on the nightstand and saw that it was seven A.M.

"You want to go decorate the fountain?" he asked. The night before, after we returned from the fundraiser at Annie's Paramount Steak House for the families of the Orlando victims, Vincent had suggested we sissify the fountain in Dupont Circle. He was primarily motivated to decorate the fountain after learning that another rainbow flag outside an Adams Morgan restaurant was set on fire. "Those bastards are not going to mess with my flag!" he exclaimed the night before, sipping a glass of vodka. "We're going to sissify the fountain."

"Isn't it raining?" I asked, looking out the window at the gray sky above. I had agreed to his plan the previous evening only if it wasn't raining.

"Not enough to stop us," he replied. "Get your ass up and come to the fountain."

"Yeah," I grumbled as I rose out of bed. "Let me put some clothes on."

"Hurry up! I ain't got all day, girl!"

I threw on a pair of shorts, tennis shoes, and the rainbow-colored glasses I had received at the Pride Parade and walked out of the room. Vincent moved throughout the apartment in fevered purpose, carrying an old brown leather suitcase. He opened the suitcase on his dining room table, hoping to fill it with various supplies. But after a minute, he changed his mind, closed the suitcase, and returned it to the closet. He then grabbed a small canvas bag and began filling it with some of the trinkets and favors left over from his Pride party: strands of brightly colored beads, rainbow paper streamers, rainbow garlands, and rainbow birthday hats. "You think I should bring some candles?" he asked.

"There are plenty of candles there, I'm sure," I replied.

"Good," he said, throwing a lighter in his bag. "Let's go sissify the fountain."

We walked south on New Hampshire Avenue. It was a gray and cool morning, the sky indicating that it might deliver a deluge at any moment. As we approached Dupont Circle, I wondered whether what we were doing was, in fact, a fool's errand. It has been a week since people started the memorial at Dupont Circle. Given the excessive heat, rain, and wind we had experienced over the last few days, I wondered whether our alterations to the fountain would last very long.

"How long do you think they will keep this memorial out there?" I asked.

"As long as people keep creating one," he replied.

We reached the Circle and noticed that much of the memorial had not survived the previous night's thunderstorm. Several of the faded posters were illegible. Messages once visible from the far edge of the Circle had faded from the harsh sun and the previous night's rainstorm. Old bouquets, dried after sitting for days in the heat, were strewn all over the fountain's base. Melted candle wax had hardened on the concrete at the base. As we walked up the stairs toward the fountain, we noticed that several candles sitting along the edge had fallen into the water, some floating upside down. As we surveyed the mess, I looked at Vincent and saw him moving items around.

"Remember," I told him, "we are adding. We're not getting rid of anything."

He went into his little bag and pulled out several strings of beads. I grabbed one of the rainbow flags, and we walked up to the fountain's base. He began wrapping the beads around the votive candles, making sure the beads draped over the ledge. "We gotta make sure people can see it." I found a taped candle among the votives and stuck the tiny rainbow flag into the hardened wax. "This will be able to withstand the elements," I said to Vincent, who nodded as he walked down the stairs to his bag. He pulled out more strings of beads and placed half of them in my hand. We continued decorating the candles until we ran out of beads. He then grabbed the brightly colored crepe paper streamers and put them in my hands. "Do something with these," he said, walking to one of the memorial panels.

Holding the crumpled rainbow streamers in my hand, I did not know what to do with them. As a light breeze began to blow, I began placing them under candles, thinking that at least they somehow were anchored. If it worked well, the streamers would billow in the breeze. I began cutting the long streamers and placing them under the candles. Vincent began cleaning up and organizing the windblown array of posters, candles, and flowers. He began throwing away some illegible posters, using a few to fish out memorabilia swimming in the fountain. He pulled out a lighter and reignited the candles sitting along the base. I grabbed the two rainbow garlands and walked over to the other side of the fountain. I wrapped one around the candles facing the south side of Dupont Circle and placed the other one underneath the candles on the north side of the Circle.

Vincent approached me with a handful of soggy paper and trash, and together we marveled at our work.

"Pretty good," he said.

"Yes," I replied. "For now."

A homeless guy approached us as we stood there, straightening up some loose swag. He was a short, rotund Black man in his forties.

"Is this for the Orlando tragedy?" he asked.

"Yes," Vincent and I said together.

"What a shame," the homeless man said. "And you know these shootings are going to continue. This is only the beginning."

"We got to do something about it, for sure," I replied, adding some stray beads to the candle altar.

"Yup," Vincent replied to him. "People are getting lathered up into a frenzy by assholes like Trump—"

"Trump?" the man responded. "We will be in big trouble if Trump doesn't get elected." Vincent and I looked at each other, realizing that the conversation had taken an unexpected turn. "He's the only one who . . ." The man trailed off when he realized we were no longer listening to him. He pulled his bag over his shoulder and walked away.

Vincent and I walked off the fountain and began taking pictures of the renewed memorial. We hugged each other as we looked at the fountain. He reached into his side pocket and pulled out two strands

FIGURE 4.5 The Pulse memorial at the Dupont Circle Fountain after a thunderstorm.

Photo by author.

of beads: one green and one gold. He put the gold one over my head and the green one over his.

"It seems like our days as altar boys paid off," he said. I laughed at his response. I looked up at the memorial and immediately understood his reference. The votives did make the fountain resemble an altar (figure 4.5). As if in an expression of prayer, I kissed the beads around my neck, pulled them off, and placed them around one of the votive candles. Vincent followed suit.

"Come on," I told him. "Let me treat you to a cup of coffee."

"Yes," he said. "Let's get some coffee, come back here for a bit, and sit in front of the fountain." I agreed. We walked along the north side of the Circle toward Starbucks. At first, he was somewhat hesitant about getting coffee at Starbucks. "Let's go to Firehook," he said. "Starbucks is so corporate."

"What difference does it make?" I asked. "Is Firehook even open?"

"Good point," he said reluctantly.

We walked into Starbucks and ordered a doppio for Vincent and a quad espresso over ice for me. After I paid for our drinks, we grabbed them and walked back down to Dupont Circle. We sat there for about ten minutes, drinking our coffees in relative silence as people moved through the Circle on their way to work. A "friend" of Vincent's, a white man in his forties, was walking through the Circle pulling a roller bag. Vincent called the man by name to say hello, but the man (in typical DC fashion) tried to ignore him. When he realized he couldn't do so anymore, he looked in our direction and acknowledged Vincent's presence. Vincent kept talking to him as though the man was interested in Vincent and what he had to say. "We are sissifying the fountain," he said. The man kept walking without any acknowledgment. Vincent looked back at his fountain, completely unfazed. After about ten minutes of sitting at the fountain, we had finished our coffee, and I suggested we get going. He agreed. "I got to get to work."

I admit to questioning the purpose of straightening the memorial after the thunderstorm. On the one hand, it did not seem like it was our job to clear out the debris from the fountain. However, as a community member of Dupont Circle, Vincent felt some responsibility for cleaning up the fountain. That sense of entitlement to preserve the remnants of the memorial was no different from that which led to the grassroots efforts of residents and vicarious citizens to create the monument in the first place. Vincent also understood what might happen if the monument remained untouched following the rain; city maintenance workers who might not have understood the importance of the memorial could have cleared everything away indiscriminately and without regard for those who continued to mourn the tragic loss. By saving what we could after the storm, we extended the life of the memorial, allowing members of the community a space in which to mourn and pay tribute to the lives lost in the tragedy.

SUNDAYS ON SEVENTEENTH STREET
WITH STONEWALL

Seventeenth Street is a quiet commercial area in the daytime during the workweek. The area restaurants bustle with energy on the weekend as patrons enjoy brunch, but even then the street culture does not particularly stand out from that of other busy streets you would find in Washington. However, Seventeenth Street really comes alive on the Sunday mornings when beautiful, athletic people in colorful t-shirts and shorts assemble in Stead Park, behind JR's, for their weekly kickball tournaments. Established in 2010, Stonewall Sports provides another opportunity for LGBTQ residents and allies to create and foster community while engaging in community service. Many develop lifelong friendships through their participation in Stonewall Sports, as many team members spend time together outside the kickball season. "I never realized that when I joined the kickball team, I would also find a family," explained Jordan (introduced in chapter 2). "We do almost everything together, and I never imagined that I would be part of such a diverse group of fun, interesting people."

During my sabbatical in 2018, I followed Jordan and his kickball team, the Swallows, as they participated in seasonal play. What struck me about the team was how kickball provided a pretense for the teams to socialize and challenge the neighborhood's postqueer culture by centering explicit discussions of sex and sexuality in public areas and local institutions. When I arrived for my first game in Stead Park one warm October morning, I was immediately struck by the team names. Each team had developed a name that combined DC culture with sexual innuendo so as to solicit chuckles even among the most seasoned players; they included Slide It in Me,

Just the Tip, Monumount Me, Choke on My Kick, and Pounding Fathers. Several teams displayed their names prominently on their sports uniforms as they walked down the street. The Real Housegays of DC distinguished themselves by wearing jackets and t-shirts with their branding, while the Slide It in Me members had their team name displayed across their booty shorts. When kickers approached the mound, few hesitated to bend over and reveal their team's name to bystanders nearby.

The teams play throughout the morning and early afternoon during the regular season. Eight teams play in the park at once, each game occupying one corner. While they take over much of the green space, they do not have exclusive park use. Nearby, parents push their children on swings and help them navigate slides. Women holding yoga mats and lattes walk through the park, passing older adults sitting on the benches next to women nursing their babies. Their presence does not prevent the teams from yelling sexually explicit messages at one another. Before every game, the Swallows yell, "Everybody swallows!" after a huddle. At one point, with the bases loaded and a team member approaching the mound, one of the Swallows yelled, "You better kick like a Dom top!" "Or a power bottom!" another teammate shouted. After one player stole a base, a team member, suggesting a specific sexual act, shouted, "You better sit on that base. Sit. On. That. Fucking. Base." These men also engage in gender play. During a pivotal moment, one player managed to kick the ball across the large field. As his team cheered, he pirouetted as he touched each base on his way to home plate.

When the games concluded, the Swallows had brunch with another team. Sometimes it was the team they played with that day. Other times the players met up with a different team after their game was over. If their brunch companions were playing an afternoon game, the Swallows usually spent the intervening time grabbing a coffee at the nearby café, where they continued their sexually explicit conversations. While I was sitting on the patio outside Java Café with the team, one of the team members blurted out the question "Which way does your dick swing?" Without skipping a beat, team members chimed in, discussing not only their own dicks but also those of men with whom they had sex. When I asked teammates about their sexually explicit conversations, many explained that they have never considered who might be listening nearby. "I don't even think about it," the Swallows cocaptain Cameron (twenty-eight, white, gay) explained. "Going from place to place, I don't think we are conscious of who is around." For many team members, the conversations not only seem natural but also seem necessary to protect Seventeenth Street as a gay area. "Who cares what people think?" Corey (twenty-seven, white, gay) asked. "There aren't many public places where we feel comfortable talking like this. We never had anyone really complain about it, but if they did, it wouldn't really matter."

These conversations would extend to brunch, where the size of the teams would often require the group to take over a section of a restaurant. Throughout the brunch, participants would move around the tables, often to ensure they could chat with multiple friends. One member pulled out a Bluetooth speaker and played popular songs on his phone. Sometimes the teams continued their conversations while eating. However, some teammates might get up and dance around if a favorite song came over the speakers. Several players began to sashay through the tables during one brunch when Beyoncé's "Formation" started to play. These activities sometimes appeared chaotic, which might have seemed frustrating to the servers waiting on the group. However, they managed to navigate the chaos professionally, never skipping a beat to provide top-notch service.

Following brunch, the teams would meet at for an evening of bar-hopping. In addition to the crowds who hit Number Nine or Trade on Sunday afternoons, you often found large groups of kickball players in Stonewall shirts who toasted shots and shared stories about their lives. By late afternoon, the kickball teams would all go to Cobalt, where the upper level had tables around the dance floor's perimeter so patrons could play drinking games. By 6:30 P.M., sweaty men in rainbow-colored Stonewall shirts would pack the dance floor, gyrating on top of each other to Ariana Grande and Lady Gaga. Some would have removed their shirts and tucked them into their pants to show off their glistening muscular torsos. The energy of the evening resembled a college fraternity party, where the athletes mingled in the spirit of building bonds of solidarity. "Those are my favorite times of the evening," Marty (thirty-two, South Asian, gay) said. "Some teams take the competition [during the daytime] more seriously than others. So by the time we are all at Cobalt, everyone has loosened up and let their hair down, so to speak. No judgment. None of the bitchy queens you might see on a Saturday night. Just a lot of guys, a lot of liquor, and good vibes all around."

As the evening wound down, many kickball players would grab a bite to eat at the McDonald's on Seventeenth Street, mirroring the production of place that one might find on a typical Saturday night (chapter 3). As adults with children sat in booths consuming their dinners, players would continue their sexually explicit discourses, sharing stories about sexual conquests or commenting on various men they found on Grindr. One evening, while I was waiting in line, a young blond man in his midtwenties entered the restaurant and approached the trio of kickball players standing in line in front of me. One of the men hugged the guy who had just entered and asked, "How did it go?" The man smiled at him.

"Did you do it?"

The blond man nodded. The trio cheered loudly, giving the blond high-fives and butt slaps. The man standing directly in front of me turned around to face the restaurant.

"May I have everyone's attention, please?" he asked. "Attention, everybody." The room went quiet except for the Britney Spears song playing in the background. "Somebody officially became a top!" The entire restaurant erupted in cheers. The blond blushed as a group of players approached him to ask for the details. I looked around at the tables containing nonplayers and saw that nobody was paying much attention to the young men cheering about the blonde's sexual conquest.

By the end of the evening, Seventeenth Street had again become a quiet street. Although stragglers continued barhopping, most participants had gone home to prepare for the workweek ahead. Yet as scholars highlight the decreasing salience of gay neighborhoods to younger generations, Stonewall Sundays highlight the importance of physical spaces in fostering community and of the efforts of these communities to challenge the sanitized culture within hegemonically gay spaces by drawing on conversations that center on gay sex. This form of place reactivation reflects another important strategy vicarious citizens can use to claim ownership over LGBTQ space on their own terms.

This chapter explores normative vicarious claims, allowing vicarious citizens to monitor behaviors and reinforce cultural and social norms consistent with their neighborhood vision. The exercise of normative vicarious claims frequently succeeds not only because these claims are often consistent with the production of gay community space but also because they play out through the routines of everyday life. However, there are times when enforcing normative vicarious claims or protecting community interests requires a more organized effort from vicarious citizens. Many vicarious claims that reflect normative cultural claims might be misinterpreted as radical because the claimants are perceived as outsiders to the local community, regardless of their identification to the local area. This is particularly true in iconic gay neighborhoods, where normative gay culture continues to privilege white, middle-class, adult, gay, cisgender males. Radical cultural claims challenge the perception of iconic gay neighborhoods as culturally homogeneous spaces, illuminating how various racial, class-based, and generational tensions shape debates among queer populations with rightful claims to ownership in iconic gay neighborhoods.

5

"PRESENTE! PRESENTE!"

Place Ruptures and the Enactment of
Radical Vicarious Claims

Black gay professor enters a gay bar along the Fourteenth Street strip for happy hour. After the burly Black doorman waves him through without checking his driver's license, he approaches the bar, standing in front of the designated service area. The bartender, a thick, muscular brunette wearing a black t-shirt leaving little to the imagination, is preparing a drink for the patron seated at the end of the bar. As the bartender muddles a lime, blueberries, and mint in a tall glass, he makes eye contact with the professor, who smiles and nods to signal that he will wait. The professor leans forward and rests his arms on the bar, observing the bartender pouring white rum into the glass of muddled fruit. His customer compliments the bartender on the drink, soliciting a smile and a brief exchange. As the bartender tops the drink with a blueberry garnish, a tall white man approaches the bar. He wedges his sinewy body between two patrons and waves at the bartender, who smiles back in recognition.

Setting the mojito in front of the seated gentleman, the bartender grabs the man's credit card and opens a tab at the cash register on the back bar. Adding the credit card to the collection sitting in a large shot glass, the bartender turns around and makes a beeline toward the white man after making brief eye contact with the professor. The gentleman orders a cosmopolitan, which the bartender prepares. The professor, slightly perplexed by being overlooked, attempts to make eye contact with the bartender to no avail. As the bartender pours the pink contents of the martini shaker into a glass, two white gay men appear at the opposite end of the bar. The bartender completes his transaction and then walks to the opposite end of the bar to take the couple's order. The professor grows impatient; surely, he thinks, the bartender sees him standing in front of the service station, an area designated for people making a drink order.

Fifteen minutes pass. The professor's mood dampens as the bartender serves the white couple, the handsome Latino who stands behind them, and a man in a dark blue suit seated at the bar. The professor is about to give up when the bartender approaches him and asks for his order. As the professor orders a Tito's-soda, he thinks about the years of treatment by bartenders and staff who bypass him for attractive white men. He remembers his twenty-first birthday when, after purchasing his first alcoholic beverage, the bartender not only accuses him of not paying for his drink but also calls for security to throw him out before the barback discovers that the money blew off the bar onto the floor. He flashes back to all the dates when men explained that, while they found him handsome, they could not date him because he was Black. At that moment, the professor, considering the various ways he has been rejected and treated as invisible by a community he has tried desperately to belong to, decides that he will not remain silent anymore.

"You do realize," the professor begins, trying to maintain composure, "that I've been standing here for twenty minutes—"

"Don't even think about it," the bartender interrupts, pouring the vodka into a glass filled with ice.

The professor is taken aback by the bartender's comments. "Pardon?"

"I know exactly what you're implying," the bartender replies, spraying soda water into the glass, refusing to make eye contact. "And don't go there. I just didn't see you. Not everything has to do with race." He squeezes a wedge of lime into the glass and pushes it toward the professor.

The professor pulls a ten out of his wallet. Before he places the money on the counter, he pauses. "You know what? No, thank you." The professor puts the money back into his wallet and makes his way toward the exit.

———

I have experienced interactions like that more times than I care to admit. Across twenty years and three cities, I have confronted examples of what the sociologist Reuben Buford May refers to as velvet rope racism: "collective practices supporting the exclusion of particular racial or ethnic groups from participation in nightclub social life."[1] Beyond waiting for bartenders to attend to white gay patrons before "seeing me," doormen and bar managers have required me to remove articles of clothing that white men got away with wearing (e.g., bandanas, backward baseball caps, and suggestive t-shirts). On the dance floor, men push through me without uttering a word of apology. And on the rare occasion that I meet someone or take a date to a bar for a nightcap, I have experienced other patrons literally cockblocking me, wedging their bodies between my date and me to flirt with my companion as if I wasn't there. And, confirming Buford May's argument, bar staff and patrons disregard my concerns when I call out the behavior, deflecting perceived allegations of racial discrimination.[2] I did not even have to make the accusation. The bartender *assumed* I would invoke the "race card" to challenge his poor service.

Ironically, I believe the bartender when he said he did not "see me." In the book *Racial Erotics*, C. Winter Han argues that sexual racism extends beyond erotic encounters. "As if being negated and ignored isn't bad enough," he writes, "sometimes the whiteness of gay spaces are actively policed to deliberately keep queers of color out."[3] As a thickly built (sometimes fat), conservatively presenting Black gay man, I tend to wield little erotic capital in spaces like these. As sexual fields,[4] gay neighborhoods and LGBTQ nightlife operate as spaces that privilege white gay desire. Even when sex is not the goal, erotic capital can shape patrons' interactions within commercial and cultural institutions. Throughout my fieldwork, I observed that white gay men receive greater sexual and romantic attention in LGBT establishments. If nightlife staff find them attractive, they might receive faster and friendlier service than do gay men of color. Conversely, gay men of color, especially Black gay men, often experience longer wait times, slower service, and a more hostile reception from staff and other patrons. In my fieldwork, I encountered several Black men who offered different strategies for mitigating these challenges. In specific spaces, I have relied on one of my white gay friends to purchase my drink at the bar, recognizing that they might grab the staff's attention far more easily than I would, especially on crowded nights.

While gay neighborhoods and LGBTQ institutions have diversified, these spaces nevertheless function as white spaces, privileging white desire. The participation of marginalized LGBTQ populations in spaces traditionally reserved for white gay cis men can create moments of cognitive dissonance. I refer to these practices as *radical vicarious claims*. They result from embodied misrecognition, and many reflect practices that reinforce the culture of a place while appearing to be foreign or disruptive due to the people performing them. Other radical vicarious claims openly challenge the predominant culture, as when marginalized groups bring in practices and traditions that make the space accessible. I refer to these practices as *place ruptures*—where different subcultural logics are reactivated on an existing production of place. Place ruptures range from a momentary and inconspicuous practice to a full-fledged takeover by patrons constituting the minority.

This chapter explores radical vicarious claims more closely. Whether reinforcing or challenging place cultures, radical vicarious claims constitute demands for recognition made by both outsiders and "outsiders within,"[5] who identify with many aspects of the area's dominant culture and yet, for various reasons, have been excluded from participation in local community life. Radical claims can potentially expand the cultural imagination of place and community in local neighborhoods through the appropriation and cultural misrecognition of local space, which at times may challenge more traditionally held perceptions of who belongs to the area and what practices are privileged as legitimate.

BY JUST BEING THERE

Troy (twenty-eight, Black, gay) is a tall, muscular man with a Harvard law degree and a conservative presentation. Despite his educational background and impeccably neat preppy attire, he encounters white gay men who expect him to play out their fantasies of the hypersexual Black buck. "I'm constantly accosted by these men who say the craziest things to me. Once, I was at this [gay bar in Dupont Circle] just minding my business when this white guy—he had to be in his early forties—just walked up to me, grabbed my crotch, and whispered in my ear, 'I'd love for you to rape me with that big black dick of yours.' That's all they see when they look at me—a walking, talking, fucking, Black dick."

Javier (twenty-five, Latino, gay) works as a congressional aide on Capitol Hill. He enjoys after-work happy hours where he can discuss politics with friends while sipping boulevardiers and apple martinis. Despite receiving significant attention from "well-meaning" white men in gay bars, he often finds himself frustrated by the stereotypes he confronts. "Guys approach me all the time with '*Hola, papi*,' or why they love 'spicy Latin men,' or how much they love uncut dick, and that shit drives me crazy." According to Javier, confronting these stereotypes accomplishes little, as most men respond with accusations that he misunderstood their "good intentions." "When I go off on them, they think I'm crazy!" he explains. "They suddenly get their feelings hurt as if they've done nothing wrong."

Challenging stereotypical images of Black and Latino queer sexuality held by white gay men, both Troy and Javier produce radical vicarious claims. However, neither of them actively seeks to do so. What distinguishes these claims as "radical" is that their presentation often conforms to the production of place within these traditionally white spaces. Gay men of color who do not embody the Eurocentric standards of beauty that structure the cultural and sexual life of gay neighborhoods must somehow conform to the sexualized fantasies of white gay men. Thus, gay, bisexual, and queer men of color who fail to perform sexual stereotypes that fulfill white sexual desire often find themselves invisible or pathologized in gay spaces, even in contexts outside of sexual interaction. Troy highlights the hypocrisy of interacting with other gay men at the bar. "I have overheard many conversations that [white gay men] have had about politics or the law. They can vehemently disagree over a political position, which seems to be a turn-on. I disagree with someone and I am 'intimidating'—another angry Black man. It makes no sense. On paper, I have everything people claim they want in a partner—smart, successful, and, yes, handsome. But because I'm Black, those qualities become a liability." Gregory (twenty-eight, Black, gay) received confirmation of this one evening. A Georgetown law student at the time of our interview, Gregory described the time he once vented his frustrations over his "nonexistent dating life" to his gay friends at a gay bar on Fourteenth Street. "One of my friends," he recalls, "this white twink who always seems to have someone at the end of the night, looked me straight in the face and said, 'Perhaps if you weren't so "articulate" and "smart" all the time, people might want to approach you.'"

The limited visibility of gay, bisexual, and queer men of color in gay bars and the lack of alternatives for GBQ men of color make interracial dating (Black men dating white men) expected or compulsory. Jayson (twenty-four, Black, gay) grew up in Southeast Washington but now lives in the trendy U Street neighborhood in Northwest Washington. On Friday or Saturday night, he often finds himself to be one of a handful of Black men in the bars he frequents, which produces assumptions among patrons about his preference for sexual partners. "Most men believe that if you're a Black gay man hanging out in a place like JR's [in Dupont Circle]," he observed, "then you must be looking for some white man to date."

Intraracial relationships between GBQ men of color, when performed in the white space, seem to be understood as what Marlon Riggs once described as Black gay love, a revolutionary act.[6] Ronaldo (thirty-five, Filipino, gay) refers to himself as "sticky rice"—an Asian gay man who prefers dating other Asian men. He describes two specific problems in searching for Asian partners in gay bars. First, the constant rejection by other Asian gay men has led him to lead with a question that always makes him cringe. "I hate that I have to ask another Asian whether he is into Asian men," Ronaldo explains. "It just supports the notion that gay Asian men are inferior to white men—or even Black men and their [big black dicks]." Second, he despises feeling like what Charles Nero refers to as a cultural impostor,[7] someone whose participation somehow feels inauthentic compared to that of their white gay counterparts. Too often he receives unwanted attention from white men when displaying affection with another man of color. "I feel like I am on some float in the Pride Parade," he explains, laughing, "or people don't think it's real. When I'm out on a date with someone, and we are dancing on the floor or cuddled up in the corner, several times white men have come up and tried to proposition one or both of us for sex. It's like, as an Asian, my relationship isn't valid unless it's with another white guy."

On too many occasions, I have observed moments when the presence of Black queer groups results in patrons using euphemisms like "It's getting a little dark in here" and "I didn't realize that it was Urban Night." The presence of other outsider groups, like queer women or trans people, also results in misinterpretations that render these populations outsiders. Cynthia (thirty, white, lesbian) and her partner, Cherie (twenty-eight, Black, lesbian), often experience hostility when they enter certain places because their feminine presentation makes them more legible as "straight women." Once while attending a drag show with a few friends, Cynthia approached a crowded bar for a drink. "I finally reached the front of the line," she explained, "when some white guy pushed me to get in front of me. I was like 'Excuse me. I was standing here.' And he whipped his head around and yelled, 'We don't want you here. You fucking bachelorettes ruin everything!'" It did not matter at that moment that Cynthia identified as a lesbian and felt she belonged there. To those who believed that space "belonged" to men, Cynthia became legible as an interloper within the space.

The perception of a critical mass of Black gay men in traditionally white bars can create divisions that manifest themselves spatially. When the city's decision to build a baseball stadium by the Anacostia River forced the closure of Black gay bars in the area, many Black patrons found a new hangout in Halo, a gay bar in the heart of Logan Circle. Opened in 2004, the chic yet predominately white Halo became popular among many Dupont Circle and Logan Circle residents as the first nonsmoking gay bar in the city. However, a critical mass of Black gay men on Friday nights diminished its popularity among many white gay patrons. Soon LGBTQ patrons began describing the bar as Gay Apartheid, as the patrons self-segregated by floor. Despite having the same music and drink specials on both floors, Black patrons assembled on the first floor, while white patrons made a beeline upstairs to the second floor. Colin (thirty, white, gay), who worked as a barback at Halo during that period, described his disappointment in seeing how "the white boys would walk into the room, see the sea of black, and walk right upstairs." "It was one of the nights that my coworkers dreaded," Colin remembered. "It was sad to see my coworkers being the typical hater in terms of the room full of Black guys." The situation became so pervasive that CNN and ESPN columnist LZ Granderson referred to the phenomenon in his response to a 2008 *Advocate* article claiming that "gay [was] the new [B]lack." "There is a bar at the heart of the nation's capital that might as well rename itself Antebellum," he writes, "because all of the white patrons tend to stay upstairs, and the black patrons are on the first floor."[8]

These spatial forms of accommodation also reveal the prejudices of bar management. The infusion of hip-hop and R&B music, often known to glorify and encourage violence, results in additional security measures when Black and Latinx queer bodies predominate. When Cobalt was still open on Seventeenth Street, police cars sat outside on Saturday nights in anticipation of unruly patrons and potentially violent altercations. "Oh, yeah, the police were only there when the Black people took over," Darius (twenty-four, Black, gay) explained. "A bouncer will tell a patron entering to take off a do-rag or pull up their pants, and they're looking over their shoulder [at the police], just waiting for someone to get out of line. But we won't give them the satisfaction because we know that means no more hip-hop nights." Patrons do not see the extra police surveillance on hip-hop nights as mere coincidence. Yet in refusing to give the police or the patrons the "satisfaction" of taking any action against them, these patrons also wage subtle forms of resistance that protect the spaces many rely on for creating and fostering community.

RUPTURING THE WHITE SPACE

One Friday evening a group of Black and Latino gay men were sipping cocktails on the second floor of Number Nine, a lounge in Logan Circle. Surrounded by clusters of white gay men chatting and watching music videos, they conspicuously expressed frustration over the heavy rotation of electronic music and pop standards on the monitors. Suddenly, the Juvenile music video "Back That Azz Up" came on. As soon as the song started, the Black and Latino men started dancing around the tables, with several jumping up on the empty benches, gyrating and twerking. As the dancing intensified and the men began shouting out the lyrics to the song, the white men standing nearby slowly backed away. Halfway through the song, a white man walked out of the restroom and approached the group. Sidestepping a husky Black man who was twerking on the bench where he had been sitting, he grabbed his drink from the table and tapped the man on his shoulder.

"Excuse me," the white man said to the dancer. "You're dancing on my seat."

The dancer looked down and smiled at him. "Don't worry, baby," he said without skipping a beat. "You can have it back when I'm done." Defeated, the man walked away. When the song transitioned into Meghan Trainor's "All About That Bass," the men stopped dancing. Resuming their conversation, they fist-bumped and snapped their fingers, congratulating each other for the minitakeover they had achieved.

This moment epitomizes a place rupture. Famous for its happy hour specials, Number Nine has long, narrow rooms that are not conducive to dancing, especially on crowded days. The music provides ambiance, which explains the white men's surprise at the impromptu dancing. However, this did not prevent the group of Black and Latinx men from dancing when their favorite song hit the monitors. At that moment, they abandoned the normative production of place in favor of practices aligned with their subcultures. In this case, the dancers infused the bar with practices that rendered the space culturally accessible.

As gay nightspots become increasingly diverse, many patrons bring experiences and cultural scripts that are associated with the norms and practices governing a particular space. Some place ruptures can reinforce the normative claims of a neighborhood or space. One Stonewall Sunday, the Swallows enjoyed brunch with the Real House Gays of DC on a patio outside a Seventeenth Street restaurant. As the surrounding tables filled with elderly couples and parents with children, one of the players pulled out a Bluetooth speaker and started playing Lady Gaga's "Born This Way." The team members began dancing and singing along as the diners seated around them began looking quizzically at one another. Although those at several of the surrounding tables asked to move inside, none of the staff approached the table of players to request that they lower the music.

These discrepant practices can create conflict between groups as people conduct their daily and nightly rounds.[9] For example, gay bars and nightclubs have become popular destinations for straight women searching for "safe spaces" to drink without fear of the aggressive advances of straight men.[10] Perceiving these spaces as welcoming and accepting, many straight women enter these establishments expecting to enjoy the same privileges they might encounter at a "straight" establishment (e.g., men will buy their drinks, hold the door for them, or dance with them). Sometimes these women will take liberties, groping gay men on the dance floor or attempting to make out with them, feeling that no consequence will befall them. In spaces where men are searching for other men for romantic and sexual encounters, these practices can pose a significant break in space. While many gay men ignore these place ruptures, others respond with another place rupture that draws on the spatial practices that motivated these women to seek safety in the bar. "Oh, I grope them back," Damion (twenty-seven, Black, gay) commented. "They think they are safe from unwanted attention, so I'll give them unwanted attention, and maybe then they'll be discouraged from coming back." Damion responded to an appropriation of space by those whose presence fundamentally alters the way of life in his vicarious community.

CHOCOLATE CITY SUNDAYS
AS PLACE RUPTURES

Inevitable place ruptures can be adopted and become routinized over time. I joined my friend Tristan on U Street every Sunday for what Black gay men call Chocolate City Sunday. This is not an organized or official event; instead, it gets its reputation from the critical mass of Black LGBTQ people hopping among the bars along the Ninth Street corridor. Tristan explained to me that the informal event began along U Street when Black people began patronizing the Brixton, an Irish pub on the corner of U and Ninth Streets. However, as the Brixton grew in popularity, leading to long lines, patrons expanded to other locations, including Dirty Goose, a hip lounge along U Street known for its signature cocktails. On Sunday afternoons, patrons would enjoy its relaxed atmosphere, sipping martinis while enjoying a little background music or a movie on the first floor and on the rooftop deck in good weather.

The takeover began with sporadic place ruptures peppered throughout the bar. One Easter Sunday I joined a group of friends at Dirty Goose. While we stood on the crowded rooftop sipping cocktails and enjoying the beautiful weather, a Black gay man pushed through the crowd, gyrating wildly to the music. When a Beyoncé song came on, the man's choreography became more elaborate, as he performed high kicks and death drops to the music. He wove his way into groups, grinding on other men and unsuccessfully trying to get them to dance. As he moved from one group to the other, he found himself rebuffed, as the men had no interest in transforming the rooftop into a dance floor. Over time, however, as more Black men came to the bar, what appeared as a sporadic place rupture became more common, with groups of Black men dancing when R&B and hip-hop hits came on. As a result, the bar began adjusting to this reality; while the second floor was not necessarily opened for dancing, R&B selections were played. And even though the bar did not market itself as a Black gay bar, the space developed enough of a reputation to become a destination on Sunday afternoons.

While consciously created, place ruptures do not intentionally challenge another group's use of space. Certain subcultures may disrupt a space to write themselves into community. The following two sections highlight place ruptures by LGBTQ subcultures traditionally excluded from normative LGBTQ spaces. In both cases, these groups challenge the production of space to create new spaces for themselves, and by doing so, they also transform the gayborhood by creating new meaningful forms that make these spaces accessible.

YOUTH PRIDE AS A RADICAL VICARIOUS CLAIM

The participation of LGBTQ youths in gay neighborhoods often constitutes radical vicarious claims because of their age. Contemporary attitudes about "the new gay teenager"[11] dismiss the role of LGBTQ youths as placemakers in gay neighborhoods. In *There Goes the Gayborhood?*, Amin Ghaziani and his respondents relegate LGBTQ youths of color to being simply "inheritors" of the gayborhood. However, their preferences for sexually diverse spaces, according to Ghaziani, might prevent them from even pursuing gay neighborhoods altogether. "The more we insist on defining gayborhoods as minority-only or separatist spaces," he concludes, "the less they will appeal to queer youth who, compared to prior generations, have more sexually mixed friendship circles. Similarly, the more we define gay neighborhoods as something that queer people 'need' in order to deal with their 'issues,' the less they will appeal to queer youth who are not burdened by their sexuality in quite the same way."[12] Later, when considering the resonance of gay neighborhoods for queer youths of color, Ghaziani reduces them to bystanders in the production and the preservation of queer culture in gay neighborhoods. "While many of these kids are too young to get into the bars," he writes, "they still come 'to bear witness to it' and 'be connected to the energy and diversity and the experience of Halsted Street.'"[13] These arguments suggest that queer youths must become adults before they can meaningfully participate in the material culture of gay neighborhoods. "There is a lag between when kids come out, and when they decide to move out of their parent's home," according to Ghaziani. "This means that the changes transpiring in gay neighborhoods right now, at this very moment, are not immediately shaped by teenagers."[14]

Several scholars have countered these observations, highlighting the value of physical spaces for LGBTQ youths, even as they rely on communication technologies to foster and maintain community. Exploring LGBTQ youths in rural areas, Mary L. Gray finds that they integrate their use of "new media" and physical spaces to create visibility and navigate the complexities of gender and sexual identities in small towns. Transforming the Walmart aisles into catwalks for doing drag might prove fleeting and fragile, as they are still subject to policing by staff and customers. Nevertheless, it also represents a vital strategy they use to "absorb, recycle, and recuperate these spaces to make them, albeit temporarily, address their needs."[15] Similarly, my work on queer street families explores how LGBTQ youths of color adopt "codes of the street" from their local neighborhoods and use them to transform the streets of Chicago's Northalsted neighborhood (formerly Boystown) into spaces where they can safely express and navigate their gender identities.[16] Even as the gayborhood's residents (many of whom are white gay men) find the presence and activities of these youths on street corners disruptive to the production of space in iconic gay neighborhoods, their various expressions of placemaking, from using storefront windows to do their makeup to "voguing the house down on sidewalks," offer powerful reminders of the value of iconic gay neighborhoods.

Today many of DC's LGBTQ youths are coming of age in a very different situation, when the locus of the gay community in Washington has shifted to other areas of the city. Because many groups can claim the traffic circle, LGBTQ youths may see Dupont Circle reactivated as an LGBTQ-specific space only on special occasions, such as the Pride Parade or the Pulse commemoration. These formal opportunities may indicate that LGBTQ youths lack the attachments to place their forebears had, potentially confirming Ghaziani's assessment that they are inheritors of queer culture. However, in the absence of informal opportunities, there are indeed moments when LGBTQ youths lay claim to Dupont Circle, developing new relationships that can perpetuate the Circle and fountain as place abeyance signifiers. The following vignette explores how the reactivation of Dupont Circle for DC's annual Youth Pride Day fills that gap, offering new ways for LGBTQ youths to access an essential anchor of the city's LGBTQ community. Returning to the Circle allowed LGBTQ youths to write themselves into place, infusing their tastes and attitudes about queer culture in ways that make the area sociocultturally meaningful while keeping the Circle's gay legacy alive.

On April 30, 2011, the Youth Pride Alliance held its fifteenth annual Youth Pride Day in Dupont Circle. The alliance was founded in 1996 by Christopher Dyer to plan and execute the daylong celebration for LGBTQ youths. "We wanted to have a celebration," Dyer explained in 1997, "a safe way for youths to check out information that might save their lives." On April 19, 1997, the first Youth Pride celebration occurred in the Circle. Drag queens and folk singers performed to the enthusiastic crowd while youths shared their coming-out experiences. The event concluded with a special appearance by openly gay skating champion Rudy Galindo, who "spoke bashfully to the crowd about his own coming out experiences." Many LGBTQ teens arrived in groups, sitting on the grass around the fountain and eating lunch. "Several young couples held hands and stole quick kisses, flanked by friends," reported Viet Dinh of the *Washington Blade*, "[while others] lay out in the sun, sharing hugs."[17] Throughout the day, volunteers distributed flyers containing available resources for LGBTQ youths.

The event proved hugely successful, providing both an affirming environment where LGBTQ youths could express their sexuality without fear of retribution and could find each other. "We had 900 people show up the first year," Dyer recalled in a 2012 *Metro Weekly* interview. "I was expecting 200 or 300."[18] The following year the festival attracted almost two thousand people. By 2001, it had outgrown the traffic circle, forcing organizer to move the event to P Street Beach, a grassy knoll that runs along Rock Creek at P and Twenty-Third Streets. It lies west of the traffic circle and the P Street strip, once home to the popular gay bars Badlands (later renamed Apex), Omega, Mr. P's, and the Fireplace (the only bar remaining in the area).

Ten years later organizers returned the event to Dupont Circle as a special commemoration that connected LGBTQ youths to their history there. Jessica Rotem, who in 2011 completed her first year as a Youth Pride Alliance board member, recalled how the board discussed the significance of returning to the roots of Youth Pride and the cultural roots of Washington's gay community. "Dupont Circle was the original location for Youth Pride," she explained, "and it was the fifteenth anniversary. So as a board, we discussed bringing it back not only out of P Street Beach, because it is a less visible location than Dupont Circle, but as kind of a memory of where we started and the founders' dream and what it was meant to be."

At the same time, in addition to increased visibility and access, the Circle provided new opportunities to draw attention to the plight of LGBTQ youths. The suicides of several bullied LGBTQ teens received national attention in late 2010 and early 2011, and organizers hoped that moving the event to a more public setting would increase contact between the LGBTQ youths and the broader community. "The underlying point is that we wanted the community to get involved," explained Franklin Johnson, another board member. "We wanted the community to realize that there were LGBTQ youth out there, who need support, who need help, who need organization, who need stability."

I arrived at the festival at noon, its scheduled start time. The traffic circle area has two concentric circular walkways separated by tree-shaded green space as well as walkways radiating from the center. Entering the Circle from the north side on Connecticut Avenue, what particularly struck me about the festival layout was its integration with the various other activities. A double-tiered, white marble fountain lies at the center of the park; the base of its reflecting pool provides additional seating for guests and serves as a popular rendezvous point for locals year-round. Walking toward the fountain, I noticed the large stage erected at the northwest end of the park; a large white banner proclaiming "Youth Pride Day" hanging from the aluminum stage backdrop swayed gently in the breeze. A few participants had clustered around the stage to listen to the official welcome while a small group of journalists scribbled furiously on their notepads. Except for the stage, the north side of the park resembled what one would likely find on any gorgeous late Saturday morning in spring: men playing chess on the built-in chess tables on the northeast side of the park; joggers, rollerbladers, and stroller-pushing parents making their way through and around the Circle; shirtless, muscular men in sunglasses and running shorts playing Frisbee with large dogs on the grass; and women sitting on park benches, chatting while sipping their postyoga iced lattes.

Around the fountain, volunteers representing forty-six local and national LGBTQ organizations had set up resource tables decorated with banners where they offered pamphlets and a variety of brightly colored souvenirs branded with organizational logos—everything from stress balls to cloth Frisbees. A police car with a rainbow flag draped over the hood sat on the southwest side on the park. Two uniformed officers wore arm patches indicating they represented the Gay and Lesbian Liaison Unit. Nearby stood a white tent where willing participants could get their faces and bodies painted with rainbow-colored flags, symbols, and queer-friendly slogans. Finally, a mobile testing center stood in the southeast part of the park, offering free HIV and STD screening throughout the day.

By 2:30 P.M., the park had come alive as hundreds of LGBTQ youths and allies, representing a healthy cross section of racial and ethnic groups, had converged in the Circle. The grassy area around the stage had filled up with groups of Black and Latinx youths cuddled up while watching performances by groups like Drag City DC, the Mpoderate! Salsa Dancers, and the DC Cowboys. Several shared testimonials of their coming-out experiences and listened to speeches from the civil rights leader Frank Kameny and DC's U.S. delegate Eleanor Holmes Norton. Christopher Dyer, wearing a rainbow boa, sunglasses, and a tall hat covered in rainbow flowers, gave a brief speech welcoming the crowd before offering an a cappella rendition of "Aquarius" from the musical *Hair*.

Around the park, racially mixed groups of teens sat under trees eating lunch while many strolled through the park openly expressing affection with their partners. Some paraded around the park holding pieces of paper with statements ranging from friendly flirtations (e.g., "Free Hugs and Kisses" and "Let's Make Out") to brief testimonials ("I Played Straight to Play in a Heavy Metal Band ☺"). Two participants approached the three women holding the "Free Hugs and Kisses" sign and asked them to take a picture. After posing provocatively, the youngsters rotated, giving each other hugs and kisses. Many visited the resource tables, perusing the pamphlets, collecting free swag, and signing up to join organizational listservs. Representatives at the Howard University table administered surveys. Youngsters at another table were spinning a brightly colored wheel for free prizes. Some parents who were invited along for the afternoon stopped at the PFLAG table to chat with the volunteers.

At the fountain's base, youths mingled with other park guests, some of whom came to enjoy the festival. One young white girl proved particularly popular among the LGBTQ youths. While walking through the Circle around noon, the young girl noticed the balloons and the Pride flag. Almost immediately, she begged her parents to stay. After having Pride flags painted on her chubby cheeks, she played hopscotch in a space near the fountain, her parents observing happily from the fountain's base. Several youths with brightly colored hair and provocative costumes approached the young girl, cheering and taking photos as she continued her game. At one point, a group of Black teens played with her. The family hung out around the Circle for about two hours. When her parents decided to leave, the young girl waved a little rainbow flag as she fist-bumped the youths along the path toward the south end of the Circle.

The festival also allowed some teens to interact with people they might otherwise have avoided outside this context. At the park's south end, three young Black women approached the flag-covered police car and asked the officer to take their pictures on the car's hood. After photographing the young women, the officer smiled and asked whether they wanted a photo taken inside the car. The young women looked at each other and shook their heads. "Oh, no, no, no!" they shouted in unison before walking away, laughing raucously.

Many participants engaged in some of the more common activities at the Circle. Teens in rainbow-colored t-shirts and sports bras played chess with the older men at the northeast end. A group of Black and Latinx teens pounded rhythmically on overturned plastic bins with a couple of Black drummers at the southwest end. Several of those passing through the park received rainbow flags from the teens while others stopped to take pictures with flamboyantly dressed attendees. The festival also attracted many older gay male allies, who sat along the benches clutching Human Rights Campaign (HRC) shopping bags while taking in the festivities. A muscular middle-aged white man was sunning himself on one of the benches when a group of teens approached him.

"*Ay, Papi!*" one of the teens yelled as he hopped on the bench next to him. "Why are you sitting here all alone?"

The man said he had been walking through the Circle when he saw the festival and wanted to see what was happening.

"Well, let's show you," the teen said, grabbing the man's hand and tugging at him gently to get up. The group took him over to the body-painting tent, where they all stepped inside. When they came out a few minutes later, the man had a huge rainbow painted across his chest with the word "Pride" underneath.

Immediately south of the fountain, youths spray-painted white t-shirts and shoes in various colors. Some of these youths even made a physical mark on Dupont Circle. After one spray-painted his boyfriend's shoe gold, the young man stepped on the grass, leaving a sparkly gold imprint. "Oops," he said, initially embarrassed by the mark he left. But when his friends expressed their fondness for the shimmering imprint, the young man looked down and smiled at his friends, admiring his handiwork. "I guess I made my mark after all," he explained. High-fiving his friends, he told his boyfriend to lift his shoe. As the young man raised his foot, Mr. Gold grabbed a spray can and began spraying the sole of his shoe red while the group continued their painting. As I passed through the space again later that afternoon, I noticed seven colorful shoe imprints next to the gold one.

By five P.M., many youths had left the Circle to attend the queer prom hosted by the Youth Pride Alliance, and people in the park had returned to their normal activities. Yet with more than eight hundred queer and allied youths in attendance, organizers hailed the return of Youth Pride Day to the Circle as one of the most successful Youth Pride festivals in years. Many attributed that success to how the festival and the youths integrated their activities with those in the Circle. "There's something about that closeness, having everybody right there, people walking through, just hanging out and everybody being involved," Nikisha Carpenter, president of the Youth Pride Alliance, told *Metro Weekly* the following year, "There's no need to be spread out."[19] The event proved so successful that the tradition continued, disrupted only by the COVID pandemic.

At some level, Youth Pride Day appears to operate under multiple seemingly paradoxical logics. On the one hand, organizers hoped to make the lives and struggles of the area's LGBTQ youths visible without disrupting the Circle's cosmopolitan setting. "We really wanted to spread out around the circle to utilize the space while respecting that it was still a community space," Jessica Rotem stated. In this way, organizers recognized the Circle as a postgay cosmopolitan canopy,[20] where racially, ethnically, sexually, and intergenerationally diverse people could mingle and cultivate a greater appreciation for one another through folk ethnography and casual interactions.[21] "Diverse people converge," writes the sociologist Elijah Anderson, "defining the setting as belonging to everyone and deemphasizing race and other particularities. No one group claims priority, a hallmark of the cosmopolitan canopy."[22]

On the other hand, by returning to the Circle as a commemoration, organizers also hoped to make the Circle culturally and politically accessible to the youths as an LGBTQ institutional anchor. Returning to the Circle linked a new generation to the local LGBTQ community's past. It also provided the youths a forum in which to make various radical vicarious claims to Dupont Circle. Inserting themselves as community stakeholders by appropriating and producing space, these youths found new ways to make the park socioculturally meaningful while keeping the Circle's gay legacy alive.

PRESENTE! PRESENTE!

Within hours of the shooting at the Pulse nightclub, various groups jumped at the chance to capitalize on the tragedy to advance their specific interests. Conservative leaders quickly labeled it an act of radical Islamic terrorism while ignoring the fact that the massacre had occurred inside a gay bar. "Appreciate the congrats for being right on radical Islamic terrorism," then presidential candidate Donald Trump tweeted. "I don't want congrats. I want toughness and vigilance. We must be smart."[23] Condemning the shooting, gun control advocates seized the opportunity to call for more comprehensive gun control legislation, while gun rights organizations went on the defensive. "Evil struck in Orlando yesterday morning," tweeted Gun Owners of America. "No matter how tragic, no amount of gun control could've stopped evil."[24]

Worldwide, LGBTQ organizations vacillated amid rumors about the shooter's internalized homophobia and proclamations about the importance of gay bars for fostering community. Many LGBTQ citizens expressed anxiety over losing gay bars and safe spaces that protected the community. "These are our spaces," Chance (thirty-six, white, gay) explained. "Everyone keeps saying we don't need them anymore. But what happened should be a *huge* wake-up call to those who colonize our spaces. We've got to protect what is ours." That the shooting occurred during Pride Month was also not lost on older generations of white gay men, who took the opportunity to highlight how their efforts to create these spaces were under threat. During one DC vigil, a white gay man in his late fifties challenged younger LGBTQ people to protect the spaces that helped anchor the LGBTQ community. "We built these spaces because we knew the importance of protecting each other," he shouted through a broken megaphone. "We've done our part. Now it's your turn. Take care of each other. Protect what [our generation] built."

As the community's response to the Pulse tragedy crystallized around protecting LGBTQ organizations, Guillermo (twenty-four, Mexican, gay) was critical. "HRC and gay white people are totally hogging the spotlight on *our* tragedy." "Like always, they have made this about themselves and completely disregarded that our community was the one under threat." "Too many people are dismissing that the shooting took place during Pride month at a Latin night event," wrote journalist Alan Pelaez Lopez. "Even friends on social media have said that this shooting has nothing to do with race because, after all, white gay people go clubbing, too. But Sunday's shooting was an attack against a primarily young crowd of Latinx and Black individuals celebrating their existence in a world that has continually tried to silence them."[25]

Meanwhile, members of the LGBTQ Muslim communities worried that framing the tragedy as an act of radical Islamic terrorism made them targets even within their LGBTQ communities. Tariq (thirty-five, Arab, Muslim, gay) recalled that while walking down Seventeenth Street the Sunday after the shooting, he heard several gay men muttering epithets as he passed them. "I felt like I had a target on my back," he explained. Although I interviewed him months after the incident, revisiting the tragedy brought tears to his eyes. "I am just as shocked and scared as anyone else by what happened," he stated, pausing to regain composure. "I have gone through a lot to come out and live my truth, and now I have to deal with my own community turning their back on me." The strong reaction also elicited anger among LGBTQ Muslims. "We are mourning," Aabirah (twenty-six, Iranian, Muslim, queer) told me. "This shooting impacts queer Muslims around the world . . . just as it does anyone else. And yet we are being attacked by members of our own [LGBTQ] community. They don't care that we are also mourning." Many who experienced abuse did not even identify as Muslim, amplifying the indiscriminate prejudice that LGBTQ non-Muslims expressed in the immediate aftermath. Justin (twenty-three, South Asian, gay) does not identify as Muslim, yet he endured multiple violent attacks by white gay men. "I was waiting in line [in a gay bar] for a drink when someone just walked up to me and told me, 'You've got some nerve being here, you fucking Arab.' I was dumbfounded because he couldn't have been more off. I'm Indian. I was raised Catholic. And I grew up in *New Jersey*, for fuck sake! He didn't even care that I went out to be with my community and mourn like everybody else."

Frustrated by their erasure, several Latinx and Muslim LGBTQ organizations collaborated in creating communitywide events to write themselves back into the conversation. While Latinx organizers hoped to elicit audience sympathy for the victims and survivors, they also wanted to create an intersectional movement, connecting their collective suffering to the abuse experienced by Muslims. "We quickly realized that our mourning was not separate from the violence against queer Muslims or trans people," said Pablo (thirty-eight, Latinx, gay). "We were not going to repeat what the white gays did to us. We are going to show them how to do it right." On Monday, the Muslim American Women's Policy Forum organized the first vigil in Dupont Circle, establishing traditions that other vigils later followed. In addition to incorporating local traditions, such as the performance of "We Shall Overcome" by the Gay Men's Chorus of Washington, DC and an open mic session during which members of the LGBTQ community could share their feeling, the organizers made sure to include elements from Latinx and Muslim tradition in the event. Toward the end, the president of Latino LGBT History Project led the participants in a call-and-response reading of the victims' names. The audience responded with *"Presente!"* as each name was called, symbolizing their presence in spirit. While establishing a tradition that would continue at other vigils throughout the weeks, *"Presente!"* also became a rallying cry for the Latinx queer community.

The monument at the Dupont Circle fountain also incorporated elements of the Latino and Muslim cultures. Along the walkways surrounding the fountain, messages in Spanish appeared. *"La determinación orgullo y amor de las personas LGBT brillará más fuerte,"*[26] written in bold-colored chalk, dominated one side of the fountain (figure 5.1). Supportive messages in Arabic soon appeared alongside the Spanish, transforming the sidewalk into a colorful mosaic of tributes. Youths chalked the surrounding sidewalk with supportive English, Spanish, and Arabic messages, including "Muslims Love Queers" and "Presente! Presente! Presente!" (figure 5.2). The display at the fountain also included objects from the curbside memorials I remembered all too well from growing up in Los Angeles. Rosaries encircled sanctuary candles with images of Our Lady of Guadalupe, Jesus, and St. Joseph overlooking color photos of the forty-nine victims. The juxtaposition of Arabic and Spanish embodied the spirit of many events led by the Latinx and Muslim queer communities that week.

Before the largest In Memoriam to the Pulse tragedy victims took place in Dupont Circle, representatives of Washington's Latinx and Muslim queer communities hosted a community dialogue on the shooting at a church on Sixteenth Street. The program included moments during which members of the audience could express their

FIGURE 5.1 Messages written in Spanish to support the Muslim and Latinx LGBT communities erased in local Pulse commemorations.

Photo by author.

feelings about the tragedy. However, the organizers made it clear from the outset that the evening's dialogue was to focus on the stories of those silenced in the public grieving. "We recognize that you all feel some personal connection to the tragedy," one of the organizers explained to the audience at the beginning of the meeting. "But this is also your time to listen to those most affected by what happened at Pulse." Throughout the program, organizers emphasized the costs of the tragedy for those in the Latinx queer and transgender

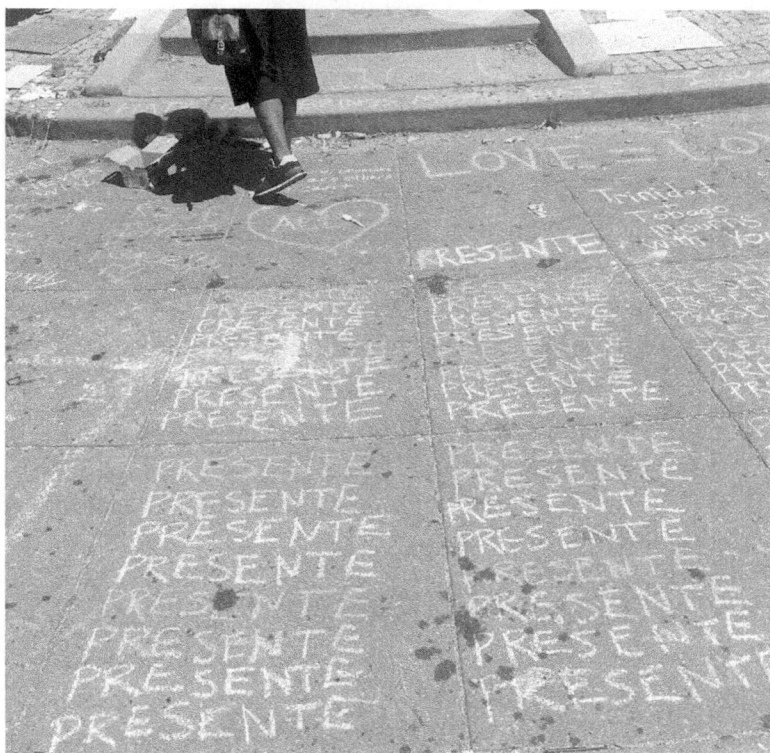

FIGURE 5.2 The rallying cry, "*Presente!*" to signal the presence of the victims in spirit written along the walkways near the fountain to support the Muslim and Latinx LGBT communities erased in local Pulse commemorations.

Photo by author.

communities. Several spoke of the friends and family members they lost. Others shared their experiences of visiting the nightclub, highlighting the tragedy of losing one of the safe spaces for the Latinx LGBTQ community. During one poignant moment, a Latinx transgender woman scolded the audience for focusing on the safety and preservation of white queer spaces at the expense of the few existing spaces for queer communities of color. "You all sit there crying about no longer feeling safe in your bars," she shouted. "Pulse wasn't even a queer Latinx nightclub. It was only Latinx once a month."

After the dialogue, the organizers invited us to participate in a candlelight procession from the church to the Dupont Circle vigil. As we walked out, we grabbed long white candles from volunteers at the doors. Lining up in front of the church, we fought the warm summer breeze to light our candles, which gave participants a chance to chat and reflect on what they heard. While I was lighting the candle of the white man standing next to me, he asked me if I was gay. I replied affirmatively. He then asked me what I thought of the evening.

"I thought it was pretty powerful," I replied.

"Yeah," the man replied, nodding. Identifying himself as straight, he described how he came to the event to get a different perspective. "We are so focused on our own pain sometimes. We have no idea who we might be hurting."

"Totally," I replied.

"I wish more people could hear that perspective," he said, "to move past their own privilege and recognize how they could be allies to others who have to suffer in silence."

Within fifteen minutes of our lining up, the president of the Latino LGBT History Project assumed his position at the front of the extensive line, and the procession began. As we walked along P Street, the president shouted the shooting victims' names through a megaphone, after which we replied with *"Presente."* Strangers walked arm-in-arm as the roll call began, reducing marchers to tears. Marchers demonstrated extraordinary kindness to each other along the six-block walk to Dupont Circle. One marcher attempted to balance his candle while walking on crutches. When a car pulled up alongside to offer him a ride to the Circle, he smiled and politely declined. "Thanks," he told the driver, "but this is something I really need to do." As the procession neared Dupont Circle and the man began feeling pain in his leg, marchers came to his aid. One grabbed his crutches and candle while two men carried him the rest of the way.

The observance in Dupont Circle had already begun by the time we arrived. As a Black minister continued a rousing sermon about the power of forgiveness, participants stopped behind the procession leader and continued their call-and-response. Our arrival barely registered among members of the crowd. A few bystanders turned around to see what was going on. Once they realized what we were doing, they returned their attention to the pastor. Undeterred by the ongoing activity, the leader continued calling out the names until he reached the end. When he had finished, the group disbanded, dispersing into the crowd to participate in the service. In the days that followed, reports on the vigil in Dupont Circle eclipsed the dialogue and funeral-like procession along P Street. Yet several things occurred during the week that became traditions in subsequent years. On the anniversary of the tragedy, a Latino LGBT History Project representative reads the victims' names during the annual commemoration in Dupont Circle, inviting the audience to respond with "Presente!" Vigils include makeshift memorials that incorporate votive candles and some visual representation of the victims' names. These events did not necessarily receive as much attention that week as the events held by mainstream organizations did. Nevertheless, enacting familiar subcultural traditions, the Latinx and Muslim LGBTQ communities translated Dupont Circle into a place where queer communities of color could mobilize to mourn, heal, and articulate their anger and grief on their own terms.

————

This chapter explored radical vicarious claims, which constitute demands for recognition made by outsiders and "outsiders within." Radical claims entail expanding the cultural imagination of place and community in local neighborhoods through the appropriation and cultural misrecognition of local space,[27] which may sometimes challenge more traditionally held perceptions of a space's or place's use and meaning. Sometimes the practices that constitute radical vicarious claims can align with normative claims made by the dominant group. At other times, community members may rupture place by imposing practices that align with aspects of their subcultures. Dancing in a bar that patrons do not view as a dance club or writing oneself into place by infusing spaces with traditions and customs associated with one's indigenous culture may seem innocuous. Nevertheless, they also constitute vital strategies for disrupting the whiteness of queer spaces.

However, the examples of placemaking evoked by the Latinx and Muslim LGBTQ communities in the wake of the Pulse tragedy extended far beyond radical vicarious claims to the Dupont Circle neighborhood. They represented a challenge to the whiteness of gay neighborhoods and the LGBTQ community more broadly. Calling attention to their collective erasure, the Latinx and Muslim LGBTQ communities also made a political claim for recognition by the mainstream communities. As I discuss in the next chapter, when vicarious citizens make political vicarious claims, they may rely on traditional political channels to protect their interests in iconic gay neighborhoods. They may draw on various strategies to insert themselves into the local political process, sometimes relying on residents to defend their political interests and enact their visions of community. Increased access to information has yielded greater involvement in the local political sphere. However, vicarious citizens also face significant challenges when exercising political claims. Many local and municipal institutions often limit the rights associated with local community decision-making to those with more significant material ties to the area.

6

POLITICAL VICARIOUS
CLAIMS AND THE ART OF
SELF-ENFRANCHISEMENT

The April 26, 1969, edition of the *Richmond Times-Dispatch* carried a rather unusual warning from the Washington gay activist Frank Kameny to Virginia's Alcohol Beverage Control (ABC) Board. Throughout much of the 1960s, the board had targeted several bars and restaurants catering to gays and lesbians along The Block, a popular destination for the city's underground gay community dating back to the 1940s. After Virginia Commonwealth University forced the ABC Board to revoke the license of Eton, a popular gay nightspot, in 1967, gay patrons shifted to two nearby establishments, Renee's Restaurant and the Rathskeller, which became anchors for the community. Frustration and anger within the gay community reached a fevered pitch two years later when both bars came under threat for violating two ABC regulations, one of which allowed suspension of a bar's license if it became a "meeting place and rendezvous for users of narcotics, drunks, homosexuals, prostitutes, pimps, panderers, gamblers, or habitual law violators."[1] When news spread that the ABC Board would hold a hearing on March 5, 1969, to consider revoking Renee's and the Rathskeller's beer licenses, several residents contacted Kameny, who lived ninety-two miles away. "At the time," Bob Swisher wrote in the *Richmond Pride* in 1989, "Kameny was one of only a handful of activists in the United States who were speaking out publicly for gay rights."[2]

Kameny attended the March 5 hearing. He heard ABC agents tes-
tifying to "men wearing makeup, embracing and kissing in [Renee's
Restaurant]." Kameny witnessed the defense challenge the board,
saying that it could not prove the bars were gay bars since the agents
failed to see any homosexual activity there. And he witnessed the
response of the board's chairman Warren Wright to the defense; he
asked, "Are you saying that any good, decent citizen of Richmond
could go in [either bar] and not be shocked by what he saw?"[3] After
the ABC Board revoked both bars' beer licenses on March 13, 1969,
resulting in their closure, Kameny wrote a letter to the editor of the
Richmond Times-Dispatch on behalf of the "justifiably outraged members of the Richmond homosexual community." Finding fault in tar-
geting homosexuals, he defined gay men and lesbians as first-class
citizens who "will not be satisfied with an iota less than any right,
freedom, liberty, benefit, and privilege enjoyed by all other citizens."
"I did not place my life in jeopardy in front-line combat over enemy
fire in World War II," he wrote, "in order to be told by a medievally-
minded ABC Board that I—and my fellow homosexuals, in any
number—cannot patronize public establishments of any kind upon a
basis equal to that of all other citizens."[4]

Citing the growing militancy of gays and lesbians across the
country, Kameny told the ABC Board that failure to reconsider its
policy toward these establishments would result in direct action. In
addition to lawsuits and peaceful picketing outside the ABC Board,
he threatened that homosexuals would protest by patronizing every
remaining bar in Richmond, forcing the ABC Board to close them
all. "Groups of homosexuals," Kameny writes, "designating themselves as such, may commence systematically to patronize other bars
in Richmond—one or two bars at a time—until the ABC Board—
acting in consistency with its regulations, has been forced to shut
down every bar in the city—or change its regulations."[5]

Kameny's threat never came to fruition. Although it helped
mobilize Richmond's LGBT community to fight for equality in the

months before the Stonewall riots, it would take the Virginia General Assembly almost twenty-five years to revise its ABC regulations to remove the offending provisions. Nevertheless, his threat of mobilizing gays and lesbians to transform every Virginia bar into a gay bar, according to the board's definition, reflects what I call a *political vicarious claim*. As a resident of Washington, DC, Kameny had little power to enact political change by following political channels available to those who lived in Virginia. Nevertheless, as a vicarious citizen, he articulated a claim to space that he would gladly have pursued, according to a 1994 interview with the historian Genny Beemyn.[6]

Kameny's threat offers a valuable entrée into how vicarious citizens mobilize cultural claims to pursue community interests through the local political process. In recent years, scholars have increasingly recognized how contemporary citizenship has expanded to accommodate a variety of formal (political) and informal (social) practices used by even the most economically and politically disenfranchised populations to claim, expand, or challenge rights in the postmodern city.[7] Yet because "political participation of the ordinary citizen in America is pretty much restricted to the intermittently recurring elections"[8] and because access to local decision-making channels remains the exclusive province of residents, vicarious citizens face various challenges when exercising political claims. Many political vicarious claims are vulnerable to exclusion or dismissal by local political actors who fail to take vicarious citizens' sense of community ownership seriously.

Vicarious citizens are not necessarily discouraged from actively pursuing their political interests by these challenges. Rather, they draw on various strategies to elicit attention to their political claims, often relying on taken-for-granted aspects of the local political process in pursuing their community interests. This chapter examines political vicarious claims more closely. By mobilizing normative or radical vicarious claims as a form of *self-enfranchisement*, not only do vicarious citizens expand the political possibilities of who can claim community membership locally, but also these political vicarious claims ultimately reinvent the notion of citizenship itself.

INSERTING ONESELF INTO THE LOCAL POLITICAL PROCESS

Recognizing their limited access to local decision-making, many vicarious citizens insert themselves into local political issues as community organizers, eliciting the support of residents to defend their political interests and enact their visions of community. In this position, vicarious citizens become implicit participants in local decision-making—unrecognized as legitimate political claims makers but influencing public discourse through their targeted interactions with residents.[9] Despite living in the same Northern Virginia apartment for nearly a decade, Esteban (thirty-one, Latino, gay) considers his residence to be nothing more than a 600-square-foot closet where he hangs his suits. "The only reason I live in Crystal City is that I could not afford to live in DC," he explained. "I really do everything [in DC]. I work in Dupont. I hang out with my friends there. I'm only home to change my clothes, shower, and sleep. And believe me, I don't always sleep [at home] if I am particularly lucky [laughs]." He describes his attachment to Dupont Circle as a "subconscious obsession." He jokes about how he always seemed to find himself in Dupont Circle, even unintentionally. "It seems my geographic compass is set toward Dupont," he says. "Sometimes [when I have nothing else to do], I just come to the city and grab a cup of coffee and *The Blade* or *Metro Weekly*, sit on a bench in [Dupont] Circle, and watch the people chilling on the lawn or hanging out at the fountain."

When news surfaced about a DC Council member introducing a same-sex marriage bill for a vote, Esteban knew he wanted to support the cause. Learning that same-sex marriage would be on the docket at a DC Board of Elections and Ethics hearing, he decided to attend.

"I wasn't sure that I should be there," he remembered. "I really wasn't a resident, but at the same time, I knew that getting same-sex marriage in DC would be really major, and I wanted to be part of it any way I can." Esteban was not alone. He was shocked to discover several self-identified Maryland residents who joined the meeting that evening, many expressing their opposition to the bill. As he heard one Maryland resident rationalizing his opposition to the members of the board, Esteban knew that he did not have to be a resident to engage in direct action. "He was one of those who grew up [in DC]," he recalled. "He was saying all sorts of crazy shit, man . . . but what got me was when he said that it was okay to discriminate against gays if it meant protecting the 'moral character of DC.' That's when I was like, if this dude could say that discriminating against gays was 'good discrimination,' then I could get my ass out there and have my say, too." He joined a volunteer organization and canvassed alongside residents in Dupont Circle and the U Street corridor to encourage other locals to sign the petition supporting same-sex marriage in the District. Although he could not sign the petition himself, he found great satisfaction in engaging residents on an issue he profoundly believed in. "Some people thought I was kinda crazy for standing out in the rain, drumming up support for a law I would not benefit from, living in Virginia. But I didn't care. I'd tell them that this is my community, too, and even though I can't vote or anything, I'm out here doing what I can to help. Then I'd ask them, 'What are you doing to help?' I think I guilted a lot of people to sign that way."

Despite Esteban's enthusiasm, neither he nor the Maryland residents who spoke up at that meeting stood to be directly affected by the decision on marriage equality in the District. Yet by participating in a local organization, Esteban embodies the spirit of Saul Alinsky's radical, establishing his political legitimacy by mobilizing a constituency that could realize his vision of community.[10] By focusing on his limited capacity to effect change through the referendum, Esteban drew on his status as a vicarious citizen to encourage residents to support his cause.

Vicarious citizens may also draw on political claims to enact normative vicarious claims. In the months following the Pulse tragedy, Vincent (forty-two, white, gay) canvassed local LGBTQ establishments on behalf of Gays Against Guns, a nonprofit organization supporting gun control laws. On the morning we painted the rainbow crosswalks on Seventeenth Street (chapter 4), Vincent decided to bring a Gays Against Guns t-shirt and stickers for the mayor. "I want her to hold up the shirt like Barack Obama did when he received shirts from organizations," he said. As we walked down the street toward JR's to meet the volunteers who would paint the crosswalks, he distributed flyers to every person we passed. When one person politely declined his flyer, he shouted at the person, a young white woman. "We've got to send a message to our mayor," he explained. "We got her back on these gun control laws. We need to keep Dupont and our LGBTQ communities safe." Sighing in defeat, she quietly nodded and took the flyer from his hand. By drawing local attention to a national public issue, Vincent believes he is challenging the apathy of LGBTQ residents who *should* have an investment in local safety. "Taking back our streets means being ready for political action," he explained. "LGBT people take for granted that our freedom is fragile. We can't stop at marriage when our community is at risk."

Local institutional actors may serve as proxies for groups of vicarious citizens, exercising political vicarious claims on their behalf. These proxies may strengthen political claims by tying them to broader political issues, especially when political opportunities coincide with other local claims. Following the passage of Proposition 8 in California in 2008, gay bars and establishments banned bachelorette parties throughout the United States. Geno Zaharakis became the first to receive national attention for implementing such a ban at his gay bar in Boystown. "Until same-sex marriage is legal everywhere," Zaharakis wrote in a prepared statement, "and same-sex couples are allowed the rights as every heterosexual worldwide, we simply do not think it's fair or just for a female bride-to-be to celebrate her upcoming nuptials here."[11] While many Washington bars did not ban bachelorette parties, they did mobilize. At drag shows at Town Discoboutique, bachelorettes and their participants had to sign a petition supporting marriage equality. Several drag performers donated the tips they received from bachelorette parties to organizations like Lambda Legal and the Human Rights Campaign. At one drag show where a bachelorette party was present, the drag queen looked down at her tip jar at the end of a set and demanded the party tip more. "Oh, no, no, no!" the performer yelled. "If you want to come in here to celebrate your wedding, you're to pay it forward." She walked up to the group and shook the tip jar with its Freedom to Marry logo displayed to the audience. The audience cheered the drag performer while the women began placing money into the tip jar.

POLITICAL VICARIOUS CLAIMS IN THE AGE OF SOCIAL MEDIA

Using protests to radicalize political vicarious claims, even when these are normative claims on space, intensifies the sense of urgency and heightens challengers' collective efficacy.[12] Despite having increased access to local political channels, vicarious citizens may initially reject operating within the routinized political process in favor of pursuing more radical political tactics. In 2007, the manager of a U Street drug store kicked out a gay Maryland couple for showing affection in the store. Two weeks later approximately fifty gay men and their supporters, including the area's gay DC Council member, convened at the drug store and staged a "hug-in," where same-sex couples lined up in front of checkout lines and hugged each other on cue for about a minute. After reading about the incident in *Metro Weekly*, protest organizers promoted the event through Facebook and local neighborhood blogs.

None of the organizers knew the couple before the incident, and the drug store was not considered a gay institutional anchor. Instead, the organizers mobilized to challenge actions inconsistent with the neighborhood's character. As one organizer, a gay-identified resident, explained in an interview with the *Washington Blade*, "I'm not one to sit around and say 'oh well' when I hear about people's rights being violated, especially when it happens to gay couples and especially in my neighborhood."[13] One of the men who had been told to leave the drug store participated in the protest, expressing pride in the community's response as well as disbelief. "It was a bit of a shock for the most part since I didn't realize that I had a support system," he explained. "I didn't know that the incident had reached a lot of people . . . I was more than glad to see that people, in general, were standing up for our rights, and it's about time."[14]

The hug-in illuminates a paradox of contemporary political claims making in the postmodern city. The hug-in seemed to be an act of disruption by marginalized outsiders who were challenging the actions of a homophobic local institution. Yet the goal of the protest was to have community insiders enforce a normative claim, thus policing behavior inconsistent with the area's local character as a gay space. In this way, large demonstrations and protests, traditionally understood by social movement scholars as the most effective tool of the powerless, also represent a performative act by urban cosmopolitans to lend a sense of cultural authenticity to political claims.[15] As with more-traditional protest activities, such protests aim to draw public and media attention and stimulate political action by others with the power and resources to realize the ultimate goals of the protest.[16] In the case of the hug-in, where protesters could have easily used any of the tactics in their arsenal to realize their political goals, they chose to activate participation from those willing to pursue their cause through the local political process. While organizers described the hug-in as a success, neither the protesters nor the organizers pursued legal action. After the Metropolitan Police Department and members of the DC Council contacted the drug store chain's corporate offices, a company representative told *Metro Weekly* that the case would be investigated, reaffirming the company's dedication to honoring the respect and dignity of all clients.[17]

The transience of the hug-in is no indication of the intensity and investment of the involved protesters in their cause. Instead, it reflects the increasing ease with which interested political actors can insert themselves into critical political debates with the help of social media. As illustrated by the hug-in, Facebook and local blogs connected a community of residentially dispersed, like-minded strangers, rapidly disseminating information and catalyzing offline political action.[18]

POLITICAL VICARIOUS CLAIMS AS EXPRESSIONS OF BLACK QUEER JOY

Social media platforms can also democratize local political partici-pation, offering new avenues for various political actors who would otherwise be excluded from the local political process. In the wake of Black Lives Matter, social media have become a powerful tool for communities of color, especially as phone technology has allowed everyday citizens to record troubling interactions with the police and security personnel. Additionally, as mainstream media outlets cre-ate narratives that criminalize and pathologize Black victims, social media have offered new ways for Black participants to reshape domi-nant narratives so as to activate Black LGBTQ communities to par-ticipate in various social justice movements against violence, racism, homophobia, and urban disinvestment. More importantly, Black digital spaces create opportunities for "expressive, resistant, and life-sustaining practices" that also celebrate the Black queer experience.[19]

In the summer of 2021, Nellie's Sports Bar faced controversy after a video surfaced of a security guard dragging twenty-two-year-old Keisha Young down the stairs by her hair during Capital Pride

Month. The altercation began as a case of mistaken identity. In the early hours of June 13, 2021, a staff member mistook the young woman for another Black woman who had allegedly brought a bottle into the bar. A fight that ensued between patrons and security spilled out into the street. The cell phone footage, which lasted around a minute, quickly went viral, motivating racial justice groups and local activists to take immediate action. Within hours of the incident, nearly one hundred demonstrators gathered outside the bar, chanting "Justice for Keisha" and "Protect Black women."[20]

Protestors used the incident to highlight long-standing issues between the bar and its patrons of color. As Preston Mitchum, a local activist, explained to the *Washington Blade*, "Over the years, the culture [at Nellie's] became one that seemed hell-bent on pushing Black patrons out and making it a bar more for straight people and white gay men. In fact, [owner] Doug Schantz has gone on record calling his bar 'straight-friendly.'"[21] Mitchum observed numerous examples of racial profiling at the bar during his time as a DC resident. Security was increased on days when Black patrons populated the bar, and the genre of music was changed from hip-hop to avoid potential "violent interactions." The prices for certain drinks "stereotyped as ordinarily purchased by Black patrons" also increased, while the prices for drinks popular among white patrons remained stable. And in 2018, Nellie's became the target of another protest by the group No Justice No Pride after a Blue Lives Matter flag was flown outside the bar. Beyond these issues, Black LGBTQ leaders wanted to draw attention to the scarcity of Black queer spaces as gentrification persisted. Mitchum spotlighted this ongoing concern for Washington's Black LGBTQ community during a virtual town hall about the incident. "This is bigger than Nellie's," he stated. "It's about the lack of Black queer spaces and safety in DC."[22]

Despite initial efforts to work with the owner of Nellie's to improve conditions for Black patrons, Mitchum contended that conditions never really changed. "Myself and others have written letters,"

Mitchum wrote in a Facebook post, "did interviews, conducted sensitivity trainings, met with the owner, and even planted ourselves as observers to document our experiences."[23] Within days of the incident, Schantz took steps to mitigate the protests. In addition to firing the independent security vendor that had been hired for the evening in question, he offered a "heartfelt apology" in a Facebook post "to all who witnessed the horrific events of this past weekend."[24] Schantz's apology further fanned the flames, as protestors recognized that his apology omitted Young. "The public didn't really get dragged down the stairs," Young explained to *DCist*. "I did. The public doesn't have bruises. I do."[25]

When the owner refused to acknowledge a list of demands from protest organizers, demonstrators returned for a protest block party every Friday for several weeks. Advertised on Facebook, these block parties drew from a few dozen to over a hundred protesters each week, standing in solidarity with Young and calling on the owner to meet their demands for tangible change. People danced in the streets, with some hitting death drops to music spun by DJs. Others lined the streets, standing in front of Nellie's entrance with bullhorns, shouting their demands. Drawing attention to the lack of spaces available for Black queer people in the District, these block parties combined the political with the pleasurable. As Makia Green, one of the protest organizers, told the *Washington Post*, "We shook not only this establishment, this neighborhood and the city. We didn't do it in the sense of what you see time and time again of the most marginalized carrying a movement or a protest on our backs like mules. . . . You can fight for freedom and have pleasure and joy at the same time." Protestors celebrated the block parties as they mixed activism with the community. One community member explained how the protest block parties created a space that supported Black women: "What the boycotts have given me, in that space that it's created, is that I can be my whole, total self in a world that continues to tell me that being that is not enough. When I see Keisha [Young], I see me."[26]

During this time, #BoycottNellies transformed from a protest into a movement. The protest block parties raised funds to support Young's recovery and encouraged protestors to hold Nellie's account-able. Their ongoing protests also sparked an investigation by the Alcoholic Beverage Control Board, the DC Metropolitan Police Department, and the Office of the Attorney General for DC Neigh-bors got involved in the protests as well. The bar closed immediately after the incident and remained closed throughout June to "evaluate this regrettable situation." However, once the bar reopened in July, the protests continued. Residents who observed patrons entering the bar on July 13 shared the information on social media using the hashtag #BoycottNellies. That same evening activists returned, forming a human chain to block people from entering.[27]

By the end of the summer, the protest block parties had ended despite vows by various organizations to continue boycotting the bar. And although Nellie's owner promised to make changes, including providing deescalation training and hiring a director of community engagement, many found the gestures hollow. In a statement on Twit-ter, Harriet's Wildest Dreams, a Black-led prison-abolitionist group, warned residents not to be fooled by the protests. "It is heartbreak-ing that Black native Washingtonians, women and GNC [gender-nonconforming] people have spent weeks on the ground to get one public apology for such a gruesome assault," the statement read. "It's even more infuriating to have our calls for Black LGBTQ led accountability, reparations, and transformation to be ignored and scapegoated by a non-Black leader in the queer community. . . . Do not be fooled. The boycott continues until all demands are met."[28]

Social media have played a decisive role in political activism, "doc-umenting and challenging episodes of police brutality and the mis-representation of racialized bodies in mainstream media."[29] Over the last decade, scholars have given increased attention to how advances in "personal, mobile, informational technology" have expanded the imagination of political possibility. Social media have been vital in producing "fresh kinds of highly informed, autonomous communities that coalesce around local lifestyle choices, global political demands, and everything in between."[30] Regarding political activity in local communities, vicarious citizens often leverage social media to participate in communities of limited liability.[31] Participants shift from being passive political actors who post on online discussion boards, financially support political causes, and offer emotional support for movements to being active political actors who protest through more direct action.[32] In the case of the Nellie's protests, Black digital spaces proved vital in fostering community building and calling attention to concerns that many local mainstream LGBTQ establishments have too long ignored.

However, social media cannot sustain political vicarious claims alone. Place mattered for these young activists, who understood that appropriating and transforming space through ephemeral placemaking was vital to writing themselves into the local community. In this case, Black protesters expressed political vicarious claims by creating the community many of them too often felt denied. In so doing, they did not just draw attention to the suffering created by the incident. They also engaged in forms of placemaking that reflect the "fun, . . . witty, . . . soulful, . . . smart, . . . biting and . . . rejuvenating" spirit that tied them to Shaw/U Street as an important cultural anchor for the city's Black communities.[33]

WHY ARE THEY PROTESTING SOMETHING HAPPENING OVER THERE OVER HERE?

Sometimes political vicarious claims reflect strategies for building necessary alliances among those under the diverse LGBTQ umbrella, even when the issues raised have little to do with what is going on in the gayborhood. By 2019, violence against LGBTQ citizens had reached epidemic proportions in the United States. In June of that year,

GLAAD reported an overall decline in LGBTQ acceptance among younger Americans and identified at least thirty-two incidents of anti-LGBTQ-related violence in the United States within the year. That same month the Human Rights Campaign highlighted the murders of at least ten transgender and gender-nonconforming people in the United States, including two transgender women of color from the DC area.[34] On March 30, 2019, twenty-seven-year-old Ashanti Carmon was shot and killed on Eastern Avenue along the DC-Maryland border, a known gathering place for sex workers and trans women. Nearly three months later, on June 13, police found the body of twenty-three-year-old Zoe Spears on the sidewalk within a few blocks of where Carmon was murdered. Reports surfaced that Spears was a good friend of Carmon, had witnessed her murder in March, and had reached out for help relocating out of the area the week before she died.[35]

Spears's death punctuated a particularly violent Pride Month in the District. Days earlier, on June 8, a man brandishing a BB gun in Dupont Circle disrupted the Pride Parade as attendees, fearing an active shooter, ran for their lives. Seven people, caught up in the stampede, required hospitalization for their injuries. A week later, on June 15, a man threatened several trans women with a gun after demanding oral sex outside Casa Ruby, the LGBTQ community center on Georgia Avenue, amplifying fear within the city's transgender community. A day later more than a dozen men attacked and robbed a gay couple outside Nellie's Sports Bar on U Street, leaving one victim with two broken teeth, a bruised lip, and a swollen eye. Across town, an altercation resulted in the stabbing of three people inside the Fireplace, Dupont Circle's last gay bar, along the P Street strip. In response to the wave of violent attacks across the city, several LGBTQ organizations organized a Vigil Against the Violence on June 21. Nearly three hundred people gathered in Dupont Circle for the sunset vigil, promoted on Facebook and in flyers distributed throughout Dupont Circle, U Street, and Logan Circle.

As I approached the Dupont Circle Fountain that evening with two friends, I overheard several conversations questioning the purpose of the vigil. The simple branding of the event left much to the imagination—rainbow stripes against a black field with "A Vigil Against the Violence" written in white and the DC flag printed in gray tones underneath. Many assumed the vigil would address the recent violence in and around Dupont Circle. However, the posters adorning the fountain centered on the violence against transgender women of color on Eastern Avenue. Poster-sized photos of Spears and Carmon lined the fountain's base along with handmade posters with messages like "Black Trans Lives Matter" and "We Will Not Be Erased." Various participants also carried signs in solidarity with the transwomen of color throughout the crowd. Near where I stood, a female-presenting participant held up a poster with a hand-drawn outline of the United States. The states where the transgender women had been murdered were outlined on the map, with the victims' names written around them. Next to the map a women held up a sign displaying the message, "Remember the Names [and Fight 4 the Living]" was written in large letters. Below the message was a list of issues affecting the lives of transgender citizens: affordable housing, health care access, employment protections, livable wages, accessible bureaucracy, sex work decriminalization, youth support, and community.

While residents waited for the vigil to begin, volunteers distributed miniature rainbow flags and 5" x 7" glossy black cards (figures 6.1 and 6.2). On the front of the card, a lit candle stood against a background of golden halos representing lit candles. The words "In Loving Memory: An Evening of Remembrance" were written at the top, and "Candlelight Vigil for 2019 Murdered Transgenders" appeared at the bottom underneath the day and time of the evening's vigil. The ten trans women who died in 2019 were listed on the back of the card in the order of their date of death:

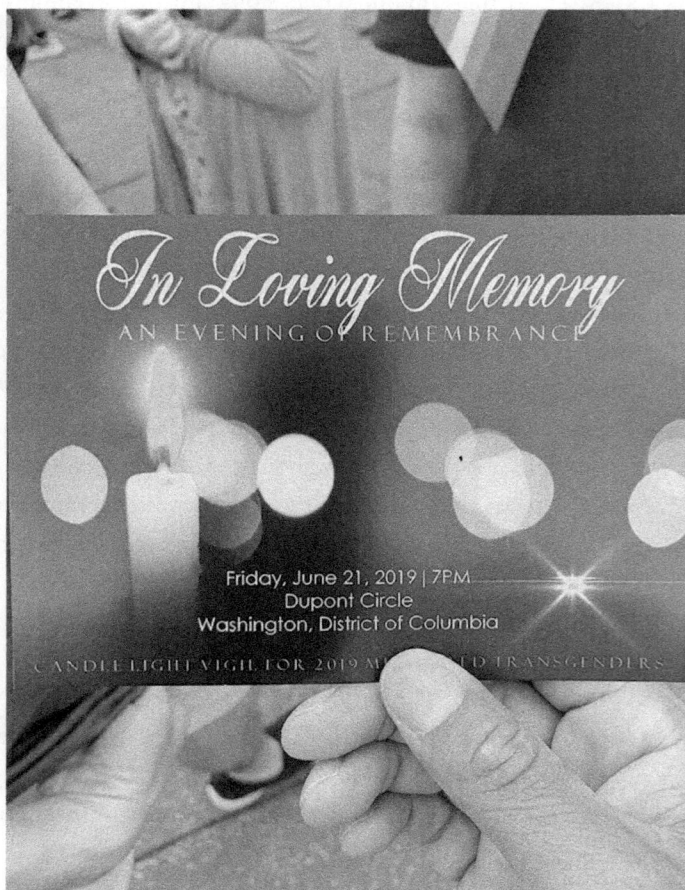

FIGURE 6.1 The front of the card distributed during the Vigil Against the Violence, showing the details of the event.

Photo by author.

Dana Martin (31), January 6, 2019

Jazzaline Ware (no age indicated), March 2019

Ashanti Carmon (27), March 30, 2019

Claire Legato (21), May 14, 2019

Muhlaysia Booker (23), May 18, 2019

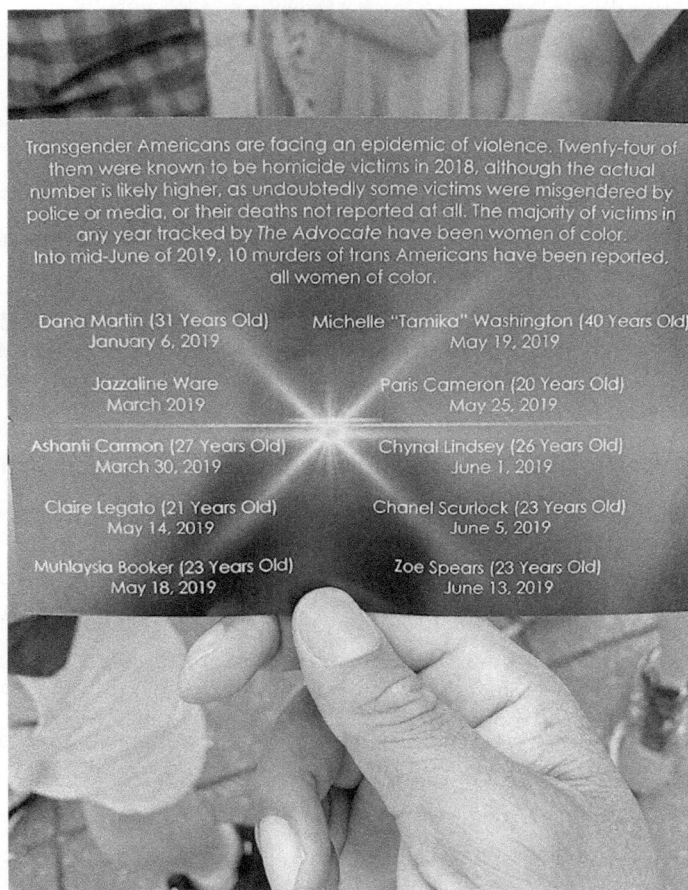

FIGURE 6.2 The back of the card distributed during the Vigil Against the Violence, highlighting the names of the victims.

Photo by Author.

Michelle "Tamika" Washington (40), May 19, 2019

Paris Cameron (20), May 25, 2019

Chynal Lindsey (26), June 1, 2019

Chanel Scurlock (23), June 5, 2019

Zoe Spears (33), June 13, 2019

While inspecting the card, I overheard a trio of white gay men in their twenties expressing their confusion and frustration over the Vigil.

"I didn't come here for this!" one said, fanning the card. "I thought this was about the violence happening here."

"Classic bait-and-switch," said another. "They say this is about protecting our community and then turn the focus on the shit happening on Eastern Avenue."

"I don't get why they are bringing something happening ten miles away from here," the third man added. "We have enough to deal with here."

Standing in front of the trio, a Black trans woman holding a "Black Trans Lives Matter" sign shook her head and sucked her teeth at their conversation. She finally had enough after one of the men made a crude joke about what the trans women were doing on Eastern Avenue.

"What's the matter with all of you!" she shouted, shaking her sign in their faces. "You need to know what's going on up there! These women were part of our community. *I'm* part of this community, and I deserve to be here!"

The men's faces reddened as nearby bystanders turned around to see the commotion. "I'm sorry," one of the men replied. "We are just trying to understand why this is relevant to us."

"If you gotta ask," she clapped back, "then you've answered your own stupid question." As she whipped back around to face the crowd, she spat out, "Y'all need to stop showing your asses and show some damn respect."

The men surveyed the spectators in search of any sign of sympathy. As the bystanders returned to their conversations, the men, finding no allies, mumbled a quick apology and pushed their way through the crowd to the other side of the fountain.

Earline Budd, a trans activist, opened the vigil. "Thank you for taking the opportunity this Friday to join us for a vigil against the violence," she said. "Not just here, but around the country." Spotlighting the recent deaths of Carmon and Spears, she described how their deaths particularly resonated because both would have celebrated birthdays in June. After thanking the DC Center (the city's LGBTQ center) for organizing the event, Budd acknowledged the city officials in Fairmount Heights and the members of the DC Council who had spoken at an earlier vigil. "We're just so thankful that things are finally starting to move," she said. "And we're going to hold you to those promises." After the audience applauded her promise of account-ability, Budd invited the crowd to bow their heads in prayer. Bishop Allyson Abrams of Empowerment Liberation Cathedral and the Reverend Elder Dyan Akousa McCray of Unity Fellowship Church offered blessings, and the Gay Men's Chorus of Washington, DC led the crowd in singing "We Shall Overcome."

Budd then announced that several trans women would share their experiences of survival. However, when Emmelia Ruiz Talarico, another trans activist, grabbed the microphone, she immediately made it clear that she had no intention of sharing her experiences for the audience's benefit. Despite experiencing a hate-related incident a few days earlier, Talarico refused to assuage the guilt of "white, cis-gender audience members" who expressed hostility toward her one moment and engaged in empty symbolic promises the next. "There are people I'm sharing the stage with," she read from her iPhone, "who tried to get me and other members of No Justice No Pride fired because we wanted the police not to march in Pride. I share this space with people who threw trash, bottles, and punches at us, who called us and our loved ones slurs. But now, two years later, that my story benefits a narrative that the establishment supports, they wish to acknowledge me." She had barely finished that sentence when the microphone malfunctioned. Undeterred, Talarico continued her speech, yelling at the crowd until one of the organizers ran up and handed her a bullhorn.

Talarico offered a "counternarrative" that placed a necessary spot-light on the white gay establishment for unapologetically supporting

the police at the expense of Black and Brown lives, ultimately silencing queer and trans communities of color. "We cannot have an hon-
est conversation about police violence against trans sex workers," she
explained, "because every time we do, the feelings of gay cops matter
more than the lives of Black and Brown people." She criticized the
police for hypercriminalizing trans women of color in crisis. "When
the police hear about a trans woman of color suffering a mental health
crisis, they send a military force because they see trans women in crisis as a threat to the neighborhood's safety. *But* when a trans woman
asks for protection, they come too little, too late."

Talarico also directed vitriol toward the mayor for lacking transparency and continuing to sweep the violence against Black and
Brown trans women under the rug. "The girls will not be safe," she
continued, "while Mayor Bowser sits on police cam footage, refusing
to give it to the families of the survivors. We will not be safe while so
many community leaders continue to remain silent, willing to work
with Mayor Bowser while she destroys DC public housing." Wrapping up, Talarico spoke of her initial reluctance to speak at another
vigil. "I'm here to talk about these attacks," she explained, "but I'm
not here to pressure the city to give more money to white cis male
LGBT groups that do not recognize that there cannot be Pride for
some without liberation for all of us." The solution, she argued, was
going out into the streets, not paying lip service through the perfor-
mativity of another vigil. "This is the last time I'm coming to a vigil,"
she concluded. "I'm not doing this no more—no more moments of
silence when we should be angry, loud, and screaming in the streets."

In sharp contrast, the two speakers who followed Ruiz Talarico
willingly shared their stories of survival. When Charmaine Eccles
grabbed the microphone, she introduced herself as lucky to stand
before the crowd to tell her story. "I am Black," she began. "I am trans.
I am a survivor. I am a victor. I'm a victor. I'm tired. I'm outraged. I'm
resilient. I'm privileged. I've had enough. I'm tired of the problems.
I'm tired of constantly being a problem." Striking an imposing figure

at six feet, seven inches, the soft-spoken Eccles choked back tears when recalling her experiences of violence as a former sex worker on Eastern Avenue. "I have been victimized," she described. "I have been damaged. I have been beaten. I almost had my throat slit with a hook knife. I've actually been shot out there. I was attacked when three men put a shotgun to my face."

Regretting the loss of so many friends who never escaped the dangerous world of "survival sex," Eccles stated that she felt inspired to speak for those who never managed to achieve their dreams as she had. "I am a living testament for the women who are no longer here to tell their stories," Eccles said. "And it hurts because Zoe was my friend. Ashante was my friend. And they deserve to be here." These losses compelled Eccles to quit her government job and become an advocate for trans women. "I knew I had a calling, and I had to sacrifice to do what I had to do," she explained. She implored the crowd to confront their prejudices against transgender people and treat them with dignity. "I'm six feet, seven inches," she explained. "And people look at me as if I am a problem when I'm a fabulous person. You don't have to accept me, but you do have to respect me."

Speaking to the crowd in Spanish to increase awareness among the Spanish-speaking residents of the Washington area, Gisselle Flores reminded the audience how the violence against trans women of color is not limited to Eastern Avenue. She described a recent incident where a security guard attacked her in a Dupont Circle restaurant after entering a bathroom. "He threatened me and beat me up," she explained. Despite feeling abandoned after the attack, Flores vowed to fight. However, due to her limited resources, the only lawyers she could secure were immigration attorneys. "Now I am looking for a lawyer to demand my rights, . . . but I have not been able to find one because most of the support is for immigration attorneys." By speaking that evening, Flores concluded, she hoped to represent those who too often must suffer alone. "We should not have to wait for a vigil for someone to hear us," she stated. "We are all human, and we all deserve to live our lives as we want to. We all must come together and show that all lives have value."

While highlighting the epidemic of violence against trans women of color, speakers also called attention to the systemic challenges transgender Americans face. After Eccles finished her testimony, Budd expressed her pride that Eccles was the first trans woman to secure a position as a 311 operator. Distinguishing herself, Eccles received numerous awards for her service and achieved the status of a 911 operator. "We never had something like that before," Budd explained. As the audience applauded Eccles's accomplishments, Budd leveraged Eccles's success to challenge the DC government to employ more transgender people. "DC should open their doors and make sure that someone else like Charmaine can take the position," she explained. "We don't want to be a token. We want jobs for all."

The next speaker, a black transwoman who identified herself as Cherise, urged the crowd to shout as a way of "rais[ing] their voices for transwomen of color," a Black transwomen Cherise. Draped in a trans flag and joined by another trans woman holding up a trans flag bearing the words "Black Trans Lives Matter," Cherise connected the murders of trans women nationwide to the lack of various protections. "Some of these cases involve clear antitransgender bias," she said, "while in others, their trans status may have put them at risk in ways such as forcing them into homelessness, trafficking, or what I like to plain call 'survival sex.'" Describing how racism, sexism, and transphobia combine and "conspire to deprive [trans women of color] of employment, housing, and health care," Cherise reminded the audience that despite the advances in LGBTQ rights, few spaces exist where trans women of color feel safe. Ending the speech on a hopeful note, she reminded the audience that their support for trans women's lives empowers them to survive. "You support us. You are what makes us survive, to do better." Leading the crowd in a call-and-response, Cherise named the ten trans women who died that year.

Local LGBTQ activists and politicians homed in on the local government's lack of transparency when these attacks occur. Rick Rosen-
dall of the Gay and Lesbian Activist Alliance described how the lack
of information on hate crimes against LGBTQ individuals prevents
leaders from doing their work effectively. "When the mayor's office
ordered the police to stop sharing information about hate crimes with
LGBT leaders," he said, "it became harder for us to reach survivors
with counseling, support, and information about their rights. The
activists who do this work need less control from our government and
more timely information." Randy Downs, a member of the Advisory
Neighborhood Commission, told the crowd that local queer politicians had sent a letter to DC leaders urging them to support the
LGBTQ community. "We were unified in our message to District
leaders," he yelled. "We've learned long ago that silence equals death.
And the silence enacted from District leaders is killing members of
our community by placing them in harm's way and hospital emer-
gency rooms." Demanding $5 million in resources from the DC gov-
ernment, Downs vowed to hold leaders accountable for turning their
backs on the LGBTQ community. "Words and friendship no longer
ring true," he stated to wild applause. "You can no longer march in our
parade, throwing beads and candy only next week to deny us funding
and resources we deserve."

Christopher Macciotte, representing the Victory Fund, encouraged voters to run for office when their leaders refused to hear them.
Highlighting the successful campaign of Danica Roem, the first
openly transgender candidate to win a seat in a state legislature, Macciotte emphasized the power of grassroots organizing. He implored
residents to act through the political process. "You see the opportunity
to challenge politicians who are just plain wrong?" he asked. "Run.
When your straight allies say they are with us, but then they don't do
anything? Run. When they say that there isn't enough money in the
budget to protect the most vulnerable among us, like Ashante and
Zoe, from hate crimes? Run."

Ruby Corado, founder and then executive director of Casa Ruby, closed the evening's vigil. As two trans women held photos of Zoe and Ashante, Corado sought to dispel the media's oversimplification of Zoe as a sex worker. "I want you to look at Zoe's picture," she stated. "This is one of the last pictures I took of her less than thirty days ago. I want you to look at her smile because I want to clarify how the media portrayed her." Corado continued, describing the Zoe Spears she knew and reading the last text exchanges they shared. "On Sunday at 12:48 A.M.," she recalled, "Zoe wrote, 'Hey Mom, I'm home. I made it safe, and I love you. Sweet dreams. And by the way, Happy Birthday!'" Challenging the media's depiction of Spears as a sex worker, Corado described how Zoe turned to survival sex only as a last resort. "She struggled to find work," Corado explained. "Many of you who lived in survival mode know what it is like to be hungry." Instead of judging her survival, Corado wanted the community to remember Zoe Spears as a woman with aspirations and ambition. "She wanted to be a lawyer," Corado stated, "and she was in school. So although [her goals] may not be accomplished because she is no longer with us, we will fight for her."

After the applause died, Corado turned her attention to the local government. She explained that in her twenty-five years as an advocate, she had always encountered resistance from local politicians when asking for recognition. Calling out the DC Council chair, who was making a hasty exit through the crowd, Corado recalled his response when she asked him why the city's budget did not include any line items for the city's LGBTQ community. "He said that we don't believe in handouts," she explained. "Gay people should be able to access and get services anywhere." Corado disagreed, arguing that although Washington had the largest residential concentration of LGBTQ residents in the country, many of its residents experienced obstacles when trying to access city services. "We have the largest concentration of LGBTQ youth in the country," she said, "but they are not able to access vital services. We have the highest unemployment rate among trans people, so clearly they cannot walk into every agency or the Department of Employment Services and access services. Today we have senior citizens, many of them like me, who are going to need services from the city, and they cannot walk in everywhere. We have the highest rate of hate crimes and violence against the LGBTQ community in this country, so we can't access services. This is our reality."

Evoking the Stonewall riots and reminding the crowd that the riots began through the efforts of trans women of color, Corado railed against the empty rhetoric of allyship. "I don't want solidarity," she explained. "I don't want your allyship if it does not mean that my survival as a trans woman of color and [that] the people [who] are served can have equity." She explained that this should not be a vigil against violence but a rally to action. "And it begins with our elected officials," she screamed through the megaphone. "It begins with the [LGBT] cop," she said, to the audience's growing approval. "If those elected officials I spoke to don't want to give us equity, they need to go." After recounting how elected officials threatened that she could lose everything she had for speaking her truth, Corado reminded the crowd that she had nothing to fear. "Try me," she said to the haters. "I started Casa Ruby with my own money. I will open it from a homeless shelter if I have to." She closed her remarks by asking the crowd to spread the hashtag #BlackTransLivesMatter" and promising elected officials that she would work to remove them from office if their inaction continued. "We must live out the spirit of Stonewall," she closed. "We cannot have another twenty-five years of inaction. If you do not give us equity, you will not be in power anymore."

After the vigil, I walked with my friends Ryan and Dan to Rosemary's Thyme on Eighteenth Street for drinks. Except for our brief exchanges on where we were heading, we largely remained silent, processing what we had just witnessed. We grabbed a table on the patio and played with our phones until the server arrived. He took our drink orders, and we returned to our phones, enabling me to jot down a few field notes about the event. Once our martinis arrived, I took a sip of liquid courage and broke the silence.

"Pretty powerful," I said. My friends nodded.

"Absolutely," Ryan responded. "But I am a little confused."

"Confused how?" Dan jumped in.

"I get that this was important," Ryan explained. "I just don't get why they are protesting about something that happened over there over here."

Ryan's comments revealed the necessity of holding the Vigil Against the Violence in Dupont Circle in the first place. In the aftermath of the shooting at the Pulse nightclub in 2016, few people hesitated to show solidarity with the victims. One of the most poignant moments in Washington came when a speaker during one of the vigils expressed not only that the city was with Orlando but also that "We *are* Orlando"—despite the fact that the tragic event occurred eight hundred miles away. As I discussed in the previous chapter, the tragedy resonated to the point that white LGBTQ Washingtonians faced accusations by LGBTQ communities of color that they were hijacking the tragedy to achieve their own ends at the expense of scapegoating queer Muslim residents. And yet many attendees at the Vigil Against the Violence failed to understand the connection between the violence in Dupont Circle and the peril trans women of color faced nearly ten miles away. And as a result, many participants who came to the vigil hoping to protest the homophobic violence occurring in Dupont Circle and Shaw/U Street could not understand what claims these women had on Dupont Circle or why they would stage their protests there.

However, the vigil highlighted how little these trans women identified with Eastern Avenue or with the sex work many were forced to do as a means of their very survival. Their presence on Eastern Avenue resulted from various policies that displaced trans sex workers from gentrifying neighborhoods in the District. The anthropologist Elijah Adiv Edelman observes how this spatial displacement, arising from the creation of "prostitution free zones" in the District, denied trans women of color the rights of urban citizenship. As a result of efforts to clear vice from gentrifying areas, trans women of color in these areas were mislabeled and misrecognized as sex workers.[36] The jurisdictional issues created by Eastern Avenue being the border between DC and Maryland further exacerbated the detachments from place, as these murders often received little (if any) coverage in the local media. Despite that sense of detachment, however, these women mobilized in Dupont Circle as both a call to build coalitions among LGBQ residents and an act of resistance. Beyond bringing the issues of Eastern Avenue to the city's LGBTQ community, these activists were connecting the violence they encountered at the hands of the police, municipal service providers, and residents with the homophobic violence in Dupont Circle and Shaw/U Street. Doing so then allowed them to insert themselves as legitimate stakeholders of the community, with every entitlement to participate in the appropriation of space and the production of its meaning. They were also mounting a significant challenge to the view that their presence in these spaces was illegitimate due to the pervasive perception, perpetuated in the local and national media, that sex work is the only avenue that trans women of color can pursue in order to exist. They had a right to participate as part of the community, and in shaping the discourse around the epidemic of transgender violence, the organizers and speakers made it clear to the community that their cries for help could not be ignored.

———

Vicarious citizens face numerous challenges when exercising political vicarious claims. Because electoral enfranchisement is almost exclusively limited to residents, many political vicarious claims are vulnerable to dismissal by those with more material ties to the area. As a result, vicarious citizens often have to develop strategies to draw attention to their political claims, relying on taken-for-granted aspects of the local political process to serve their community interests. Drawing on various resources, including social media, vicarious citizens can influence critical decision makers, build coalitions, and shape local debates about pressing political issues that impact the production of space and the maintenance of local community. The increasing presence and involvement of vicarious citizens in local community affairs make it clear that critical local decision makers can no longer afford to ignore the concerns of vicarious citizens solely on the basis of absence of residential proximity.

CONCLUSION

Place Reactivation and Vicarious Citizenship
Beyond the Gayborhood

M ake no mistake: gay neighborhoods and the institutions that once distinguished these geographies are changing. Amin Ghaziani states it most eloquently in *There Goes the Gayborhood?* "It is quixotic to think that gayborhoods have always been around," he observes, "that they will remain stable in their character and composition, or that they will never change."[1] Numerous changes have impacted the evolution of gay neighborhoods in the decades since scholars first studied them. By the late 1970s, soaring real estate prices in the Castro forced working- and middle-class residents to seek affordable housing in surrounding neighborhoods. The influx of upscale shops also priced out gay small businesses in the area, including Supervisor Harvey Milk's camera shop, which for many years functioned as the headquarters of San Francisco's burgeoning gay rights movement.[2] In the early days of the AIDS epidemic, city governments shut down gay bathhouses in the name of public safety.[3] The culture clashes resulting from the influx of straight residents and their families in iconic gay neighborhoods have "sanitized" the explicit sexual cultures that once characterized these areas, impacting the content we observe on the street, from sex shop window displays to Pride Parade floats.[4] We have witnessed the closure of LGBTQ bookstores as queer literature and scholarship have become readily available to consumers in mainstream bookstores and, subsequently, through Amazon. And over the last decade, scholars have noted the role sex and dating apps like Grindr have played in the closure of gay bars and nightclubs worldwide, signaling to journalists and academics the end of LGBTQ culture as we know it.[5] And with the closure of public spaces during the COVID pandemic in 2020 and 2021, journalists and academics have expressed little faith in these trends reversing course.[6]

Not in My Gayborhood! derives a different truth from the overwhelming evidence signaling the decline and "plateauing" of gay neighborhoods.[7] Scholarly emphasis on residency as a defining feature of gay neighborhoods overlooks the role of residential outsiders whose participation in the cultural, economic, and political life of the gayborhood reflects vital strategies for maintaining community investment, attachment, and belonging. Residential relocation or displacement does not necessarily diminish one's connection to the gayborhood. Many return, playing out the routines of their queer lives within them. And as numerous institutions that once anchored their sense of community close or disappear, LGBTQ communities develop various strategies for keeping alive the traditions associated with their vision of community. The cultural moments perpetuating an area's reputation as a gay neighborhood, from Pride Parades to street festivals and political rallies, reflect bursts of placemaking that flourish and ebb, only to regenerate when the event reoccurs. How owners market an LGBTQ bookstore, community center, or nightclub may contrast with the various meanings, practices, and reputations that consumers map onto them. The reputation of a gay bar may easily outlast the building it once occupied as patrons and business owners transfer the activities and traditions associated with that bar to different spaces, transforming the vestiges of nightlife into containers for multiple, sometimes competing places. Participants in gay neighborhoods are more than passive consumers of LGBTQ culture and institutions. Instead, by their participation, whether as residents or as vicarious citizens and whether for a fleeting moment or for a lifetime, they define what makes a gay neighborhood.

Extending these practices of ephemeral placemaking, place reactivation, and vicarious citizenship to iconic gay neighborhoods complicates the normativity of gay neighborhoods advanced in the scholarly and popular imaginations. These practices are not ancillary to the creation and evolution of gay neighborhoods; they are constitutive of them. These practices have always represented vital strategies for community building and maintenance. Despite the stigma attached to homosexuality during the first half of the twentieth century, gay men and women developed a variety of highly sophisticated social worlds where their extensive social networks flourished and where they cultivated different forms of community identification and attachment. Although gay worlds varied in size and visibility, the communities that emanated from them highlight important ways in which gay men and women "reterritorialize[d] the city in order to construct a gay city in the midst of (and often hidden from) the normative city."[8] We have considered examples of gay and lesbian vicarious communities outside of Washington, DC. In New York, for example, patrons of the Greenwich Village bars and restaurants were predominantly gay residents; however, these establishments "also provided a home-away-from-home for gay visitors from other parts of town, a place where people who had no private space of their own in the neighborhood could gather nightly and construct a social world for themselves."[9] In his 1942 master's thesis, Earle W. Bruce observes that the Chicago gay men in his sample, "regardless of place of residence, frequented the 'social world of the homosexuals, where they have their particular status, participate in common activities, . . . [and] can express themselves in their particular fashion.'"[10] For those living outside of the gay enclaves and those living double lives, access to gay institutions has proved to be essential to one's sense of community as residential proximity.

These practices have also proven vital for creating and producing geographies of LGBTQ communities of color. Legacies of racial and economic segregation within cities have resulted in a different spatial imagination. Black gays and lesbians depended on ephemeral placemaking to develop vibrant communities that mirrored (and at times rivaled) those of their white gay counterparts. Private house parties, cookouts, and drag balls enabled these communities to foster relationships and maintain a certain degree of visibility within the proximity of their families. Economic disinvestment in Black neighborhoods, propelled by rioting and the out-migration of the Black middle class in the 1950s and 1960s, did not eliminate the Black queer spatial imagination. In the face of racial and sexual discrimination in iconic gay neighborhoods and white gay establishments, Black queer culture persisted in predominately Black residential areas as Black gays and lesbians navigated a terrain where their sexuality may have been known but was never discussed. They sat in church pews and sang in the choir while listening to sermons demonizing homosexuality.[11] Many developed distinct relational orders where their sexuality was performed privately or in spaces outside their neighborhoods. The spaces that foster these communities often have proved to be ephemeral. Gay nightlife may constitute a single night in a straight club venue; festivals in local parks may create a safe "queer space" for an afternoon or a weekend. Nevertheless, these communities marshal their available resources to carve out spaces where they are visible to one another and can leverage economic opportunities that mitigate the effects of poverty and hypersegregation.[12]

Drawing attention to these practices, this book writes Black queer subjects into the narrative of LGBTQ geographies within cities. Challenging conventional scholarship on gay neighborhoods, which too often characterizes Black queer geographies as oppositional to more mainstream LGBTQ places, *Not in My Gayborhood!* legitimates these practices as creative forces within urban placemaking. From the house parties and drag balls in the early twentieth century to the queer ballroom scenes and public spaces occupied by queer youths experiencing homelessness, these geographies speak to the resilience and resourcefulness of LGBTQ people in their search for affirming spaces for queer gender and sexual expression. Black queer subjects are not merely additive to the story of LGBTQ geographies. Instead, their practices constitute vital strategies for constructing and maintaining queer geographies in American cities.

Many examples I present in this book highlight how vicarious citizens protect their vision of community through placemaking practices that are legible to others as normative to the cultural production of place within a neighborhood. Engaging in public displays of affection, patronizing a gay bar, or attending a Pride Parade aligns in some fashion with the expected production of space within a gay neighborhood. However, various trends that once distinguished gay neighborhoods culturally have disappeared or evolved, reflecting the changing values of new generations of LGBTQ citizens. For example, the evolution of gay neighborhoods into sites of cultural consumption has virtually erased the public sexual cultures that once distinguished these areas. Yet the "sexy communities" emerging in certain gay nightclubs and bars reflect the use of explicit sex and sexual cultures to reclaim the gayborhood as a site of sexual exploration and experimentation from the straight newcomers and homonormative residents who minimize elements of queer sexuality in favor of diversity consumption.[13] Additionally, fetish and kink events, like the Mid-Atlantic Leather Weekend in Washington, DC, and the Folsom Street Fair in San Francisco, reflect forms of ephemeral placemaking that allow LGBTQ people to temporarily celebrate these explicit subcultures away from the prying eyes of homonormative queers and heterosexuals "on safari" in mainstream gay nightclubs.

Of course, not all exercises of vicarious citizenship resemble traditional placemaking practices. Many who identify with a neighborhood's local reputation may find themselves excluded from traditional modes of community participation, thus requiring them to develop a different repertoire of placemaking practices to render the local community accessible. In my work on queer street families in Chicago, I consider how LGBTQ youths of color travel hours from their South Side and West Side neighborhoods to Boystown to seek spaces that may affirm their sexual and gender-variant identities.[14] Often finding themselves excluded from traditional LGBTQ institutions due to age and economic restrictions, these youths develop a public relational order that mirrors the "street corner societies" in inner cities.[15] They gather on street corners around institutional anchors, use storefront windows and café bathrooms to apply makeup, and transform sidewalks into makeshift catwalks to "vogue the house down." Sometimes they draw on the "codes of the street," using violence as both a form of play and a way to mediate internal conflicts and external threats. White residents and traditional vicarious citizens may find the presence of Black and Latinx youths on street corners to be a threat to public safety, but these youths rely on these practices to make these areas socially and culturally resonant to them and legitimate their claim as community stakeholders. Their presence and practices also highlight the enduring value of gay neighborhoods as cultural, social, and political centers that foster the safe exploration of sexuality and gender expression.

While we cannot predict how gay neighborhoods will evolve, we have seen evidence from other neighborhoods of how their reputations may endure irrespective of their residential and cultural transformations. I discovered one such example in Shaw at the end of my fieldwork in Washington, DC While I have described Shaw/U Street as a gayborhood in this book, it still retains its value as the heart of a chocolate city for generations of Black residents who have since been displaced by the neighborhood's economic transformation. Although the Shaw/U Street area has gentrified in the past few decades, many Black residents throughout the city still return to the area to participate in traditions associated with their vision of Black Broadway. And when white residential newcomers have challenged long-standing traditions in the community, these vicarious citizens have mobilized to defend one of the last existing cultural and institutional remnants of chocolate city. By presenting the story of #DontMuteDC, I hope not only to highlight the enduring value of neighborhoods for vicarious citizens but also to draw attention to the utility of this book's framework beyond the context of gay neighborhoods.

#DontMuteDC

Nothing about the MetroPCS store on the corner of Seventh Street and Florida Avenue NW screams subtle. Painted cherry red, the brick building is a stark contrast to the graffiti-covered walls of neighboring businesses and the crisp industrial designs of new condo buildings constructed in recent years. Since 1995, the store's local trademark been the loud go-go music emanating from the bright red building. Go-go is a "mixture of relaxed funk, gospel, jazz, call and response, and Afro-Caribbean beats" that originated in the Washington, DC, area in the 1970s with the music of Chuck Brown, known as the godfather of go-go.[16] And for anyone growing up in the area, go-go music reflects the heartbeat of Washington, DC. "You want to know what go-go music is?" Lawrence responded to my question. "DC is go-go. Go-go is DC. That's all you need to know." For Donald Campbell, the MetroPCS store owner, playing the music extends a bygone era when go-go clubs flooded the area. To longtime Black residents of the area, the infectious beats blasting out of a building on a street corner and commemorating the architect of go-go are one of the remaining holdovers of Shaw's Black history and culture as the Shaw/U Street area continues gentrifying at a "dizzying pace."[17] The store's identity has become so intertwined with playing go-go music that several Yelp reviews of the business highlight the go-go music as a benefit. "I cannot speak on the phone services," a reviewer wrote about the store in a five-star Yelp review. "My two visits were to buy music that I've heard playing. . . . But hey, [MetroPCS] keeps the tradition [of go-go] alive. I am glad that they do and I got a lot of love and respect for them for doing so."[18]

In early April 2020, news reports surfaced that T-Mobile, which had recently acquired MetroPCS, contacted Campbell and told him he had to cease playing music outside his shop. In an interview with DCist, Campbell explained that a resident in The Shay, a luxury, mixed-use development located nearby, had threatened to sue T-Mobile due to the noise.[19] Although no official complaints had emerged about the volume of the music playing outdoors, residents had grumbled about the music for the last several years. "People have complained to me about this over the years," tweeted Brianne Nadeau, the DC Council member for Ward 1, "but I've always said that a small business playing go-go in Ward 1 is a thing we should celebrate. They only do it during business hours, and there are always people outside enjoying it." "There have been complaints about the music being extremely loud," a representative for The Shay told DCist, "but it's not just The Shay. It's people who live all over or are visiting the area."[20]

Campbell complied, moving his speakers inside. And while people reported that he continued playing go-go music inside the store, many Black residents lamented that Chuck Brown Way—the honorary name given to the block of Seventh Street where MetroPCS (now Metro by T-Mobile) was located—no longer felt the same. "Every day all day," Campbell explained, "people think we are closed. People have been complaining, asking what's going on."[21] Social media exploded, with people using the hashtag #DontMuteDC to discuss the silencing of the go-go music. "Shutting down the Go-Go music piping out of Metro PCS on Georgia Avenue makes Shaw a less lively and vibrant place," tweeted Derek Brown, a local business owner. Many connected the silencing of MetroPCS to the gentrification of Washington more broadly. "If you choose to live in the U street area," another person tweeted, "and complain about the gogo [sic], you are an awful, entitled dork who shouldn't be given any voice or power." Local politicians also chimed in on the debate, expressing their support for MetroPCS. "When I drive down [Florida] Ave," tweeted Robert White, also a member of the DC Council, "I turn off my radio & roll down my window to hear gogo as I pass the corner of Georgia & Florida. I love that people move here from around the globe. But welcoming the new can't come at the expense of our culture."[22]

Several community activists organized to champion Campbell's right to play music outside his business. A petition supporting his continuing to play the music on the street garnered over sixty thousand signatures. Over the next several days, Black residents throughout the Washington area converged outside MetroPCS to protest. They blasted go-go music from speakers throughout the day and carried signs saying "Are you funkin' kidding me?" while Campbell worked quietly in his store. People speaking to the crowds expressed the importance of go-go music to Washington, DC, as a chocolate city. "This is the sound of Florida and Georgia Avenues," one attendee stated. "This is probably one of the last things out here on U Street that is still DC."[23] Throughout the city, go-go protests and performances took place in support of MetroPCS, including a performance outside the Reeves Center at Fourteenth and U Streets, a town hall meeting at Check It Enterprises, and a series of press conferences held outside the store, calling on T-Mobile to "bring back the music."[24] The protesters garnered support from members of the DC Council and Mayor Muriel Bowser, who tweeted, "I'm with you #DontMuteDC."[25]

Days after the protests began, the CEO of T-Mobile reversed the decision to silence the music at the store. "I've looked into the issue myself and the music should NOT stop in DC!" CEO John Legere tweeted. "@TMobile and @MetroByTMobile are proud to be part of the Shaw community—the music will go on and our dealer will work with the neighbors to compromise volume."[26] While Black Washington celebrated the return of go-go music outside MetroPCS, the battle that go-go represented had only begun. #DontMuteDC became a movement as organizers planned protest rallies throughout the Washington area. The most prominent event occurred on May 7, 2019, as nearly five thousand area residents came together at the intersection of Fourteenth and U Streets for Moechella, a musical rally that "reinforced the importance of DC's musical heartbeat."[27] To those who participated, the event reinvigorated the fight by displaced Black residents to preserve their chocolate city against the "cultural genocide" resulting from demographic and economic changes that had swept the city.[28] "It was beautiful, man," Clayton (thirty-nine, Black, straight) told me about the rally. "We showed up, and we showed out. These white people need to learn that they can take our homes and whiten our streets with their wine bars and yoga studios. But they can't take away the heart of what makes DC As long as the heart of go-go beats on, DC will always be Chocolate City."

The success of these rallies led to calls to make go-go the official music of Washington, DC, a step that was taken the following year when Mayor Bowser signed the Go-Go Music of the District of Columbia Designation Act on February 19, 2020. "Today, we are proud to say that DC's official music will always be Go-Go, because there is no DC without Go-Go and there is no Go-Go without DC!" said Mayor Bowser. "Go-Go music is a creative force that has inspired generations of Washingtonians socially, culturally, and artistically, and this legislation will empower us to preserve and celebrate our native sound."[29]

WRITING THEMSELVES BACK IN

#DontMuteDC also animates *Not in My Gayborhood!* As scholars have observed the decline of Washington's Black population in the last twenty years, many have expressed concerns over the city's reputation as a chocolate city. The sociologist Derek Hyra, in his study

on the gentrification of U Street, referred to Washington as a cappuccino city to express the displacement of Black residents by young,
white, moneyed gentrifiers who also aestheticize the "codes of the
streets" as a strategy for renewal.[30] Similarly, the geographer Brandi
Thompson Summers uses the term *post–chocolate city* to consider
the deployment of Black culture and history as an economic growth
strategy along the H Street NE corridor.[31] However, for the hundreds
of Black residents who protested the silencing of MetroPCS, Washington remains Chocolate City. Black residents have not necessarily
relinquished ownership over their neighborhoods. Without residency
claims, Black residents exercise vicarious citizenship, recreating and
sustaining communities by reactivating place and culture.

The battle over MetroPCS playing loud go-go music reflects two
competing relational orders. On one side, residents viewed the practice of playing go-go music as disruptive to the private relational order
of their residential community. Opponents of the music hoped to celebrate the area's diversity while calling attention to the fact that residents should not have to compromise their quality of life in order to
do so. Citing the music among the top long-standing complaints she
received from her constituents, Anita Norman, the area's representative on the Advisory Neighborhood Commission, described how the
music disrupted the ability of community members to navigate their
daily rounds. "I don't have a problem with the music," she explained
to DCist. "I have a problem with anything that disturbs the quality of
life of residents, whether it's music coming from them or a nightclub.
I'm all for them playing music, but at a reasonable volume."[32]

Conversely, supporters of the music challenged the eradication of
Black places at the hands of neoliberalism and gentrification. Despite
the neighborhood's shifting residential composition, many displaced
Black residents often return to Washington to participate in the
neighborhood's lingering cultural, institutional, and spiritual life. Like
Councilmember White, many viewed the music and the store as place
abeyance signifiers. "The history of music in this corridor in particular

is so important to our heritage, our history, and our present," Councilmember Nadeau explained in an interview, "but we see less and less of it as the neighborhood changes. This corner has been one of the places we all know we can come and hear some go-go during the course of our day, and I think that's reassuring and comforting to some people that miss that about this area." As rallies and protests spread throughout the city in support of #DontMuteDC, Black residents drew on acts of ephemeral placemaking to protect the vision of place they align with the city's authentic community. Blasting go-go music out of one's car in front of the store or holding an impromptu music rally may not seem like a political act. "When we move to a neighborhood," White explained during one of the rallies, "we have to embrace what the neighborhood is. We can't feel like we discovered these neighborhoods like these neighborhoods, didn't have a culture, a sound, a vibe before we got there. One of the things that makes change in DC so difficult is a lack of respect for what is and what was before a lot of people got here."[33]

Scholars continue to exclude Black spatial practices from these conversations on the relationship between various forms of placemaking and new expressions of urban citizenship in the postmodern or postindustrial city. Although gentrification and economic restructuring have resulted in new, flexible forms of citizenship employed by diverse actors through the appropriation of space and the production of its meaning,[34] urban scholars have yet to extend this framing to the practices typically associated with the iconic ghetto.[35] They have long maligned street corner culture and underground economies as consequences of urban blight and economic disinvestment. However, these practices can also reflect expressions of agency, resistance, and play in a society where Black citizens endure racial profiling, hypercriminalization,[36] and violence in public spaces at the hands of ordinary white citizens and the institutions that support white supremacy. As Black residents are pushed out of the historically Black neighborhood of Shaw/U Street, many return as vicarious citizens to attend their places of worship on Sundays, triple parking as they always have, to the exasperation of the new residents. They get their double smokes from Ben's Chili Bowl on U Street. They hang out on the street corners, playing music loudly as people walk by. Student bands practice their formations in the quiet tree-lined residential streets near their high schools. While often misrecognized as pathological—a product of the institutional and economic isolation characteristic of Black urban communities—these moments combine celebration and politics to protect the meaningful spaces that mobilize Washington's Black communities.[37] At the same time, they highlight the transformative potential of spatial practices that Black people have relied on for their very survival in a white world.

BEYOND WASHINGTON, DC

Communities do not disappear because a neighborhood gentrifies. Instead, as place entrepreneurs increasingly rely on cultural and historic preservation efforts as strategies for revitalizing neighborhoods, cultural residues from former communities—commercial or cultural institutions, public monuments, street iconography, and public rituals and festivals—remain potent symbols of community identification. Vicarious citizens are able to access and activate these spaces when they need them to carry out the functions of community. Drawing attention to these practices, *Not in My Gayborhood!* highlights how contemporary neighborhoods encompass diverse social worlds with reputations that shift depending on the community occupying these spaces at any given time. Additionally, this book reinforces the enduring value of iconic urban neighborhoods (i.e., historical racial, ethnoreligious, and sexual enclaves) as sites of collective identification, community mobilization, and citizenship formation. It draws attention to a class of neighborhood-level stakeholders, overlooked in urban and community scholarship, who articulate legitimate claims to local neighborhoods through the appropriation of space and the (re)production of its meaning through place reactivation and vicarious citizenship.

These dynamics also extend well beyond the practices of marginalized communities. In the book *Music/City*, the sociologist Jonathan Wynn observes how municipalities promote annual musical festivals as engines of economic growth. Attracting participants from around the world, these festivals also epitomize place reactivation. The practices, traditions, and cultural representations mobilized throughout these festivals differ from the sense of place developed by locals, many of whom leave town during these events.[38] In recent years, the transformation of many New England towns into "entertainment machines"[39] has also shifted understandings of place. During the summer months, millions of tourists who pass through Portland, Maine, reshape the local economy and destabilize distinctions between city and town as the momentary population increases disrupt the traditional *Gemeinschaftlich*, or community-centered, relationships many locals enjoy throughout the year. The growing popularity of New England towns, now buoyed by creative industries, has resulted in the displacement of residents by people who live in Portland only four months out of the year, either in short-term rentals or in newly purchased second homes. Nevertheless, many displaced locals have found meaningful ways to foster attachment to the area as vicarious citizens. And as the murders of George Floyd and Brianna Taylor reignited debates over removing Confederate monuments, we continue to understand how they operate as place abeyance signifiers. Supporters of the statues defended their importance as emblems of Southern pride only after protesters called for their removal. However, for many Black communities in the South, they stood as quiet emblems of white supremacy and white terror.

Not in My Gayborhood! demonstrates the vital role of cities as sites where the symbolic ownership of local space can translate into meaningful political participation on the municipal, national, and transnational levels. These claims are made by diverse global actors who converge in cities—individuals who find themselves disenfranchised by more traditional forms of political participation. Sometimes these challenges take on very visible forms, including cultural jamming tactics and antigentrification graffiti in Capitol Hill and counterprotests by queer youths of color against the residents of Boystown. However, many expressions of resistance take on more subtle forms, enacted through living out the routines of everyday life. Practices like attending church on Sundays in your "old neighborhood," expressing same-sex affection on a street corner, and patronizing local commercial establishments identified with traditional communities may often go unnoticed. Still, for many who cannot claim neighborhood ties through residency, these practices can represent the community ownership and investment that enables them to preserve vital ties to the local community and pursue political and cultural interests there. Exemplified by the protesters who opposed the construction of a mosque near 9/11's Ground Zero,[40] who erected shantytowns in downtown business districts during the Occupy Wall Street demonstrations,[41] who organized peaceful marches in numerous American cities to call attention to police brutality in Ferguson, Missouri,[42] and who participated in the Capital Riots on January 6, 2021, neighborhood stakeholders are not necessarily confined to the boundaries of neighborhood, city, and state. Indeed, these examples demonstrate how forms of extralocal participation, such as place reactivation and vicarious citizenship, reflect vital processes by which individuals understand and construct community, neighborhood, socioeconomic, and political membership.

Much remains to be learned about how urban citizens articulate legitimate stakes to placemaking in contemporary cities, particularly how they may draw on a neighborhood's culture and reputation to make these claims.[43] Contemporary urban scholarship underscores the ubiquity of "communities without propinquity,"[44] where "durable networks of *Gemeinschaftlich* social relations [are] maintained over great distances" with the assistance of contemporary communication technologies.[45] *Not in* My *Gayborhood!* indicates that local neighborhoods in the postindustrial city have significance because of their symbolic content and their residential and institutional infrastructure. Residues of individual and community identities may persist in a place's history and culture, even long after those residents leave the area. Place reactivation and vicarious citizenship raise important questions about who belongs to neighborhood-based communities and what functions urban neighborhoods serve. While scholars tend to consider an urban neighborhood to have a single or dominant reputation, neighborhoods may, in fact, constitute time-contingent, segmented social orders, in which the identity and reputation of the neighborhood shift depending on the community that occupies the area at any given moment.

As a final note on the future of gay neighborhoods, place reactivation and vicarious citizenship do not suggest that the changing cultural landscape of LGBTQ spaces does not negatively impact the communities these spaces serve. Indeed, the factors contributing to the closure of gay bars in cities and towns, from gentrification to the proliferation of communication technologies, are rightly a cause for concern. Yet the fact that LGBTQ communities continue to reproduce the meaningful spaces that mobilize their sense of community also suggests the constant value of gay nightlife for anchoring LGBTQ communities. Thus, while the future of gay neighborhoods remains uncertain, it is evident that many participants will find new ways to make gay neighborhoods culturally relevant to themselves.

APPENDIX A

Map of Washington, DC, Gayborhoods Referenced

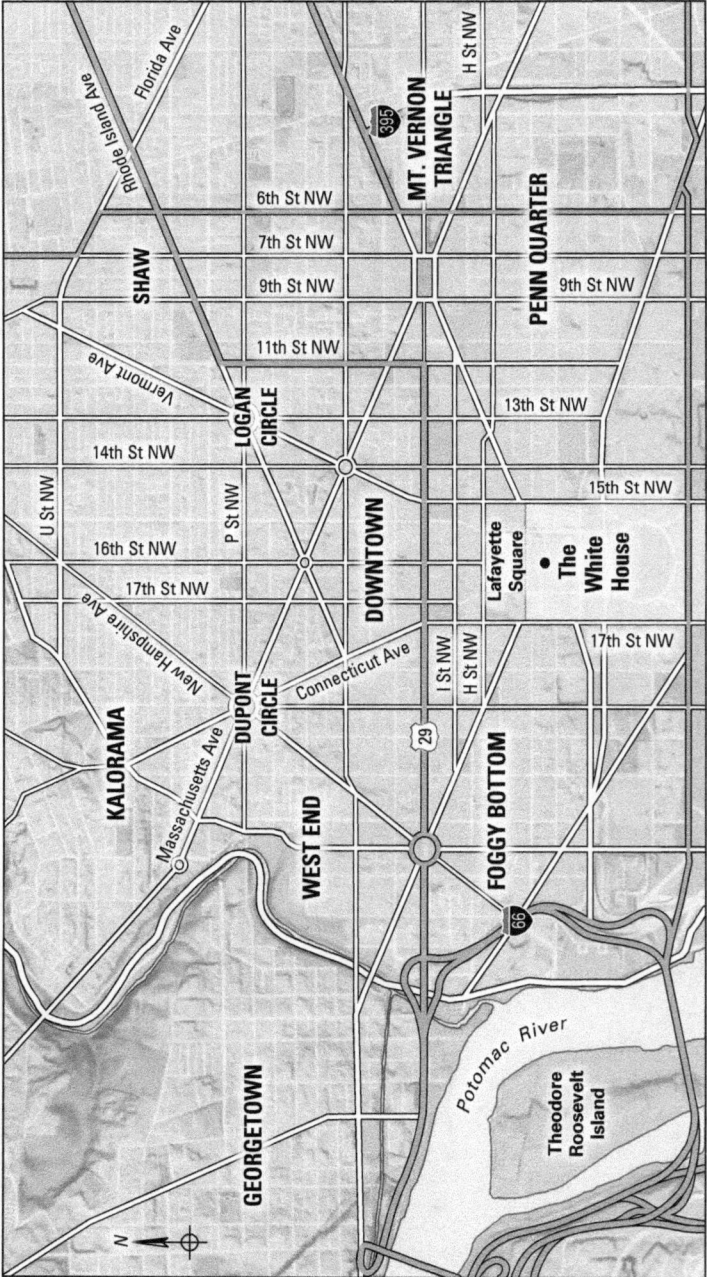

APPENDIX B

Washington, DC, LGBTQ Places Referenced

Place	Address	Neighborhood	Opened	Closed	Gender Served	Race/ethnicity	Comments
Strand Theater	811 D St., NW	Downtown	1916	1965	M	White	
Krazy Kat	3 Green Ct., NW	Thomas Circle	1920	1922	M	White	
Howard Theater	620 T St., NW	Shaw/U Street	1910		M	Black	
Lincoln Theater	1215 U St., NW	Shaw/U Street	1922 1994	1968		Black	Renovated and reopened in 1994.
YMCA Central Branch		Downtown				White	
Twelfth Street YMCA	1816 Twelfth St., NW	Shaw/U Street	1912	1982	M	Black	Now the Thurgood Marshall Center.
Chicken Hut	1720 H St., NW	Downtown	1948	1970	M	White	
Carroll Tavern	510 Ninth St., NW	Downtown	1934	1986	M	White	
Mayflower Hotel	1127 Connecticut Ave., NW	Downtown/White House	1925		M	White	Covert cruising site for white professional men in the 1930s and 1940s.
Statler Hotel	1001 Sixteenth St., NW	Downtown/White House	1943	1977	M	White	Covert cruising site for white professional men in the 1940s. Renamed the Capitol Hilton Hotel in 1977.
The Showboat	1303 H St., NW	H Street	1936	1947	F	White	Later moved to 1310 H St., NW. A popular site for lesbians in the 1930s and 1940s.
Maystat Tavern	1628 L St., NW	Downtown/White House	1945	1950	MF	White	
Redskin Lounge	1628 L St., NW	Downtown/White House	1952	1958	M	White	

(continued)

Republic Gardens	1355 U St., NW	Shaw/U Street	1929		M	Interracial	One of the few interracial establishments in the 1920s and 1930s.
Cozy Corner Bar & Grill	708 Florida Avenue NW	Shaw/U Street	1949	1968	M	Black	
Crystal Caverns	2011 Eleventh St., NW	Shaw/U Street	1939	1941	MF	Black	
Britt's Café	1211 Wisconsin Ave., NW	Georgetown	1928	1967	M	White	
Nob Hill Restaurant	1101 Kenyon St NW	Columbia Heights	1957	2004	M	Black	
Johnnie's	500 Eighth St., SE	Capitol Hill	1949	1974	M	White	
Hideaway	303 Ninth St., NW	Downtown	1963	1983	M	White	
Club Washington	20 O St., SE	Navy Yard	1972	2006	M	White	
Ziegfeld's	1345 Half St., SE	Navy Yard	1980	2006	M	White	
Lost & Found	56 L St., SE	Navy Yard	1971	1991	M	White	
Delta Elite	3734 Tenth St., NE	Brookland	1976	2014	M	Black	
Zodiac	221 Riggs Rd., NE	Fort Totten	1969	1971	MF	Black	
Third World	221 Riggs Rd., NE	Fort Totten	1972	1976	MF	Black	
ClubHouse	1296 Upshur St., NW	Petworth	1975	1990	MF	Black	
Tracks	1111 First St., SE	Navy Yard	1984	1999	MF	Black	
Paramount Steak House	1518 Seventeenth St., NW	Dupont Circle	1948	1985	MF		
Community Building	1724 Twentieth St., NW	Dupont Circle	1971	1980s			Housed several countercultural organizations and became the first location of Lambda Rising.

Place	Address	Neighborhood	Opened	Closed	Gender Served	Race/ethnicity	Comments
Mr. P's	2147 P St., NW	Dupont Circle	1976	2004	M		
Fraternity House	2122 P St., NW	Dupont Circle	1976	1997	M		
JR's Bar & Grill	1519 17th Street NW	Dupont Circle	1986		M		
Rascals	1520 Connecticut Ave., NW	Dupont Circle	1979	1992	M		
Halo	1435 P St., NW	Dupont Circle	2004	2010	M		
Local 16	1602 U St., NW	U Street Corridor		2021	MF		Restaurant popular with gay men as U Street began gentrifying in the early 2000s.
El Faro	2411 Eighteenth St., NW	Adams Morgan	1991	1995	MF	Latino	
Escandalo	2122 P St., NW	Dupont Circle	1994	1997	MF	Latino	
Chaos	1603 Seventeenth St., NW	Dupont Circle	1998	2008	MF	Latino	
Club Fuego	1438 U St., NW	Shaw/U Street	2003		MF	Latino	A dance night that had multiple iterations in locations throughout the DC area, beginning at the Four Points Sheridan Hotel in 2003 and moving to Cada Vez restaurant in 2005. Also located at the Tequila Grill on K and Twentieth Streets in 2004 before residential complaints over noise forced its relocation.
Pitchers Bar	2317 Eighteenth St., NW	Adams Morgan	2018		M		

Name	Address	Neighborhood				Description
A League of Her Own	2317 Eighteenth St., NW	Adams Morgan	2018		F	Opened by owner Dave Peruzza on the lower level of 2317 Eighteenth Street, below Pitchers Bar, to cater to primarily an LBQ clientele
Earthworks	1724 Twentieth St., NW	Dupont Circle	1971	(?)	MF	A headshop/paraphernalia store opened by Deacon Maccubbin that began selling gay and lesbian literature. Due to its popularity, Maccubbin spun off the book and periodical section as Lambda Rising.
Lambda Rising	1724 Twentieth St., NW	Dupont Circle	1974	1978	MF	Began as part of Deacon Maccubbin's paraphernalia store Earthworks. Became an important community anchor as both an independent business and an ersatz community center.
Lambda Rising	2012 S St., NW	Dupont Circle	1978	1984	MF	Lambda Rising's second location, where Maccubbin hosted the first Pride Festival in Washington, DC in 1975.
Lambda Rising	1625 Connecticut Ave., NW	Dupont Circle	1984	2010	MF	Lambda Rising's final location.
McDonald's	1619 Seventeenth St., NW	Dupont Circle			MF	A popular hangout spot for LGBTQ partiers after the bars closed. Was open twenty-four hours on the weekends before it remodeled in 2018.

(continued)

Place	Address	Neighborhood	Opened	Closed	Gender Served	Race/ethnicity	Comments
Annie's Paramount Steak House	1609 Seventeenth St., NW	Dupont Circle	1985		MF		Formerly Paramount Steak House but was later named for longtime bartender Annie Kaylor, the owner's sister, in the 1960s. A popular hangout among LGBTQ residents.
Town Discoboutique	2009 Eighth St., NW	Shaw/U Street Corridor	2007	2018	M		Spacious gay nightclub with multiple dance floors on two levels and a lounge. Hosted drag shows, Latinx Prides, and Bear Crüe Happy Hours.
Uproar Restaurant & Lounge	639 Florida Avenue NW	Shaw/U Street	2016		M		
Be Bar/EFN Lounge	1318 Ninth St., NW	Ninth Street Corridor/ Downtown	2006	2009	M		Opened as Be Bar in the predominately Black neighborhood after various unsuccessful protests by Black churches. Rebranded itself as EFN Lounge after several incidents of antigay violence. Later closed and reopened as a straight bar.
Nation (Velvet Nation)	South Capitol and K Sts., SE	Navy Yard	1999	2006	MF		A venue that hosted Velvet Nation, a popular gay dance club, on Saturday nights. Closed in 2006 to make way for new baseball stadium.
Lizard Lounge	1223 Connecticut Ave., NW	Dupont Circle	1998	2006	M		Popular gay party held on Sundays. Shut down by owner Mark Lee when the city banned indoor smoking.

Cobalt	1639 and 1641 R St., NW	Dupont Circle	2001	2018		Multilevel establishment consisting of three distinct spaces: the third-floor dance floor/nightclub space; Lower Level, the restaurant bar on the basement level; and 30 Degrees, the second-floor lounge area known for its happy hour specials.
Trade	1410 Fourteenth St., NW NW	Fourteenth Street Corridor	2015		M	
Dirty Goose	913 U St., NW	Shaw/U Street Corridor	2016		M	
Nellie's Sports Bar	900 U St., NW	Shaw/U Street Corridor	2008		M	

Note. These placed are listed in order of first appearance. The data included are drawn primarily from the Rainbow History Archive's Places and Spaces Database (http://rainbowhistory.org/places-and-spaces/); Genny Beemyn's *A Queer Capital: A History of Gay Life in Washington, D.C.* (New York: Routledge, 2015); and issues of the *Washington Blade* (https://www.washingtonblade.com).

NOTES

INTRODUCTION: MAKING DUPONT GAY AGAIN

1. Andrew Giambrone, "D.C. No Longer Has a Central Gay Neighborhood. Does It Matter?," *Washington City Paper*, June 2, 2016, http://www.washingtoncity paper.com/news/article/20781582/dc-no-longer-has-a-central-gay-neighborhood -does-that-matter.

2. *Gayborhood* is the portmanteau of *gay* and *neighborhood*. Commonly used within the LGBTQ communities, sociologists have largely attributed the concept to Amin Ghaziani's *There Goes the Gayborhood?* (Princeton, NJ: Princeton University Press, 2014). I will use the terms interchangeably.

3. Giambrone, "D.C. No Longer Has a Central Gay Neighborhood."

4. LGBTQ refers to lesbian, gay, bisexual, transgender, and queer communities. Although the acronym has expanded to include explicitly various gender non-conforming, asexual, questioning, two-spirited, and same-gender loving communities, this book will use LGBTQ as a shorthand, whereby the "Q" functions as an (admittedly imprecise) stand-in for the various diverse communities not included under the LGBT umbrella. I do so for the sake of legibility. However, in cases when authors or interlocutors use LGBT or LGBTQ+ to reflect these communities, I will remain faithful to their terminology.

5. Giambrone, "D.C. No Longer Has a Central Gay Neighborhood." (The comments are no longer available online.)

6. Christopher Ingraham, "In the Modern History of Mass Shootings in America, Orlando Is the Deadliest," *Washington Post*, June 12, 2016, https://www.washingtonpost.com/news/wonk/wp/2016/06/12/in-the-modern-history-of -mass-shootings-in-america-orlando-is-the-absolute-worst/; Eyder Peralta,

"Putting 'Deadliest Mass Shooting in U.S. History' Into Some Historical Context," NPR, June 13, 2016, https://www.npr.org/sections/thetwo-way/2016/06/13/481884291/putting-deadliest-mass-shooting-in-u-s-history-into-some-historical-context; Laura J. Nelson, "The Worst Mass Shooting? A Look Back at Massacres in U.S. History," *Los Angeles Times*, June 14, 2016, https://www.latimes.com/nation/la-na-mass-shooting-20160614-snap-story.html. Much debate exists over how to classify the Pulse shootings, given the history of massacres in the United States, including, according to Nelson, "race riots, labor disputes in the early 1900s and massacres perpetrated by the U.S. Army or settlers in the American West." Consistent with the definition developed by the criminologist Grant Duwe in *Mass Murder in the United States: A History* (Jefferson, NC: McFarland, 2007), the Pulse shootings constitute a "mass public shooting," denoting an act of violence taking place in public or semi-public spaces where murder is the ultimate goal" (see Nelson, "The Worst Mass Shooting?"; Peralta, "Putting 'Deadliest Mass Shooting in U.S. History' Into Some Historical Context").

7. Dan Reed, "DC's Gay Neighborhoods Are Disappearing. How Do We Feel About That?," *Washingtonian*, October 6, 2017, https://www.washingtonian.com/2017/10/06/dcs-gayborhoods-disappearing-feel/.

8. Japonica Brown-Saracino, "Aligning Our Maps: A Call to Reconcile Distinct Visions of Literatures on Sexualities, Space, and Place," *City & Community* 18, no. 1 (2019): 38.

9. Pew Research Center, *A Survey of LGBT Americans: Attitudes, Experiences and Values in Changing Times* (Washington, DC: Pew Research Center, June 13, 2013), http://www.pewsocialtrends.org/2013/06/13/a-survey-of-lgbt-americans/.

10. Amin Ghaziani, "Post-gay Collective Identity Construction," *Social Problems* 58, no. 1 (2011): 99–125.

11. John Paul Brammer, "Commentary: Pulse, and the Beautiful, Sad Joyful Tradition of Queer Grief," NBC News, June 12, 2017, https://www.nbcnews.com/feature/nbc-out/commentary-pulse-beautiful-sad-joyful-tradition-queer-grief-n770936.

12. Evan Sernoffsky, Lizzie Johnson, and Nanette Asimov, "Vigil in SF's Castro Mourns Orlando Massacre Victims," *SFGate*, June 12, 2016, https://www.sfgate.com/news/article/SF-vigil-planned-for-Orlando-massacre-victims-8081843.php.

13. Gillian Edevane, "LGBT Community in SF Shows Allegiance with Orlando Through 'Kiss-In,' " *NBC News Bay Area*, June 15, 2016, https://www.nbcbayarea

.com/news/local/LGBT-Community-in-SF-Shows-Allegiance-with
-Orlando-through-Kiss-In—383175001.html.

14. Ben Quinn and Nadia Khomani, "Orlando Shooting: World Pays Tribute to
Victims with Vigils and Rainbow Flags," *The Guardian*, June 13, 2016, https://
www.theguardian.com/us-news/2016/jun/13/orlando-nightclub-shooting
-world-in-mourning-for-victims.

15. Max Bearak, "The World Reacts to the Mass Shooting in Orlando," *Washington
Post*, June 12, 2016, https://www.washingtonpost.com/news/worldviews/wp
/2016/06/12/the-world-reacts-to-the-mass-shooting-in-orlando/.

16. Marcus Anthony Hunter, "The Nightly Round: Space, Social Capital, and
Urban Black Nightlife," *City & Community* 9, no. 2 (2010): 165–86; Ryan Still-
wagon and Amin Ghaziani, "Queer Pop-Ups: A Cultural Innovation of Urban
Life," *City & Community* 18, no. 3 (2019): 874–95; Theodore Greene, "'You're
Dancing on My Seat!': Queer Subcultures and the Production of Places in
Contemporary Gay Bars," *Studies in Symbolic Interaction* 54 (2022): 137–65.

17. Thomas F. Gieryn, "A Space for Place in Sociology," *Annual Review of Sociology* 26 (2000): 465.

18. Gieryn, "A Space for Place in Sociology"; Krista E. Paulsen, "Making Character Concrete: Empirical Strategies for Studying Place Distinction," *City &
Community* 3, no. 3 (2004): 243–62.

19. Henri Lefebvre, *Writings on Cities* (Cambridge: Blackwell, 1996).

20. For scholarship exploring the importance of gay districts in what Amin Ghaziani refers to as "the coming out era," see Elizabeth Armstrong, *Forging Gay
Identities: Organizing Sexuality in San Francisco, 1950–1994* (Chicago: University of Chicago Press, 2002); Ghaziani, *There Goes the Gayborhood?*; Manuel
Castells, *The City and the Grassroots* (Berkeley: University of California Press,
1983); and Manuel Castells and Karen Murphy, "Cultural Identity and Urban
Structure: The Spatial Organization of San Francisco's 'Gay Community,'"
in *Urbanism Under Capitalism*, ed. Norman Fainstein and Susan Fainstein
(Beverly Hills, CA: SAGE, 1982), 237–59.

21. Examples of these forms of placemaking include Genny Beemyn, "A Queer
Capital: Race, Class, Gender, and the Changing Social Landscape of Wash-
ington's Gay Communities, 1940–1955," in *Creating a Place for Ourselves: Les-
bian, Gay, and Bisexual Community Histories*, ed. Genny Beemyn (New York:
Routledge, 1997), 183–210; George Chauncey, *Gay New York: Gender, Urban
Culture, and the Making of the Homosexual* (New York: Basic Books, 1994);
Allen Drexel, "Before Paris Burned: Race, Class, and Male Homosexuality

on the Chicago South Side, 1935–1960," in *Creating a Place for Ourselves: Lesbian, Gay, and Bisexual Community Histories*, ed. Genny Beemyn (New York: Routledge, 1997), 119–44; and David K. Johnson, "The Kids of Fairytown: Gay Male Culture on Chicago's Near North Side in the 1930s," in *Creating a Place for Ourselves: Lesbian, Gay, and Bisexual Community Histories*, ed. Genny Beemyn (New York: Routledge, 1997), 97–118.

22. Johnson, "The Kids of Fairytown."

23. Chauncey, *Gay New York*; Chad Heap, *Slumming: Sexual and Racial Encounters in American Nightlife, 1885–1940* (Chicago: University of Chicago Press, 2009).

24. Chauncey, *Gay New York*, 4.

25. Elizabeth Lapovsky Kennedy and Madeline D. Davis, "I Could Hardly Wait to Get Back to That Bar: Lesbian Bar Culture in Buffalo in the 1930s and 1940s," in *Creating a Place for Ourselves: Lesbian, Gay, and Bisexual Community Histories*, ed. Genny Beemyn (New York: Routledge, 1997), 27–72.

26. Laud Humphreys, *Tearoom Trade: Impersonal Sex in Public Places* (Hawthorne, NY: Aldine de Gruyter, 1975).

27. Ann Forsyth, "Sexuality and Space: Nonconformist Populations and Planning Practice," *Journal of Planning Literature* 15, no. 3 (2001): 339–58. See also Ghaziani, *There Goes the Gayborhood?*

28. Genny Beemyn, "A Queer Capital: Lesbian, Gay, and Bisexual Life in Washington, DC 1890–1955" (PhD diss., University of Iowa, 1997), 20.

29. Beemyn, "A Queer Capital," 20.

30. Beemyn, "A Queer Capital," 19.

31. Esther Newton, "The 'Fun Gay Ladies': Lesbians in Cherry Grove, 1936–1960," in *Creating a Place for Ourselves: Lesbian, Gay, and Bisexual Community Histories*, ed. Genny Beemyn (New York: Routledge, 1997), 147.

32. Genny Beemyn, interview with Haviland Ferris, May 16, 1994, Genny Beemyn Queer Capital Oral History Collection, Raibow History Project, https://archives .rainbowhistory.org/collections/browse.

33. Ghaziani, *There Goes the Gayborhood?*

34. Johnson, "The Kids of Fairytown," 97, 101.

35. Genny Beemyn, "The Geography of Same-Sex Desire: Cruising Men in Washington, DC in the Late Nineteenth and Early Twentieth Centuries," *Left History* 9, no. 2 (Spring 2004): 157n38. See also David K. Johnson, *The Lavender Scare: The Cold War Persecution of Gays and Lesbians in the Federal Government* (Chicago: University of Chicago Press, 2004).

36. Johnson, "The Kids of Fairytown," 97.

37. Johnson, *The Lavender Scare*, 47.

38. John D'Emilio, *Sexual Politics, Sexual Communities: The Making of a Homosexual Minority in the United States 1940–1970* (Chicago: University of Chicago Press, 1983); Martin Duberman, *Stonewall* (New York: Penguin, 1993); David Carter, *Stonewall: The Riots That Sparked the Gay Revolution* (New York: St. Martin's, 2004).

39. Carter, *Stonewall*, 88.

40. Nancy Achilles, "The Development of the Homosexual Bar as an Institution," in *Social Perspectives in Lesbian and Gay Studies*, ed. Peter M. Nardi and Beth E. Schneider (London: Routledge, 1967), 182.

41. Alan Lew, "Tourism Planning and Place Making: Place-Making or Placemaking?," *Tourism Geographies* 19, no. 3 (2017): 449.

42. Carter, *Stonewall*, 80.

43. Accounts of Stonewall include terms for transidentified people long considered outdated in the public and scholarly imagination, including *transsexuals* and *transvestites*. While contemporary convention might necessitate identifying these participants as transgender, I retain the historically correct terms whenever possible out of respect for the way individuals self-identified at the time.

44. "Lovers' lane" refers to Kew Gardens, a public park and convenient trysting place for gay men in Queens. In late June 1969, a group of neighborhood vigilantes cut down the trees in Kew Gardens. Several citizens reported the park's destruction to the police, "only to see the police cars drive, up, and an officer get out and chat with the vigilantes, then leave without taking any action." Carter, *Stonewall*, 123.

45. Carter, *Stonewall*, 143.

46. Carter, *Stonewall*, 148.

47. Lucian Truscott IV, "Gay Power Comes to Sheridan Square," *Village Voice*, July 3, 1969, 18.

48. Carter, *Stonewall*, 157.

49. Donn Teal, *The Gay Militants* (New York: Stein and Day, 1971), 20.

50. Carter, *Stonewall*, 183.

51. Truscott, "Gay Power Comes to Sheridan Square," 18.

52. Duberman, *Stonewall*, 204.

53. Amin Ghaziani, *The Dividends of Dissent: How Conflict and Culture Work in Lesbian and Gay Marches on Washington* (Chicago: University of Chicago Press, 2008); Lillian Faderman, *Odd Girls and Twilight Lovers: A History of Lesbian Life in Twentieth-Century America* (New York: Penguin, 1991); Allan

Bérubé, *Coming Out Under Fire: The History of Gay Men and Women in World War II* (New York: Free Press, 1990); Duberman, *Stonewall*.

54. Armstrong, *Forging Gay Identities*, 63.

55. Carter, *Stonewall*, 178.

56. Castells, *The City and the Grassroots*, 138.

57. Tim Davis, "The Diversity of Queer Politics and the Redefinition of Sexual Identity and Community in Urban Spaces," in *Mapping Desire: Geographies of Sexualities*, ed. David Bell and Gill Valentine (London: Routledge, 1995), 286. See also Martin P. Levine, "Gay Ghetto," *Journal of Homosexuality* 4, no. 4 (1979): 363–77; Stephen O. Murray, "The Institutional Elaboration of a Quasi-Ethnic Community," *International Review of Modern Sociology* 9 (July 1979): 165–77;

58. Castells, *The City and the Grassroots*; Castells and Murphy, "Cultural Identity and Urban Structure," 237–59; Lawrence Knopp, "Gentrification and Gay Neighborhood Formation in New Orleans: A Case Study," in *Homo Economics: Capitalism, Community, and Lesbian and Gay Life*, ed. Amy Gluckman and Betsy Reed (New York: Routledge, 1997), 45–63; Lawrence Knopp, "Some Theoretical Implications of Gay Involvement in an Urban Land Market," *Political Geography Quarterly* 9, no. 4 (1990): 337–52; Mickey Lauria and Lawrence Knopp, "Toward an Analysis of the Role of Gay Communities in the Urban Renaissance," *Urban Geography* 6, no. 2 (1985): 152–69.

59. Edmund White, *States of Desire: Travels in Gay America* (New York: Dutton, 1980), 321.

60. Amin Ghaziani, "Cultural Archipelagos: New Directions in the Study of Sexuality and Space," *City & Community* 18, no. 1 (2019): 1–19.

61. Castells, *The City and the Grassroots*, 156.

62. Knopp, "Gentrification and Gay Neighborhood Formation in New Orleans," 49.

63. Levine, "Gay Ghetto," 372.

64. Kyra Kyles, "Boystown Shifting as More Families Move In," *RedEye*, December 10, 2007, http://articles.chicagotribune.com/2007-12-10/news/0712100253_1_gay-men-calendars-culture-clash; Ghaziani, *There Goes the Gayborhood?*

65. Jason Orne, *Boystown: Sex and Community in Chicago* (Chicago: University of Chicago Press, 2017).

66. Greene, "'You're Dancing on My Seat!'"

67. Lefebvre, *Writings on Cities*. See also Mark Purcell, "Excavating Lefebvre: The Right to the City and Its Urban Politics of the Inhabitant," *GeoJournal* 58, no. 2–3 (2002): 99–108.

68. Theodore Greene, "Queer Street Families: Place-Making and Community Among LGBT Youth of Color in Iconic Gay Neighborhoods," in *Queer Families and Relationships After Marriage Equality*, ed. Michael Yarborough, Angela Jones, and Joseph Nicholas DeFilippis (New York: Routledge, 2018), 168–81; Theodore Greene, "Aberrations of 'Home': Gay Neighborhoods and the Experiences of Community Among GBQ Men of Color," in *The Handbook of Research for Black Males: Quantitative, Qualitative, and Multidisciplinary*, ed. Theodore Ransaw, Richard Majors, and Charles Gause (East Lansing: Michigan State University Press, 2019), 189–209.

69. Lew, "Tourism Planning and Place Making," 449.

70. Lefebvre, *Writings on Cities*; Henri Lefebvre, *The Production of Space* (Cambridge: Blackwell, 1991); Purcell, "Excavating Lefebvre."

71. Lew, "Tourism Planning and Place Making," 449.

72. Harvey W. Zorbaugh, *The Gold Coast and the Slum* (Chicago: University of Chicago Press, 1929), 105, 115.

73. Dwight Conquergood, "Life in Big Red: Struggles and Accommodation in a Chicago Polyethnic Tenement," in *Structuring Diversity*, ed. Louise Lamphere (Chicago: University of Chicago Press, 1992); Sudhir Venkatesh, *American Project: The Rise and Fall of a Modern Ghetto* (Cambridge, MA: Harvard University Press, 2000); Sudhir Venkatesh, *Off the Books: The Underground Economy and the Urban Poor* (Cambridge, MA: Harvard University Press, 2006).

74. Hunter, "The Nightly Round."

75. Kevin Fox Gotham and Krista Brumley, "Using Space: Agency and Identity in a Public-Housing Development," *City & Community* 1, no. 3 (2002): 267–89.

76. Examples of the spatial practices aligned with the "creative class" include Japonica Brown-Saracino, *A Neighborhood That Never Changes: Gentrification, Social Preservation, and the Search for Authenticity* (Chicago: University of Chicago, 2009); Ryan Centner, "Places of Privileged Consumption Practices: Spatial Capital, the Dot-Com Habitus, and San Francisco's Internet Boom," *City & Community* 7, no. 3 (September 2008): 193–223; Terry Nichols Clark, ed., *The City as an Entertainment Machine* (Amsterdam: Elsevier, 2004); Richard Florida, "Cities and the Creative Class," *City & Community* 2, no. 1 (2003): 3–19; Richard Lloyd, *Neo-Bohemia: Art and Commerce in the Postindustrial City*, 2nd ed. (New York: Routledge, 2006); and Sharon Zukin, *Naked City: The Death and Life of Authentic Urban Places* (Oxford: Oxford University Press, 2010).

77. Jonathan R. Wynn, *Music/City: American Festivals and Placemaking in Austin, Nashville, and Newport* (Chicago: University of Chicago Press, 2015).

78. Gordon C. C. Douglas, *The Help-Yourself City* (Oxford: Oxford University Press, 2018).

79. Centner, "Places of Privileged Consumption Practices."

80. Gregory J. Snyder, *Skateboarding L.A.: Inside Professional Street Skateboarding* (New York: New York University Press, 2017); Jeffrey L. Kidder, *Parkour and the City: Risk, Masculinity, and Meaning in a Postmodern Sport* (New Brunswick, NJ: Rutgers University Press, 2017).

81. Derek Hyra, *Race, Class, and Politics in the Cappuccino City* (Chicago: University of Chicago Press, 2017).

82. Elijah Anderson, "The Iconic Ghetto," *Annals of the American Academy of Political and Social Science* 642 (2012): 8–24.

83. Chris Myers Asch and George Derek Musgrove, *Chocolate City: A History of Race and Democracy in the Nation's Capital* (Chapel Hill: University of North Carolina Press, 2017); Marcus Anthony Hunter and Zandria F. Robinson, *Chocolate Cities: The Black Map of Urban Life* (Berkeley: University of California Press, 2018).

84. Jackelyn Hwang, "The Social Construction of a Gentrifying Neighborhood," in "Reifying and Redefining Identity and Boundaries in Inequality," *Urban Affairs Review* 52, no. 1 (2016): 98–128.

85. Don Taylor, "DC Store Blasting Go-Go Music Sparks Neighborhood Controversy," *Patch*, April 10, 2019, https://patch.com/district-columbia/washingtondc/dc-store-blasting-go-go-music-sparks-neighborhood-controversy.

86. Tiffany Muller Myrdahl, "Ordinary (Small) Cities and LGBQ Lives," *ACME* 12, no. 9 (2013): 279–304; Jennifer Robinson, *Ordinary Cities: Between Modernity and Development* (London: Routledge, 2006); Amy L. Stone, "The Geography of Research on LGBTQ Life: Why Sociologists Should Study the South, Rural Queers, and Ordinary Cities," *Sociology Compass* 12, no. 11 (2018), https://doi.org./10.1111/soc4.12638.

87. LGBT Demographic Data Interactive, Williams Institute, UCLA School of Law, January 2019, https://williamsinstitute.law.ucla.edu/visualization/lgbt-stats/?topic=LGBT&area=27#about-the-data; Pew Research Center, *A Survey of LGBT Americans*; Perry Stein, "D.C.: The Gayest City in America," *Washington City Paper*, January 6, 2014, https://www.washingtoncitypaper.com/news/city-desk/blog/13068165/d-c-the-gayest-city-in-america; Mariah Cooper, "D.C. Has the Highest LGBTQ Population in the U.S.," *Washington Blade*, March 6, 2019, https://www.washingtonblade.com/2019/03/06/d-c-has-highest-LGBTQ+-population-in-the-u-s/; Jeremy W. Peters, "The Gayest Place in America?,"

New York Times, November 15, 2013, https://www.nytimes.com/2013/11/17/fashion /Washington-DC-has-thriving-gay-lesbian-and-transgender-population.html; Zach Stafford, "Even Under Donald Trump, Washington D.C. Is the Gayest Place in America," *The Advocate*, March 5, 2019, https://www.advocate.com/news /2019/3/05/even-under-donald-trump-washington-dc-gayest-place-america.

88. Johnson, *The Lavender Scare*.

89. Michael Alison Chandler, "Street Fest Lets Gays Revel in Freedom," *Washington Post*, June 11, 2007.

90. Dudley Clendinen and Adam Nagourney, *Out for Good: The Struggle to Build a Gay Rights Movement in America* (New York: Simon & Schuster, 1999).

91. Article 1, section 8 of the U.S. Constitution bestows on Congress exclusive jurisdiction over the District of Columbia in "all cases whatsoever." Congress transferred some of its powers to local government in the 1973 Home Rule Act; however, Congress maintains the right to review and veto all legislation approved by the mayor and the thirteen-member City Council. Congress also maintains authority over the District's operating budget. Despite the city's four electoral votes, District residents have no voting representation in either chamber of Congress.

92. Leah Asmelash, "Capitol Rioters Shouted 'This Is Our House.' But the Capitol Was Built by Enslaved Black Americans," CNN, January 12, 2021, https:// www.cnn.com/2021/01/12/us/capitol-riot-history-trnd/index.html.

93. Carol Morello and Tim Craig, "In Sign of Rebound, DC Population Set to Surpass 600,000," *Washington Post*, December 31, 2009, www.washingtonpost. com/wp-dyn/content/article/2009/12/31/AR2001231101310_pf.html; "District of Columbia: Census 2000 Profile" (Washington, DC: United States Census Bureau, August 2002); "District of Columbia Population 2019," World Population Review, accessed June 5, 2019, http://worldpopulationreview.com /states/district-of-columbia/.

94. Hyra, *Race, Class, and Politics in the Cappuccino City*; Carol Morello and Dan Keating, "Number of Black DC Residents Plummets as Majority Status Slips Away," *Washington Post*, March 24, 2011, http://www.washingtonpost.com/local /black-dc-residents-plummet-barely-a-majority/2011/03/24/ABtlgJQB_print .html; Hunter and Robinson, *Chocolate Cities: The Black Map of Urban Life*.

95. Ghaziani, "Cultural Archipelagos"; Theodore Greene, "Queer Cultural Archipelagos Are New to US," *City & Community* 18, no. 1 (2019): 23–29.

96. Elijah Anderson, "The White Space," *Sociology of Race and Ethnicity* 1, no. 1 (2015): 10–21.

97. Patricia Hill Collins, "Learning from the Outsiders Within: The Sociological Significance of Black Feminist Thought," *Social Problems* 33, no. 6 (1986): S14–32.

1. STILL "A VERY GAY CITY": A HISTORICAL IMPRESSION OF WASHINGTON'S LGBTQ COMMUNITIES

The chapter title is a play on "'This Used to Be a Very Gay City': Lafayette Park and the Sex Crime Panic," the title of chapter 2 of David K. Johnson's book *The Lavender Scare: The Cold War Persecution of Gays and Lesbians in the Federal Government* (Chicago: University of Chicago Press, 2004). His title comes from a quotation given by one of his interview subjects to highlight how, before World War II, the federal government employed many homosexuals: "'This used to be a very gay city,' friends told Ramon G. when he moved to Washington in 1951. 'People would practically carry on on park benches . . . the agencies here were filled with gays. Nobody bothered them, nobody cared" (39). In titling this chapter "Still 'a Very Gay City,'" I hope to convey how DC's contemporary queer landscape reflects a legacy of queer placemaking that endured despite local and federal governmental efforts to eradicate public expressions of queer life in employment and in public spaces.

1. Brock Thompson, "There Goes the Gayborhood?," *Blot Magazine*, August 3, 2015, https://www.theblot.com/there-goes-the-gayborhood-7748649.

2. Jack Lait and Lee Mortimer, *Washington Confidential* (New York: Crown, 1951), 90.

3. The question of Von Steuben's sexual predilections remains a subject for debate. Randy Shilts alleges Von Steuben, once a close aide to Prussia's King Frederick II, had taken "familiarities with young boys," creating such a scandal as to influence his decision to come to America. Randy Shilts, *Conduct Unbecoming: Lesbians and Gays in the U.S. Military: Vietnam to the Persian Gulf* (New York: St. Martin's, 1993), 7–10. Other historians, however, have dismissed these claims as circumstantial at best. The Von Steuben biographer Paul Lockhart writes, "There is little evidence to prove one or the other. Steuben enjoyed the company of women, in social settings at least, but like many soldiers of his day, he spent nearly all of his time in the exclusively male society of the army. Whether Steuben was homosexual or heterosexual, or asexual, for that matter, may never be known without any certainty." Paul

Lockhart, *The Drillmaster of Valley Forge: The Baron de Steuben and the Making of the American Army* (New York: Harper Collins, 2008), 204.

4. Despite his empirical focus on Chicago's Boystown, Amin Ghaziani historicizes gay neighborhoods nationally, focusing primarily on the formation of gay neighborhoods in the "great cities." See Amin Ghaziani, *There Goes the Gayborhood?* (Princeton, NJ: Princeton University Press, 2014).

5. Amin Ghaziani, "Cultural Archipelagos: New Directions in the Study of Sexuality and Space," *City & Community* 18, no. 1 (2019): 1–19.

6. For a discussion of communities of interest, see Melvin Webber, "Order in Diversity: Community Without Propinquity," in *Cities and Space: The Future Use of Urban Land*, ed. Lowdon Wingo, Jr. (Baltimore, MD: Johns Hopkins University Press, 1963), 23–56.

7. Marcus Anthony Hunter, "All the Gays Are White and All the Blacks Are Straight: Black Gay Men, Identity, and Community," *Sexuality Research and Social Policy* 7, no. 2 (2010): 81–92.

8. Marcus Anthony Hunter and Zandria F. Robinson, *Chocolate Cities: The Black Map of Urban Life* (Berkeley: University of California Press, 2018).

9. Keith Boykin, *One More River to Cross: Black and Gay in America* (New York: Doubleday, 1996); Theodore Greene, "Queer Cultural Archipelagos Are New to US," *City & Community* 18, no. 1 (2019): 23–29.

10. Marcus Anthony Hunter, "The Nightly Round: Space, Social Capital, and Urban Black Nightlife," *City & Community* 9, no. 2 (2010): 165–86.

11. Amy L. Stone, "The Geography of Research on LGBTQ Life: Why Sociologists Should Study the South, Rural Queers, and Ordinary Cities," *Sociology Compass* 12, no. 11 (2018), https://doi.org/10.1111/soc4.12638.

12. See George Chauncey, *Gay New York: Gender, Urban Culture, and the Making of the Homosexual* (New York: Basic Books, 1994). Chauncey describes how the repeal of Prohibition laws in the United States resulted in the creation of local laws in New York City that banned gay bars. This chapter highlights how, despite the various laws banning bars in Washington, DC (where all bars were banned outright), a distinct local context allowed gay men (and to a lesser extent lesbians) spaces to congregate in the 1930s and 1940s.

13. Genny Beemyn, *A Queer Capital: A History of Gay Life in Washington, D.C.* (New York: Routledge, 2015); *Annual Report of the Chief of Engineers, United States Army to the Secretary of War for the Year 1887, Part III* (Washington, DC: Government Printing Office, 1887), 2078. The report indicates that before

1886 the parks had been open until eleven P.M., providing ample opportunity for men to seek same-sex companionship before the parks closed.

14. Genny Beemyn, "A Queer Capital: Lesbian, Gay, and Bisexual Life in Washington, DC 1890–1955" (PhD diss., University of Iowa, 1997), 18.

15. Carter Newman Bealer's diaries have also been published under the pseudonym "Jeb Alexander" in the edited collection *Jeb and Dash: A Diary of Gay Life, 1918–1945*, ed. Ina Russell (Boston: Faber and Faber, 1993). In *A Queer Capital*, historian Genny Beeman reveals Jeb Alexander's identity. This chapter draws on excerpts from both Beemyn's book (for which they had access to Bealer's complete diary) and the edited version of his accounts from *Jeb and Dash*. However, for the sake of consistency, I will refer to Bealer by his real name.

16. Russell, *Jeb and Dash*, 227.

17. Beemyn, *A Queer Capital*, 21.

18. Beemyn, *A Queer Capital*, 20–21.

19. Irving Rosse, "Sexual Hypochondriasis and the Perversion of the Genetic Instinct," *Journal of Nervous and Mental Disease* 17, no. 11 (1892): 806. The use of "moral hermaphrodites" refers to sodomites or men-women, which aligns with the practice in that period of defining homosexuality through gender presentation rather than object choice. For additional information on the use of "moral hermaphrodite," see Chantal Zabus, *Out in Africa: Same-Sex Desire in Sub-Saharan Literatures and Cultures* (Suffolk, UK: James Currey, 2013). For discussions of the definition of homosexuals through gender presentation, see Chauncey, *Gay New York*.

20. Beemyn, *A Queer Capital*, 23.

21. Genny Beemyn, "The Geography of Same-Sex Desire: Cruising Men in Washington, DC in the Late Nineteenth and Early Twentieth Centuries," *Left History* 9, no. 2 (Spring 2004): 157n38.

22. Robert Scully, *A Pansy*, ed. Robert J. Corber (New York: Fordham University Press, 2016), 114.

23. Beemyn, "A Queer Capital," 23–24.

24. Beemyn, *A Queer Capital*, 24.

25. Chad Heap, *Slumming: Sexual and Racial Encounters in American Nightlife, 1885–1940* (Chicago: University of Chicago Press, 2009); Chauncey, *Gay New York*.

26. Kwame Holmes, "Chocolate to Rainbow City: The Dialectics of Black and Gay Community Formation in Postwar Washington, D.C. 1946–1978" (PhD diss., University of Illinois, 2011).

27. Blair Ruble, *Washington's U Street: A Biography* (Washington, DC: Woodrow Wilson Center Press, 2010); Sandra Fitzpatrick and Mara Goodwin, *The Guide to Black Washington: Places and Events of Historical and Cultural Significance in the Nation's Capital* (New York: Hippocrine, 2001); Beemyn, *A Queer Capital*, 26.

28. Beemyn, *A Queer Capital*, 25.

29. Beemyn, *A Queer Capital*, 26.

30. Beemyn, *A Queer Capital*, 37.

31. William Henry Jones, *The Housing of Negroes in Washington, D.C.: A Study in Human Ecology* (Washington, DC: Howard University Press, 1929), 135, 137.

32. Charles H. Hughes, "Postscript to Paper on 'Erotopathia,'—An Organization of Colored Erotopaths," *Alienist and Neurologist* 14, no. 4 (October 1893): 731–32.

33. Rosse, "Sexual Hypochondriasis and the Perversion of the Genetic Instinct," 802.

34. "In Female Attire: A Man Caught Masquerading in Woman's Attire Sent to the Workhouse," *Evening Star*, January 1, 1886.

35. "A Negro Dive Raided: Thirteen Black Men Dressed as Women Surprised," *Washington Post*, April 13, 1888.

36. See also Beemyn, *A Queer Capital*; Jeffrey C. Stewart, *The New Negro: The Life of Alain Locke* (Oxford: Oxford University Press, 2018).

37. Beemyn, *A Queer Capital*, 84.

38. Chauncey, *Gay New York*, 358.

39. Haviland Ferris, "Has Gay Life Changed Much in Fifty Years?," *Washington Blade*, October 1, 1982, 16.

40. Johnson, *The Lavender Scare*. For discussions of queer life in New York and Chicago, see Chauncey, *Gay New York*; Heap, *Slumming*; and Allen Drexel, "Before Paris Burned: Race, Class, and Male Homosexuality on the Chicago South Side, 1935–1960," in *Creating a Place for Ourselves: Lesbian, Gay, and Bisexual Community Histories*, ed. Genny Beemyn (New York: Routledge, 1997), 119–44.

41. Ladd Forrester, "Rollerskating 'Round the '30s Grapevine in D.C.," *Washington Blade*, September 26, 1986.

42. Ladd Forrester, "D.C. Bars: From Parody to Poetry," *Washington Blade*, September 5, 1986, 1.

43. Genny Beemyn, interview with Frank Kameny, March 20, 1994, Genny Beemyn Queer Capital Oral History Collection, https://archives.rainbow history.org/collections/browse.

44. Beemyn, interview with Frank Kameny.

45. Genny Beemyn, interview with Haviland Ferris, May 16, 1994, Genny Beemyn Queer Capital Oral History Collection, https://archives.rainbowhistory.org/collections/browse.

46. Forrester, "D.C. Bars."

47. Beemyn, "A Queer Capital."

48. Both New York and Chicago experienced a "Negro craze" during the 1920s, where participation in Harlem and Bronzeville, respectively, provided middle- and upper-class whites the kind of separation from their daily lives they needed to explore their nonnormative sexual appetites. See Chauncey, *Gay New York*; Heap, *Slumming*. Washington did not experience this. Although the city's southern culture might explain the absence of a "Negro craze" in Washington, historical evidence suggests that white gay men could create the spatial distinction necessary to safely explore their sexuality in white spaces. At any rate, it is valuable to realize that whites enjoyed the spatial freedom to explore their sexuality as they pleased, while Blacks remained relegated to their own communities.

49. Forrester, "D.C. Bars," 11.

50. Beemyn, interview with Haviland Ferris.

51. Forrester, "D.C. Bars," 11.

52. Beemyn, *A Queer Capital*, 110.

53. Beemyn, interview with Frank Kameny.

54. Lait and Mortimer, *Washington Confidential*, 10.

55. Johnson, *The Lavender Scare*; Keith Melder and Melinda Young Stuart, *City of Magnificent Intentions: A History of Washington, District of Columbia* (Washington, DC: Intac, 1983).

56. John D'Emilio, *Sexual Politics, Sexual Communities: The Making of a Homosexual Minority in the United States 1940–1970* (Chicago: University of Chicago Press, 1983), 24.

57. Beemyn, *A Queer Capital*; Johnson, *The Lavender Scare*.

58. Beemyn, *A Queer Capital*, 100–101.

59. Beemyn, interview with Haviland Ferris.

60. Beemyn, *A Queer Capital*, 108.

61. Beemyn, *A Queer Capital*, 114.

62. Holmes, "Chocolate to Rainbow City," 45.

63. Beemyn, *A Queer Capital*, 106.

64. Genny Beemyn, interview with Esther Smith, June 9, 1994, Genny Beemyn Queer Capital Oral History Collection, https://archives.rainbowhistory.org/collections/browse.

65. Beemyn, "A Queer Capital," 187.

66. Genny Beemyn, interview with Pat Hamilton, January 13, 1995, Genny Beemyn Queer Capital Oral History Collection, https://archives.rainbowhistory.org /collections/browse.

67. Louis Lautier, "The Capital Spotlight," *Washington Afro-American*, January 28, 1933, 1.

68. Holmes, "Chocolate to Rainbow City," 46.

69. Beemyn, interview with Pat Hamilton.

70. Ulf Hannerz, *Soulside: Inquiries Into Ghetto Culture and Community* (Chicago: University of Chicago Press, 1969), 29.

71. Ben W. Gilbert and the Staff of the *Washington Post*, *Ten Blocks from the White House: Anatomy of the Washington Riots of 1968* (New York: Praeger, 1968).

72. Holmes, "Chocolate to Rainbow City," 51.

73. Tom Zito, "Anything's Cool at the Discos," *Washington Post*, October 17, 1974, E-1, E-11; Chris DeForrest, "The Washington Post: A Response to 'Anything's Cool at the Discos,'" *Gay Blade*, November 1974, 8.

74. Paul Schwartzman, "DC Gay Clubs' Vanishing Turf; City Earmarks Block of O Street SE for Stadium," *Washington Post*, June 8, 2005.

75. Angie Crouch and Bill French, "'Flaunting It': Gay Bar Bans Straight Bachelorette Parties," *NBC News*, May 25, 2012, https://www.nbcnews.com/news /world/flaunting-it-gay-bar-bans-straight-bachelorette-parties-flna794647; Caryn Rousseau, "Gay Bar Bans Brides to Be," Associated Press, June 16, 2009, https://pantagraph.com/news/bride-ban-gay-bar-says-i-dont-to-bachelorettes /article_7c9e0847-a619-52e1-878f-946ccc2a18f2.html; Jason Steele, "Should Gay Bars Ban Bachelorette Parties?," *Chicago Tribune*, March 25, 2009, http://articles .chicagotribune.com/2009-03-25/news/0903250117_1_gay-bar-gay-marriage-gay -man; Aylin Zafar, "L.A. Bar Bans Bachelorette Parties Until Gay Marriage Is Legal," *Time*, May 26, 2012, http://newsfeed.time.com/2012/05/26/l-a-gay -bar-bans-bachelorette-parties-until-gay-marriage-is-legal/.

76. Zito, "Anything's Cool at the Discos," E-11.

77. DeForrest, "The Washington Post: A Response to 'Anything's Cool at the Discos,'" 8.

78. Steve Martz, "Our Tenth Anniversary," *The Blade*, October 25, 1979.

79. Ernie Acosta, "Emerging Dialogue Between Races," *The Blade*, December 6, 1979, B-1.

80. Acosta, "Emerging Dialogue Between Races," B-1.

81. E. A. Acosta, "Black Gays Endorse Tucker for Mayor," *The Blade*, August 1978, 3.

82. ClubHouse advertisement, *Blacklight*, October 1982; Sidney Brinkley, "The Clubhouse Plans on 'Going Out in Style,'" *Washington Blade*, May 25, 1990.

83. Holmes, "Chocolate to Rainbow City," 51.

84. *The Club House Trailer* (Washington, DC: Small Wonder Media, 2021), https://www.youtube.com/watch?v=cXwkWwJ77FQ.

85. Amber Bailey, "1296 Upshur St, NW (The Clubhouse)," no. DC-884, Historic American Buildings Survey, Library of Congress, Washington, DC, 2016, https://www.nps.gov/places/upload/The-ClubHouse-1.pdf.

86. *The Club House—History: Origins and Location.*

87. John P. Olinger, "The ClubHouse, a Remarkable LGBTQ Gathering Spot," DC History Center, April 12, 2021, http://dchistory.org/the-clubhouse/.

88. ClubHouse advertisement.

89. Phil Lapadula, "Dupont Circle: A Totally Urban Experience," *Washington Blade—Supplement*, July 26, 1985, 1.

90. National Park Service, "Striver's Section: Historic District," National Register of Historic Places Travel Itinerary, 2010, accessed September 21, 2010, http://www.nps.gov/nr/travel/WASH/dc49.htm.

91. Linda Wheeler, "Dupont Circle," in *Washington at Home: An Illustrated History of Neighborhoods in the Nation's Capital*, ed. Kathryn Schneider Smith (Baltimore, MD: Johns Hopkins University Press, 2010), 187.

92. Wheeler, "Dupont Circle."

93. Lapadula, "Dupont Circle," 1.

94. Wheeler, "Dupont Circle," 191.

95. Lapadula, "Dupont Circle," 5.

96. "Lambda Rising Bookstore Moves to Connecticut Ave.; First Satellite Store Also Opens in Baltimore," *Washington Post*, December 10, 1984.

97. Lapadula, "Dupont Circle," 6.

98. Linda Wheeler, "Transformation of a Drug-Ridden Street," *Washington Post*, November 26, 1983, B-1. As is the case with areas like Logan Circle, Mount Vernon has historically been considered part of the greater Shaw neighborhood. With the construction of the Walter E. Washington Convention Center and the increased influx of white gentrifiers in the area, Mount Vernon has been distinguished as a separate area in recent years to escape the negative reputation typically associated with Shaw.

99. Wheeler, "Transformation," B-1.

100. Wheeler, "Transformation."

101. Wheeler, "Transformation."

102. Wheeler, "Transformation."

103. Wheeler, "Transformation."

104. Chibbaro, "Gentrification."

105. Chibbaro, "Gentrification," 27.

106. Jose Antonio Vargas, "In Shaw, Pews vs. Stools," *Washington Post*, April 20, 2006.

107. Gerard Martin Moeller and Christopher Weeks, *AIA Guide to the Architecture of Washington, DC*, 4th ed. (Baltimore, MD: Johns Hopkins University Press, 2006).

108. Melissa Castro, "After Gay Migration, 17th Street Seeks a New Identity," *Washington Business Journal*, July 28, 2008, http://washington.bizjournals.com; Fritz Hahn, "The Halo Effect," *Washington Post*, September 23, 2004, http://www.washingtonpost.com/wp-dyn/articles/A44741-2004Sep23.html; Anne Hull, "Palace of Plenty: Food, Class and the Coming of Fresh Fields to Logan Circle," *Washington Post*, April 1, 2001; Jura Kornicus, "Household Names," *Washington Post*, May 16, 2007, http://www.washingtonpost.com/wp-dyn/content/article/2007/05/16/AR2007051600342.html.

109. Lou Chibbaro Jr., "Council Gives Final Approval to Marriage Bill," *Washington Blade*, December 18, 2009, http://www.washingtonblade.com/2009/12/18/council-gives-final-approval-to-marriage-bill/; Yusef Najafi, "Fenty Signs D.C. Marriage Bill," *Metro Weekly*, December 18, 2009, http://www.metroweekly.com/2009/12/fenty-signs-dc-marriage-bill/.

110. Bill Roundy, "Does Dupont Circle Remain the Center of DC?," *Washington Blade*, September 24, 1999, 12.

111. Annys Shin, "From Georgetown to Adams Morgan, Liquor License Moratoriums Face Incremental Criticism," *Washington Post*, February 7, 2014, http://www.washingtonpost.com/local/from-georgetown-to-adams-morgan-liquor-license-moratoriums-face-increasing-criticism/2014/02/07/61fc0c74-7a21-11e3-8963-b4b654bcc9b2_story.html.

112. Alcohol Beverage Regulation Administration Alcoholic Beverage Control Board, "Notice Announcing the Expiration of The East Dupont Circle Moratorium Zone," August 21, 2017, accessed December 28, 2023, https://abra.dc.gov/sites/default/files/dc/sites/abra/publication/attachments/Notice%20Announcing%20the%20Expiration%20of%20the%20East%20Dupont%20Circle%20Moratorium%20Zone%20-%209%2027%2020%202017.pdf

113. Schwartzman, "DC Gay Clubs' Vanishing Turf."

114. Kim Krisberg, "Is Dupont Neighborhood Losing Its Gay-Mecca Status?," *Washington Blade*, January 25, 2001.

115. Bryan Anderton, "Capital Pride's Colorful History," *Washington Blade*, June 4, 2004.

116. Lou Chibbaro Jr., " 'Kameny Way' Ceremony Highlights Capital Pride Events," *Washington Blade*, June 8, 2010, http://www.washingtonblade.com/2010/06/08/%E2%80%98kameny-way%E2%80%99-ceremony-highlights-capital-pride-events/.

2. *"J'AI DEUX AMOURS"*: THE PROMISCUITY OF COMMUNITY ATTACHMENTS IN THE POSTMODERN CITY

1. Various scholars have considered how living in suburban or small-town communities allows same-sex couples to minimize or mute their sexual identities in order to assimilate within their respective communities. See Wayne Brekhus, *Peacocks, Chameleons, and Centaurs: Gay Suburbia and the Grammar of Social Identity* (Chicago: University of Chicago Press, 2003); Japonica Brown-Saracino, *How Places Make Us: Novel LBQ Identities in Four Small Cities* (Chicago: University of Chicago Press, 2017).

2. Brekhus, *Peacocks, Chameleons, and Centaurs*.

3. Morris Janowitz, *The Community Press in an Urban Setting: The Social Elements of Urbanism* (Chicago: University of Chicago Press, 1952); see also Albert Hunter and Gerald Suttles, "The Expanding Community of Limited Liability," in *The Social Construction of Communities*, ed. Gerard Suttles (Chicago: University of Chicago Press, 1972), 45–81.

4. Amin Ghaziani, *There Goes the Gayborhood?* (Princeton, NJ: Princeton University Press, 2014), 2.

5. Ghaziani, *There Goes the Gayborhood?*, 2.

6. Amin Ghaziani, "Cultural Archipelagos: New Directions in the Study of Sexuality and Space," *City & Community* 18, no. 1 (2019): 1–19.

7. Brekhus, *Peacocks, Chameleons, and Centaurs*.

8. Brown-Saracino, *How Places Make Us*.

9. Herbert Gans, "Urbanism and Suburbanism as Ways of Life: A Reevaluation of Definitions," in *Readings in Urban Sociology*, ed. R. E. Pahl (Oxford: Pergamon, 1968), 95–118.

10. Amin Ghaziani, "Post-gay Collective Identity Construction," *Social Problems* 58, no. 1 (2011): 99–125.

11. Albert Hunter, "Persistence of Local Sentiments in Mass Society," in *Handbook of Contemporary Urban Life*, ed. David Street and Associates (San Francisco: Jossey-Bass, 1978), 133–62.

12. Hunter, "Persistence of Local Sentiments in Mass Society," 145.

13. Janowitz, *The Community Press in an Urban Setting*; Gregory P. Stone, "City Shoppers and Urban Identification: Observations on the Social Psychology of City Life," *American Journal of Sociology* 60, no. 1 (1954): 36–45.

14. Walter Firey, "Sentiment and Symbolism as Ecological Variables," *American Sociological Review* 10, no. 2 (April 1945): 140–48.

15. Japonica Brown-Saracino, *A Neighborhood That Never Changes: Gentrification, Social Preservation, and the Search for Authenticity* (Chicago: University of Chicago, 2009).

16. Michael Bennett and Juan Battle, "We Can See Them, But We Can't Hear Them," in *Queer Families, Queer Politics*, ed. Mary Bernstein and Renate Remain (New York: Columbia University Press, 2001); Keith Boykin, *Beyond the Down Low: Sex, Lies, and Denial in Black America* (New York: Carroll and Graf, 2006); Irene Monroe, "The Garden of Homophobia," *The Advocate*, December 9, 1999.

17. Joshua Lynsen and Lou Chibbaro Jr., "Be Bar Liquor License Fight Goes Before Board," *Washington Blade*, April 21, 2006; Greg Marzullo, "Church Leader Challenges DC Gay Bar: ANC Protests Be Bar License After Anti-Gay Pastor Complains," *Washington Blade*, March 17, 2006, http://www.washblade.com/print.cfm?content_id=7870; Will O'Bryan, "D.C. Community Mourns Annie Kaylor: Namesake of Annie's Paramount Steakhouse Dies at 85," *Metro Weekly*, July 25, 2013, http://www.metroweekly.com/news/?ak=8498.

18. Kevin Naff, "Blade Blog: Where Is the Outrage Over Black Pastor's Homophobia?," *Washington Blade*, April 21, 2006, accessed December 1, 2007, http://washblade.com.

19. Japonica Brown-Saracino, "Virtuous Marginality: Social Preservationists and the Selection of the Old-Timer," *Theory and Society* 36, no. 5 (2007): 437–68.

20. See Nan Alamilla Boyd, "San Francisco's Castro District: From Liberation to Tourist Destination," *Journal of Tourism and Cultural Change* 9, no. 3 (2011): 237–48; Manuel Castells, *The City and the Grassroots* (Berkeley: University of California Press, 1983); Lawrence Knopp, "Gentrification and Gay Neighborhood Formation in New Orleans: A Case Study," in *Homo Economics: Capitalism, Community, and Lesbian and Gay Life*, ed. Amy Gluckman and Betsy Reed (New York: Routledge, 1997), 45–63; Christina Hanhardt, *Safe Space: Gay Neighborhood History and the Politics of Violence* (Durham, NC: Duke University Press, 2013).

3. PLACES IN ABEYANCE: PLACEMAKING AND THE CONSTRUCTION OF COMMUNITY IN INSTITUTIONAL ANCHORS

1. Sue Levin, *In the Pink: The Making of Successful Gay- and Lesbian-Owned Businesses* (Binghamton, NY: Harrington Park Press, 1999).

2. Genny Beemyn, interview with Deacon Maccubbin, Part 1, May 27, 1998, Genny Beemyn Queer Capital Oral History Collection, Rainbow History Project, https://archives.rainbowhistory.org/collections/browse.

3. The *Washington Blade* has undergone numerous name changes over its forty-plus-year history. Originally the *Gay Blade*, its publishers dropped the word *Gay* from its title in June 1975 after learning that a New York paper held rights to the name. In October 1980, the paper was renamed the *Washington Blade* after the company reincorporated as a for-profit, employee-formed business (Chris Johnson, "From Modest Beginnings to Paper of Record, *Washington Blade*, October 16, 2009, 6). The paper retained its name after it was purchased by Windows Media in 2001. After Windows Media abruptly ceased operation of the *Washington Blade* in 2009, staffers launched *DC Agenda*, which would eventually be renamed the *Washington Blade* in April 2010 after *DC Agenda* acquired the assets of the *Washington Blade* through the U.S. Bankruptcy Court (Dan Zak, "Gay Weekly DC Agenda Sets a Memorable Date: The Return of Washington Blade, *Washington Post*, April 27, 2010, https://www.washingtonpost.com/wp-dyn/content/article/2010/04/26/AR2010042602653.html). I will use the title appropriate to the historical moment in which the article was written: the *Gay Blade* (1969–1975), the *Blade* (1975–1980), the *Washington Blade* (1980-2009; 2010–present), and *DC Agenda* (2009–2010).

4. Beemyn, interview with Deacon Maccubbin, Part 1.

5. Beemyn, interview with Deacon Maccubbin, Part 1.

6. Levin, *In the Pink*; Yusef Najafi, "Lambda Rising, DC's Only All-LGBT Bookstore, to Close After the Holiday Season," *Metro Weekly*, December 10, 2009, https://www.metroweekly.com/2009/12/book-ends/.

7. Beemyn, interview with Deacon Maccubbin, Part 1.

8. Beemyn, interview with Deacon Maccubbin, Part 1.

9. "Lambda Rising Bookstore Moves to Connecticut Ave.; First Satellite Store Also Opens In Baltimore," *Washington Post*, December 10, 1984,

10. Levin, *In the Pink*.

11. Rainbow History Project, "Community Pioneers: Deacon Maccubbin," 2012, accessed May 25, 2019, https://archives.rainbowhistory.org/exhibits/show /pioneers/maccubbin.

12. Will O'Bryan, "Firmly Rooted: From Its Grassroots Beginnings to Its Current Magnificence, Pride Has Always Been a Day of Affirmation for the LGBT Community," *Metro Weekly*, June 8, 2005, https://www.metroweekly.com/2005 /06/firmly-rooted/.

13. Rainbow History Project, "Places in Our History: The Community Building, 1724 20th St. NW," 2010, accessed May 21, 2012, http://www.rainbowhistory.org /html/1724.html.

14. Najafi, "Lambda Rising."

15. Najafi, "Lambda Rising."

16. Guy Raz, "DC Gay Bookstore Latest to Close," National Public Radio, December 26, 2009, http://www.npr.org/templates/story/story.php?storyid=121933065.

17. Najafi, "Lambda Rising."

18. Lou Chibbaro, Jr. End of an era, as Lambda Rising to Close," *DC Agenda*, December 11, 2009, accessed January 31, 2010, https://www.washingtonblade .com/2009/12/11/end-of-an-era-as-lambda-rising-to-close/.

19. Najafi, "Lambda Rising."

20. Amin Ghaziani, "Measuring Urban Sexual Cultures," *Theory and Society* 43, no. 3–4 (2014): 373.

21. Albert Hunter, "Persistence of Local Sentiments in Mass Society," in *Handbook of Contemporary Urban Life*, ed. David Street and Associates (San Francisco: Jossey-Bass, 1978) 133–62.

22. Christopher Reed, "We're from Oz: Marking Ethnic and Sexual Identity in Chicago," *Environment and Planning D: Society and Space* 21 (2003): 425–40.

23. Emile Durkheim, *Elementary Forms of Religious Life*, trans. Karen Fields (New York: Free Press, 1912).

24. Ghaziani, "Measuring Urban Sexual Cultures," 373.

25. Dereka Rushbrook, "Cities, Queer Space, and the Cosmopolitan Tourist," *GLQ: A Journal of Lesbian and Gay Studies* 8, no. 1–2 (2002): 183.

26. Japonica Brown-Saracino, *A Neighborhood That Never Changes: Gentrification, Social Preservation, and the Search for Authenticity* (Chicago: University of Chicago Press, 2009); Richard Lloyd, "Neo-Bohemia: Art and Neighborhood Redevelopment in Chicago," *Journal of Urban Affairs* 24, no. 5 (2002): 517–32; David Grazian, *On the Make: The Hustle of Urban Nightlife* (Chicago: University of Chicago Press, 2008); Sharon Zukin, *The Culture of Cities* (Malden. MA: Blackwell, 1995).

27. Amin Ghaziani, *There Goes the Gayborhood?* (Princeton, NJ: Princeton University Press, 2014), 198–202.

28. Verta Taylor, "Social Movement Continuity: The Women's Movement in Abeyance," *American Sociological Review* 54 (1989): 761–66.

29. Verta Taylor and Alison Dahl Crossley, "Abeyance," in *The Wiley-Blackwell Encyclopedia of Social and Political Movements*, ed. David A. Snow, Donatella della Porta, Doug McAdam, and Bert Klandermans (Malden, MA: Blackwell, 2013), accessed March 1, 2023, https://doi.org/10.1002/9780470674871.wbespm001.

30. Will O'Bryan, "Forever Annie's: The Steakhouse That Transformed 17th Street," *Metro Weekly*, March 1, 2006, https://www.metroweekly.com/2006/03/forever -annies/.

31. David K. Johnson, *The Lavender Scare: The Cold War Persecution of Gays and Lesbians in the Federal Government* (Chicago: University of Chicago Press, 2004).

32. O'Bryan, "Forever Annie's."

33. Erving Goffman, *The Presentation of Self in Everyday Life* (New York: Doubleday, 1959), 17–18.

34. Lou Chibbaro Jr., "Annie Kaylor of Annie's Paramount Steakhouse Dies at 86," *Washington Blade*, July 25, 2013, https://www.washingtonblade.com/2013 /07/25/annie-kaylor-of-annies-paramount-steakhouse-dies-at-86-washington -dc-gay-news/.

35. O'Bryan, "Forever Annie's."

36. O'Bryan, "Forever Annie's."

37. O'Bryan, "Forever Annie's."

38. Doug Rule, "Upstairs Haven—17th Street's Landmark Steakhouse, Annie's, Adds an Upscale Lounge Upstairs," *Metro Weekly*, August 6, 2008, https:// www.metroweekly.com/2008/08/upstairs-haven/.

39. Will O'Bryan, "DC Community Mourns Annie Kaylor: Namesake of Annie's Paramount Steakhouse Dies at 85." *Metro Weekly*, July 25, 2013, https://www. metroweekly.com/2013/07/dc-community-mourns-annie-kayl/

40. Joe Crea, "Arrest Made in Killing of Annie's Waiter," *Washington Blade*, September 3, 2004.

41. Lou Chibbaro Jr., "Gay Waiter Killed After Leaving Annie's," *Washington Blade*, August 27, 2004.

42. Crea, "Arrest Made in Killing of Annie's Waiter."

43. Although the question of what constitutes a *bear* remains widely contested, general answers suggest that gay bears reject the stereotypical association of homosexuality with effeminacy in favor of a more natural and rugged masculinity (in contrast to the "self-conscious and exaggerated masculinity" characteristic

of the gay leather subculture) (Peter Hennen, "Bear Bodies, Bear Masculinity: Recuperation, Resistance, or Retreat," *Gender and Society* 19, no. 1 (2006): 26. Body attributes commonly associated with bears include stockiness, burliness, and hairiness. A bear can carry such modifiers as "daddy bear" (an older man), "muscle bear" (a man whose size derives from muscle and not body fat), and "black bear" (a bear of African descent). "Cub" commonly refers to younger and younger-looking bears and can also refer to the more submissive partner in a bear relationship. "Chaser" refers to a man who do not necessarily identify with the bear culture but who seeks a "bear" or a "cub" as a romantic or sexual partner.

44. Ghaziani, *There Goes the Gayborhood?*; Brian C. Kelly et al., "Exploring the Gay Community Question: Neighborhood and Network Influences on the Experiences of Community Among Urban Gay Men," *Sociological Quarterly* 55 (2014): 23–48; Greggor Mattson, "Style and the Fate of Gay Nightlife: Homonormative Placemaking in San Francisco," *Urban Studies* 52, no. 16 (2015): 3144–59; Cassie Owens and Mark Dent, "Straightwashing: Woody's and How Philly's Gay Bars Are Less Gay," Billy Penn, June 16, 2017, https://billypenn.com/2017/06/16/straightwashing-woodys-and-how-phillys-gay-bars-are-less-gay/; Michael Sibalis, "Urban Space and Homosexuality: The Example of the Marais, Paris' 'Gay Ghetto,'" *Urban Studies* 41, no. 9 (August 2004): 1739–58; Stacy Vanek Smith, "Gay Bars Adjusting to a New Reality," Marketplace, April 25, 2008, http://www.marketplace.org/topics/life/gay-bars-adjusting-new-reality; Robert David Sullivan, "Last Call—Why the Gay Bars of Boston Are Disappearing, and What It Says About the Future of City Life," *Boston Globe*, December 2, 2007; June Thomas, *The Gay Bar: Its Riotous Past and Uncertain Future* (Washington, DC: Slate Magazine, 2014); Daniel Villareal, "What the F*ck Is Killing Our Gay Bars, and Is It Our Own Fault?," Hornet, January 3, 2020, https://hornet.com/stories/gay-bar-decline-apps/; Esther Webber, "Why Are London's Gay Bars Disappearing?," BBC, August 29. 2015, https://www.bbc.com/news/uk-england-london-33608000.

45. The sociologist Greggor Mattson notes a 37 percent decline in gay bar listings in the United States from 2007 to 2019, with the most significant periods of decline occurring between 2012 and 2017 (18.6 percent decline) and 2017 to 2019 (14.4 percent). Lesbian bars decreased by 52 percent in the same period, while "cruisy bars," serving men engaging in various sexual acts on the premises, declined by nearly 60 percent. Mattson also observed a 60 percent decline of bars supporting LGBTQ communities of color.

46. Ryan Stillwagon and Amin Ghaziani, "Queer Pop-Ups: A Cultural Innovation of Urban Life," *City & Community* 18, no. 3 (2019): 874–95.

47. Teo Armus, "'You're Welcome Here': Revelry and Sadness at a Gay Mainstay's Final Weekend," *Washington Post*, July 1, 2018, https://www.washingtonpost .com/local/youre-welcome-here-revelry-and-sadness-at-a-gay-mainstays-final -weekend/2018/07/01/45d63e56-7b26-11e8-aeee-4d04c8ac6158_story.html; Melissa Lang, "DC Gay Nightclub Cobalt Closes with Little Warning," *Washington Post*, March 5, 2019, https://www.washingtonpost.com/local/dc -gay-nightclub-cobalt-closes-with-little-warning/2019/03/05/895b758c-3f85 -11e9-922c-64d6b7840b82_story.html.

48. Emma Spruce, "LGBTQ Situated Memory, Place-Making and the Sexual Politics of Gentrification," *Environment and Planning D: Society and Space* 38, no. 5 (2020): 962, https://doi.org/10.1177/0263775820934819.

49. Sidney Brinkley, "The Clubhouse Plans on 'Going Out in Style,'" *Washington Blade*, May 25, 1990.

50. Amber Bailey, "1296 Upshur St, NW (The Clubhouse)," no. DC-884, Historic American Buildings Survey, Library of Congress, Washington, DC, 2016, 3, accessed January 15, 2023, https://www.nps.gov/places/upload/The-ClubHouse-1 .pdf.

51. John P. Olinger, "The ClubHouse, a Remarkable LGBTQ Gathering Spot," DC History Center, April 12, 2021, http://dchistory.org/the-clubhouse/.

52. See Katherine McFarland Bruce, *Pride Parades: How a Parade Changed the World* (New York: New York University Press, 2016).

53. "ClubHouse Advertisement," *Blacklight*, October 1982.

54. "ClubHouse Reunion 2019," press release, 2019, https://www.instagram.com /p/CWkAQcyL126/.

55. Japonica Brown-Saracino, "From Situated Space to Social Space: Dyke Bar Commemoration as Reparative Action," *Journal of Lesbian Studies*, 24, no. 3 (2020): 312. https://doi.org/10.1080/10894160.2019.1684753.

56. Walter Firey, "Sentiment and Symbolism as Ecological Variables," *American Sociological Review* 10, no. 2 (April 1945): 140–48; Gerald Suttles, "The Cumulative Texture of Local Urban Culture," *American Journal of Sociology* 90, no. 2 (1984): 283–304.

4. HETEROS, BEWARE!: MONITORING AND PRESERVING QUEER CULTURE THROUGH NORMATIVE VICARIOUS CLAIMS

1. Adriana Brodyn and Amin Ghaziani, "Performative Progressiveness: Accounting for New Forms of Inequality in the Gayborhood," *City & Community* 17, no. 2 (2018): 307–29.

2. Manuel Castells, *The City and the Grassroots* (Berkeley: University of California Press, 1983). See also Manuel Castells and Karen Murphy, "Cultural Identity and Urban Structure: The Spatial Organization of San Francisco's 'Gay Community,'" in *Urbanism Under Capitalism*, ed. Norman Fainstein and Susan Fainstein (Beverly Hills, CA: SAGE, 1982), 237–59.

3. See also Jeffrey Escoffier, *American Homo: Community and Perversity* (Berkeley: University of California Press, 1998).

4. Some scholars like Tim Davis argue that the visibility of gay neighborhoods made LGBT people targets for antigay violence. This argument became the focus of debates in Chicago over the installation of streetscapes that would permanently mark Boystown as the city's official gay neighborhood. See Tim Davis, "The Diversity of Queer Politics and the Redefinition of Sexual Identity and Community in Urban Spaces," in *Mapping Desire: Geographies of Sexualities*, ed. David Bell and Gill Valentine (London: Routledge, 1995), 284–303; Christopher Reed, "We're from Oz: Marking Ethnic and Sexual Identity in Chicago," *Environment and Planning D: Society and Space* 21 (2003): 425–40.

5. Amin Ghaziani, *There Goes the Gayborhood?* (Princeton, NJ: Princeton University Press, 2014), 81.

6. Lou Chibbaro Jr., "Former Blade Employee Victim of Anti-Gay Attack," *Washington Blade*, November 15, 2010, http://www.washingtonblade.com/2010/11/15/former-blade-employee-victim-of-anti-gay-attack.

7. Michelangelo Signorile, "What My Partner and I Did When an Anti-Gay Bigot Called Us 'Disgusting,'" *The Blog, Huffington Post*, January 7, 2013, updated February 2, 2016, http://www.huffingtonpost.com/michelangelo-signorile-what-my-partner-and-i-did_b_2424253.html.

8. Will O'Bryan and Chris Geidner, "Frank Kameny Dies at 86," *Metro Weekly*, October 11, 2011, https://www.metroweekly.com/2011/10/frank-kameny-dies-at-86/; "Part of 17th Street Named 'Frank Kameny Way' for Gay Rights Activist," *Borderstan* (blog), June 10, 2010, https://www.borderstan.com/2010/06/10/part-of-17th-street-frank-kameny-way-for-gay-activist/#disqus_thread.

9. Brock Thompson, "Time to Make 17th Street Our Official Gay Street," *Washington Blade*, October 20, 2016, https://www.washingtonblade.com/2016/10/20/time-make-17th-street-official-gay-street/.

10. Lou Chibbaro Jr., "'Kameny Way' Street Signs Updated, Two Removed on 17th Street?," *Washington Blade*, March 24, 2021, https://www.washingtonblade.com/2021/03/24/kameny-way-street-signs-updated-two-removed-on-17th-street/.

11. Lou Chibbaro Jr., "Petition Seeks Rainbow Crosswalks on 17th Street," *Washington Blade*, April 6, 2017, https://www.washingtonblade.com/2017/04/06/petition-seeks-rainbow-crosswalks-17th-street/.

12. Canaan Merchant, "Dragons and Zodiac Symbols Will Decorate Chinatown's Streets," Greater Greater Washington, May 10, 2016, https://ggwash.org/view/41616/dragons-and-zodiac-symbols-will-decorate-chinatowns-streets.

13. Lou Chibbaro Jr., "D.C. to Install Rainbow Crosswalk Near Dupont Circle," *Washington Blade*, June 24, 2020, https://www.washingtonblade.com/2020/06/24/d-c-to-install-rainbow-crosswalk-near-dupont-circle/.

14. For more on DIY urbanism, see Gordon C. C. Douglas, *The Help-Yourself City* (Oxford: Oxford University Press, 2018).

5. *"PRESENTE! PRESENTE!"*: PLACE RUPTURES AND THE ENACTMENT OF RADICAL VICARIOUS CLAIMS

1. Reuben Buford May, "Velvet Rope Racism, Racial Paranoia, and Cultural Scripts: Alleged Dress Code Discrimination in Urban Nightlife, 2000–2014," *City & Community* 17, no. 1 (2018): 45.

2. Buford May, "Velvet Rope Racism."

3. C. Winter Han, *Racial Erotics: Gay Men of Color, Sexual Racism, and the Politics of Desire* (Seattle: University of Washington Press, 2021), 28.

4. Adam Isaiah Green, "The Social Organization of Desire: The Sexual Fields Approach," *Sociological Theory* 26, no. 1 (2008): 25–50.

5. The sociologist Patricia Hill Collins uses "outsiders within" to describe Black women (specifically Black women in the academy) who simultaneously occupy positions of privilege and marginalization and explain how they draw on their outsider status in order to generate distinct standpoints on existing sociological paradigms. Patricia Hill Collins, "Learning from the Outsiders Within: The Sociological Significance of Black Feminist Thought," *Social Problems* 33, no. 6 (1986): S14–32. This chapter elaborates this work to consider how certain groups of vicarious citizens who identify with the dominant group along one axis of identity but differ along others use their outsider status to challenge the dominant culture's claims on who belongs and who has rightful claims to access community in a particular area.

6. *Tongues Untied*, directed by Marlon Riggs (San Francisco: Frameline and California Newsreel, 1989).

7. Charles I. Nero, "Why Are the Gay Ghettos White?," in *Black Queer Studies: A Critical Anthology*, ed. E. Patrick Johnson and Mae G. Henderson (Durham, NC: Duke University Press, 2005), 228–45.

8. LZ Granderson, "Commentary: Gay Is Not the New Black," CNN, July 16, 2009, http://www.cnn.com/2009/POLITICS/07/16/granderson.obama.gays /index.html.

9. Marcus Anthony Hunter, "The Nightly Round: Space, Social Capital, and Urban Black Nightlife," *City & Community* 9, no. 2 (2010): 165–86.

10. See Tyler Baldor, "No Girls Allowed? Fluctuating Boundaries Between Gay Men and Straight Women in Gay Public Space," *Ethnography* 20, no. 4 (2019): 419–42; Amin Ghaziani, *There Goes the Gayborhood?* (Princeton, NJ: Princeton University Press, 2014); Theodore Greene, "Gay Neighborhoods and the Rights of the Vicarious Citizen," *City & Community* 13, no. 2 (2014): 99–118; Jason Orne, *Boystown: Sex and Community in Chicago* (Chicago: University of Chicago Press, 2017).

11. Ritch Savin-Williams, *The New Gay Teenager* (Cambridge, MA: Harvard University Press, 2005).

12. Ghaziani, *There Goes the Gayborhood?*, 116.

13. Ghaziani, *There Goes the Gayborhood?*, 178.

14. Ghaziani, *There Goes the Gayborhood?*, 115–16. Ghaziani does caution against overgeneralizing "the post-gay teen" across all queer youths. He particularly notes how gay neighborhoods still hold some resonance for queer and trans youth populations of color in Chicago, who face homophobia and violence in their own residential communities. In describing the role of the Center on Halsted as a haven for queer and trans youths of color, Ghaziani argues, "The bustling Center and its well-used services demonstrate that while sexuality may be less central for some youth as they come of age, for other teenagers, being gay or trans remains crucial to their identity—and just as fraught as it was in previous eras" (179).

15. Mary L. Gray, "From Websites to Wal-Mart: Youth, Identity Work, and the Queering of Boundary Publics in Small Town, USA," *American Studies* 48, no. 2 (2007): 57.

16. Theodore Greene, "Queer Street Families: Place-Making and Community Among LGBT Youth of Color in Iconic Gay Neighborhoods," in *Queer Families and Relationships After Marriage Equality*, ed. Michael Yarborough, Angela Jones, and Joseph Nicholas DeFilippis (New York: Routledge, 2018), 168–81.

17. Viet Dinh, "The Kids Are All Right—Youth Pride Day Brings Out Youths of All Ages," *Washington Blade*, April 25, 1997, 12.

18. Will O'Bryan, "Youth Pride: Youthful Measures," *Metro Weekly*, April 26, 2012, https://www.metroweekly.com/2012/04/youth-pride-2012-youthful-meas/.

19. Will O'Bryan, "Sweet 16: Youth Pride Day Returns to the Circle in 2012," *Metro Weekly*, April 19, 2012, http://www.metroweekly.com/2012/04/sweet-16-in-dupont/.

20. Elijah Anderson, *The Cosmopolitan Canopy: Race and Civility in Everyday Life* (London: Norton, 2011); Ghaziani, *There Goes the Gayborhood?*

21. Anderson describes how the intimate settings of the cosmopolitan canopy enable individuals to relax enough to engage in casual conversation with complete strangers and to engage in folk ethnography and develop their own folk theories about those with whom they share public space. Folk ethnography, according to Anderson, "serves as a cognitive and cultural base on which people construct behavior in public." Anderson, *The Cosmopolitan Canopy*, 14.

22. Anderson, *The Cosmopolitan Canopy*, 5.

23. Sam Frizell, "Donald Trump Faces Backlash for Tweets About Orlando Shooting," *Time*, June 12, 2016, https://time.com/4365411/orlando-shooting-donald-trump-tweet-congrats/.

24. Alison Kanski, "LGBT, Gun-Control Groups Respond Quickly to Orlando Mass Shooting," *PR Week* June 13, 2016, https://www.prweek.com/article/1398477/lgbt-gun-control-groups-respond-quickly-orlando-mass-shooting.

25. Alan Pelaez Lopez, "It's Not Safe to Be a Queer Person of Color in America," *Splinter*, June 13, 2016, https://splinternews.com/its-not-safe-to-be-a-queer-person-of-color-in-america-1793857466.

26. The sentence is translated as "The determination, pride, and love of LGBT people will shine brighter."

27. Ryan Centner, "Places of Privileged Consumption Practices: Spatial Capital, the Dot-Com Habitus, and San Francisco's Internet Boom," *City & Community* 7, no. 3 (September 2008): 193–223.

6. POLITICAL VICARIOUS CLAIMS AND THE ART OF SELF-ENFRANCHISEMENT

1. Cindy Bray, "Developing Identity: A Prelude to Activism," OutHistory, accessed March 16, 2022, https://www.outhistory.org/exhibits/show/rainbow-richmond/developing-identity.

2. Bob Swisher, "Anger Surfaced Here Months Before Stonewall," *Richmond Pride*, June 1, 1989, 13.

3. Swisher, "Anger Surfaced Here," 13.

4. Franklin Kameny, "State ABC Board's Action Criticized," *Richmond-Times Dispatch*, April, 26, 1969, 14.

5. Kameny, "State ABC Board's Action Criticized, 14."

6. Genny Beemyn, interview with Frank Kameny, March 20, 1994, Genny Beemyn Queer Capital Oral History Collection, https://archives.rainbowhistory.org /collections/browse.

7. Engin Isin, ed., *Democracy, Citizenship, and the Global City* (London: Routledge, 2000); Nikolas Rose, "Governing Cities, Governing Citizens," in Isin, *Democracy, Citizenship, and the Global City*, 95–109; Saskia Sassen, "The Repositioning of Citizenship and Alienage: Emergent Subjects and Spaces for Politics," *Globalizations* 2, no. 1 (2005): 79–94; Saskia Sassen, "Whose City Is It? Globalization and the Formation of New Claims," in *Cities and Citizenship*, ed. James Holston (Durham, NC: Duke University Press, 1999), 177–94.

8. Gunnar Myrdal, *An American Dilemma: The Negro Problem and Modern Democracy* (New York: Harper and Row, 1944), 717.

9. Sassen, "The Repositioning of Citizenship and Alienage."

10. Saul Alinsky, *Reveille for Radicals* (New York: Vintage, 1946).

11. Dawn Turner Trice, "Gay Rights Battle Puts Strain on Parties," *Chicago Tribune*, March 23, 2009, 15.

12. Robert Sampson, Stephen W. Raudenbush, and Felto Earls, "Neighborhoods and Violent Crime: A Multilevel Study of Collective Efficacy," *Science* 22, no. 5328 (1997): 918–24; Robert Sampson, *Great American City: Chicago and the Enduring Neighborhood Effect* (Chicago: University of Chicago Press, 2012).

13. Amy Cavanaugh, "Gays Stage 'Hug-In' to Protest Couple's Eviction from Rite Aid," *Washington Blade*, November 2, 2007.

14. Cavanaugh, "Gays Stage 'Hug-In.'"

15. See Michael Lipsky, "Protest as a Political Resource," *American Political Science Review* 62 (1968): 1144–58; Michael Lipsky, *Protest in City Politics: Rent Strikes, Housing and the Power of the Poor* (Chicago: Rand McNally, 1970); Frances Fox Piven and Richard A. Cloward, *Regulating the Poor: The Functions of Public Welfare* (New York: Vintage, 1971).

16. Lipsky, *Protest in City Politics*.

17. Yusef Najafi, "Animus in the Aisles: Gay Couple Claims to Have Been Kicked Out of the U Street Rite Aid for 'Hugging,'" *Metro Weekly*, October 24, 2007, https://www.metroweekly.com/2007/10/animus-in-the-aisles/.

18. Summer Harlow, "Social Media and Social Movements: Facebook and an Online Guatemalan Justice Movement That Moved Offline," *New Media & Society* 14, no. 2 (2011): 225–43.

19. Marcus Anthony Hunter et al., "Black Placemaking: Celebration, Play, and Poetry," *Theory, Culture, and Society* 33, no. 7–8 (2016): 31–56, 16.

20. Anna Gawel, "Investigation Into Violent Night at Nellie's Sports Bar Goes to DC Attorney General's Office," WTOP News, June 30. 2021, https://wtop .com/dc/2021/06/investigation-into-brawl-at-nellies-sports-bar-goes-to-dc -attorney-generals-office/; Catherine Whelan, "Nellie's Sports Bar Fires Con-tracted Security Company After Bouncer Dragged a Black Woman Down a Flight of Stairs," DCist, June 14, 2021, https://dcist.com/story/21/06/14/dc -protesters-nellies-sports-bar-security-dragged-woman-stairs-keisha-young/.

21. Prince Chingarande, "D.C. LGBTQ Community Reckons with Anti-Blackness, Gentrification After Nellie's Incident," *Washington Blade*, June 24, 2021, https:// www.washingtonblade.com/2021/06/24/d-c-lgbtq-community-reckons -with-anti-blackness-gentrification-after-nellies-incident/.

22. Jasmine Hilton, "Protests to Boycott Nellie's Sports Bar Created Summer-Long 'Joy Space' for Black LGBTQ Community," *Washington Post*, August 31, 2021, https://www.washingtonpost.com/local/nellies-bar-dc-protest-block -party/2021/08/30/d1e56f1c-0678-11ec-a654-900a78538242_story.html. See also Chingarande, "D.C. LGBTQ Community Reckons with Anti-Blackness."

23. Chingarande, "D.C. LGBTQ Community Reckons with Anti-Blackness."

24. Whelan, "Nellie's Sports Bar Fires Contracted Security Company."

25. Whelan, "Nellie's Sports Bar Fires Contracted Security Company."

26. Hilton, "Protests to Boycott Nellie's Sports Bar."

27. Colleen Grablick, "Demonstrators Formed a Human Chain to Stop Nellie's from Opening on Tuesday," DCist, July 14, 2021, https://dcist.com/story/21 /07/14/nellies-shut-down-by-demonstators-months-after-assault/.

28. Harriet's Dreams, "Do Not Be Fooled. The Boycott Continues Until All Demands Are Met," Twitter, July 16, 2021, https://twitter.com/HarrietsDreams/status /1416135875189252102.

29. Yarimar Bonilla and Jonathan Rosa, "#Ferguson: Digital Protest, Hashtag Ethnography, and the Racial Politics of Social Media in the United States," *American Ethnologist* 42, no. 1 (2015): 4–17, https://doi.org/10.1111/amet.12112.

30. Richard Kahn and Douglas Kellner, "New Media and Internet Activism: From the 'Battle of Seattle' to Blogging," *New Media & Society* 6, no. 1 (2004): 87–95.

31. Albert Hunter and Gerald Suttles, "The Expanding Community of Limited Liability," in *The Social Construction of Communities*, ed. Gerard Suttles (Chicago: University of Chicago Press, 1972), 45–81; Morris Janowitz, *The Community Press in an Urban Setting: The Social Elements of Urbanism* (Chicago: University of Chicago Press, 1952).

32. Jyunjin Seo et al., "Teens' Social Media Use and Collective Action," *New Media & Society* 16, no. 6 (2013): 883–902.

33. Hunter et al., "Black Placemaking: Celebration, Play, and Poetry," 56.

34. GLAAD, "Incidents of Anti-LGBTQ Hate Violence," June 24, 2019, accessed January 21, 2021, https://www.glaad.org/blog/incidents-anti-lgbtq-hate-violence-2019.

35. Natalie Delgadillo, "Community Mourns Zoe Spears, Second Trans Woman Killed on Eastern Avenue This Year," DCist, June 17, 2019, https://dcist.com/story/19/06/17/community-mourns-zoe-spears-second-trans-woman-killed-on-eastern-avenue-this-year/.

36. Elijah Adiv Edelman, "'This Area Has Been Declared a Prostitution Free Zone': Discursive Formations of Space, the State and Trans 'Sex Worker' Bodies," *Journal of Homosexuality* 58 (2011): 848–64.

CONCLUSION: PLACE REACTIVATION AND VICARIOUS CITIZENSHIP BEYOND THE GAYBORHOOD

1. Amin Ghaziani, *There Goes the Gayborhood?* (Princeton, NJ: Princeton University Press, 2014), 133.

2. Frances Fitzgerald, *Cities on a Hill* (New York: Simon and Schuster, 1986), 59.

3. Stephen M. Engel and Timothy S. Lyle, *Disrupting Dignity: Rethinking Power and Progress in LGBTQ Lives* (New York: New York University Press, 2021).

4. Kyles, Kyra. "Boystown Shifting as More Families Move In," *RedEye*, December 10, 2007. http://articles.chicagotribune.com/2007-12-10/news/0712100253_1_gay-men-calendars-culture-clash; Ghaziani, *There Goes the Gayborhood?*; Jason Orne, *Boystown: Sex and Community in Chicago* (Chicago: University of Chicago Press, 2017); Katherine McFarland Bruce, *Pride Parades: How a Parade Changed the World* (New York: New York University Press, 2016).

5. Patricia Leigh Brown, "Gay Enclaves Face Prospect of Being Passé," *New York Times*, October 30, 2007, http://www.nytimes.com/2007/10/30/us/30gay

.html/; Sean Cahill, "Op-Ed: The Slow Death of Gay Gathering Places May Be Aiding HIV," *The Advocate*, March 27, 2015, http://www.advocate.com /commentary/2015/03/27/op-ed-slow-death-gay-gathering-places-may -be-aiding-hiv; Bryce Renninger, "Grindr Killed the Gay Bar, and Other Attempts to Blame Social Technologies for Urban Development: A Democratic Approach to Popular Technologies and Queer Sociality," *Journal of Homosexuality* 66, no. 12 (2019): 1736–55, https://doi.org/10.1080/00918369.2018 .1514205; June Thomas, *The Gay Bar: Its Riotous Past and Uncertain Future* (Washington, DC: Slate Magazine, 2014).

6. Greggor Mattson, "Are Gay Bars Closing? Using Business Listings to Infer Rates of Gay Bar Closure in the United States, 1977–2019," *Socius* 5, no. 1–2 (2020), https://doi.org/10.177/2378023119894832; Greggor Mattson, "Shuttered by the Coronavirus, Many Gay Bars—Already Struggling—Are Now on Life Support," *Slate*, May 1, 2020, https://slate.com/human-interest/2020/05/gay -bars-struggling-reopen-coronavirus.html; Rachel Savage, Matthew Lavietes, and Enrique Anarte, "'We'll Die': Gay Bars Worldwide Scramble to Avert Coronavirus Collapse," Reuters, May 13, 2020, https://www.reuters.com/article /us-health-coronavirus-lgbt-nightlife-trf-idUSKBN22P1Z5; Amin Ghaziani, "Culture and the Nighttime Economy: A Conversation with London's Night Czar and Culture-at-Risk Officer," Metropolitics, November 12, 2019, https:// metropolitics.org/Culture-and-the-Nighttime-Economy-A-Conversation -with-London-s-Night-Czar-and.html.

7. Daniel Baldwin Hess and Alex Bitterman, "Who Are the People in Your Gayborhood? Understanding Population Change and Cultural Shifts in LGBTQ+ Neighborhoods," in *The Life and Afterlife of Gay Neighborhoods: Renaissance and Resurgence*, ed. Daniel Baldwin Hess and Alex Bitterman (New York: Springer, 2021), https://doi.org/10.1007/978-3-030-66073-4.

8. George Chauncey, *Gay New York: Gender, Urban Culture, and the Making of the Homosexual* (New York: Basic Books, 1994), 23; see also Martin P. Levine, "Gay Ghetto," in *Sociology of Homosexuality*, ed. Wayne Dynes and Stephen Donaldson (New York: Garland, 1992), 196–218; and Stephen O. Murray, "Components of Gay Community in San Francisco," in *Gay Culture in America: Essays from the Field*, ed. Gilbert Herdt (Boston: Beacon, 1992), 107–46.

9. George Chauncey, *Gay New York*, 239.

10. David K. Johnson, "The Kids of Fairytown: Gay Male Culture on Chicago's Near North Side in the 1930s," in *Creating a Place for Ourselves: Lesbian, Gay, and Bisexual Community Histories*, ed. Genny Beemyn (New York: Routledge, 1997), 102.

11. Michael Bennett and Juan Battle, "We Can See Them, But We Can't Hear Them," in *Queer Families, Queer Politics*, ed. Mary Bernstein and Renate Remain (New York: Columbia University Press, 2001); Irene Monroe, "The Garden of Homophobia," *The Advocate*, December 9, 1999; Keith Boykin, *One More River to Cross: Black and Gay in America* (New York: Doubleday, 1996).

12. Marcus Anthony Hunter, "The Nightly Round: Space, Social Capital, and Urban Black Nightlife," *City & Community* 9, no. 2 (2010): 165–86.

13. Orne, *Boystown*.

14. Theodore Greene, "Queer Street Families: Place-making and community Among LGBT Youth of Color in Iconic Gay Neighborhoods," in *Queer Families and Relationships After Marriage Equality*, ed. Michael Yarborough, Angela Jones, and Joseph Michael DeFlilippis (New York: Routledge, 2018), 168–181.

15. Elijah Anderson, *Code of the Streets: Decency, Violence, and the Moral Life of the Inner City* (New York: Norton, 1999).

16. Sarah Hotchkiss, "Don't Mute DC: How Go-Go Music Inspires the Beat Ya Feet Dance Movement," KQED, May 5, 2020, https://www.kqed.org/arts/13879679/dont-mute-dc-how-go-go-music-inspires-the-beat-ya-feet-d%20ance-movement.

17. Rachel Kurzius, "Shaw's Metro PCS Store Has Been Forced to Turn Off Its Go-Go Music, Owners Say," DCist, April 9, 2019, https://dcist.com/story/19/04/08/shaws-metro-pcs-store-has-been-forced-to-turn-off-its-go-go-music-owner-says/.

18. Wilson B., "Yelp Review: Metro PCS," Yelp, 2017, https://www.yelp.com/biz/central-communications-washington?osq=central+communications. (Campbell's store is incorporated as Central Communications.)

19. Kurzius, "Shaw's Metro PCS Store Has Been Forced to Turn Off Its Go-Go Music."

20. Kurzius, "Shaw's Metro PCS Store Has Been Forced to Turn Off Its Go-Go Music."

21. Kurzius, "Shaw's Metro PCS Store Has Been Forced to Turn Off Its Go-Go Music."

22. Kurzius, "Shaw's Metro PCS Store Has Been Forced to Turn Off Its Go-Go Music."

23. Rachel Kurzius, "'This Is the Sound of Florida and Georgia Avenue': Go-Go Fans Are Trying to Bring the Music Back to Metro PCS," DCist, April 9, 2019, https://dcist.com/story/19/04/09/this-is-the-sound-of-florida-and-georgia-avenue-go-go-fans-are-trying-to-bring-the-music-back-to-metro-pcs/.

24. Kurzius, "Shaw's Metro PCS Store Has Been Forced to Turn Off Its Go-Go Music."

25. Kurzius, "'This Is the Sound of Florida and Georgia Avenue.'"

26. Rachel Kurzius, "Go-Go Music Is Back at Shaw's Metro PCS Store," DCist, April 10, 2019, https://dcist.com/story/19/04/10/go-go-music-is-back-at-shaws -metro-pcs-store/.

27. Steven Kiviat, "The #DontMuteDC Go-Go Protests Aren't Done. They're Expanding," DC Line, May 27, 2019, https://thedcline.org/2019/05/27/the -dontmutedc-go-go-protests-arent-done-theyre-expanding.

28. Elliott Williams, "Why Last Night's #Moechella Protest Was a Big Deal for DC," *Washingtonian*, May 8, 2019, https://www.washingtonian.com/2019/05/08 /why-last-nights-moechella-protest-was-a-big-deal-for-dc/.

29. Executive Office of the Mayor, "Mayor Muriel Bowser Signs Bill to Designate Go-Go Music as the Official Music of DC," news release, February 19, 2020, https://mayor.dc.gov/release/mayor-bowser-signs-bill-designate-go-go -music-official-music-dc.

30. Derek Hyra, *Race, Class, and Politics in the Cappuccino City* (Chicago: University of Chicago Press, 2017).

31. Brandi Thompson Summers, *Black in Place: The Spatial Aesthetics of Race in a Post-chocolate City* (Chapel Hill: University of North Carolina Press, 2019).

32. Kurzius, "Shaw's Metro PCS Store Has Been Forced to Turn Off Its Go-Go Music."

33. Kurzius, "'This Is the Sound of Florida and Georgia Avenue.'"

34. Mark Purcell, "Excavating Lefebvre: The Right to the City and Its Urban Politics of the Inhabitant," *GeoJournal* 58, no. 2–3 (2002): 99–108; Henri Lefebvre, *Writings on Cities* (Cambridge: Blackwell, 1996).

35. Elijah Anderson, "The Iconic Ghetto," *Annals of the American Academy of Political and Social Science* 642 (2012): 8–24.

36. Victor M. Rios, *Punished: Policing the Lives of Black and Latino Boys* (New York: New York University Press, 2011).

37. Marcus Anthony Hunter et al., "Black Placemaking: Celebration, Play, and Poetry," *Theory, Culture, and Society* 33, no. 7–8 (2016): 31–56; Marcus Anthony Hunter and Zandria F. Robinson, *Chocolate Cities: The Black Map of Urban Life* (Berkeley: University of California Press, 2018).

38. Jonathan Wynn, *Music/City: American Festivals and Placemaking in Austin, Nashville, and Newport* (Chicago: University of Chicago Press, 2015).

39. Terry Nichols Clark, ed., *The City as an Entertainment Machine* (Amsterdam: Elsevier, 2004).

40. Laurie Goodstein, "Across Nation, Mosque Projects Meet Opposition," *New York Times*, August 7, 2010, https://www.nytimes.com/2010/08/08/us /08mosque.html?pagewanted=all /.

41. Michael Muskal, "Occupy Wall Street Camps Are Today's Hoovervilles," *Los Angeles Times*, November 15, 2011, http://latimesblogs.latimes.com/nationnow /2011/11/occupy-wall-street-hoovervilles.html; Lee Romney and Maria L. La Ganga, "Oakland Site Cleared, But Protest Lives," *Los Angeles Times*, November 15, 2011, http://www.latimes.com/local/la-me-occupy-oakland-20111115-story .html; Ashley Winchester, "Exploring the 'Occupy' Protest," *New York Times*, March 20, 2015, http://intransit.blogs.nytimes.com/2015/03/20/exploring-the -occupy-protest/.

42. Steve Almasy and Holly Yan, "Protesters Fill Streets Across Country as Ferguson Protests Spread Coast to Coast," November 26, 2014, http://www.cnn .com/2014/11/25/us/national-ferguson-protests/.

43. Kevin Fox Gotham and Krista Brumley, "Using Space: Agency and Identity in a Public-Housing Development," *City & Community* 1, no. 3 (2002): 267–89.

44. Melvin Webber, "Order in Diversity: Community Without Propinquity," in *Cities and Space: The Future Use of Urban Land*, ed. Lowdon Wingo Jr. (Baltimore: Johns Hopkins University Press, 1963), 23–56.

45. Hilary Silver, "Editorial: Communities and Neighborhoods," *City & Community* 13, no. 2 (2014): 97.

REFERENCES

Achilles, Nancy. "The Development of the Homosexual Bar as an Institution." In *Social Perspectives in Lesbian and Gay Studies*, ed. Peter M. Nardi and Beth E. Schneider, 175–82. London: Routledge, 1967.

Acosta, E. A. "Black Gays Endorse Tucker for Mayor." *The Blade*, August 1978.

Acosta, Ernie. "Emerging Dialogue Between Races." *The Blade*, December 6, 1979.

Alinsky, Saul. *Reveille for Radicals*. New York: Vintage, 1946.

Almasy, Steve, and Holly Yan. "Protesters Fill Streets Across Country as Ferguson Protests Spread Coast to Coast," November 26, 2014. http://www.cnn.com /2014/11/25/us/national-ferguson-protests/.

Anderson, Elijah. *Code of the Streets: Decency, Violence, and the Moral Life of the Inner City*. New York: Norton, 1999.

——. *The Cosmopolitan Canopy: Race and Civility in Everyday Life*. London: Norton, 2011.

——. "The Iconic Ghetto." *The Annals of the American Academy of Political and Social Science* 642 (2012): 8–24.

——. "The White Space." *Sociology of Race and Ethnicity* 1, no. 1 (2015): 10–21.

Anderton, Bryan. "Capital Pride's Colorful History." *Washington Blade*, June 4, 2004.

Annual Report of the Chief of Engineers, United States Army to the Secretary of War for the Year 1887, Part III. Washington, DC: Government Printing Office, 1887.

Armstrong, Elizabeth. *Forging Gay Identities: Organizing Sexuality in San Francisco, 1950–1994*. Chicago: University of Chicago Press, 2002.

Armus, Teo. "'You're Welcome Here': Revelry and Sadness at a Gay Mainstay's Final Weekend." *Washington Post*, July 1, 2018. https://www.washingtonpost.com /local/youre-welcome-here-revelry-and-sadness-at-a-gay-mainstays-final-weekend /2018/07/01/45d63e56-7b26-11e8-aeee-4d04c8ac6158_story.html.

Asch, Chris Myers, and George Derek Musgrove. *Chocolate City: A History of Race and Democracy in the Nation's Capital*. Chapel Hill: University of North Carolina Press, 2017.

Asmelash, Leah. "Capitol Rioters Shouted 'This Is Our House.' But the Capitol Was Built by Enslaved Black Americans." CNN, January 12, 2021. https://www.cnn.com/2021/01/12/us/capitol-riot-history-trnd/index.html.

Bailey, Amber. "1296 Upshur St, NW (The Clubhouse)." No. DC-884. Historic American Buildings Survey. Library of Congress, Washington, DC, 2016. Accessed January 20, 2022. https://www.nps.gov/places/upload/The-ClubHouse-1.pdf.

Baldor, Tyler. "No Girls Allowed? Fluctuating Boundaries Between Gay Men and Straight Women in Gay Public Space." *Ethnography* 20, no. 4 (2019): 419–42.

Barnard, Anne. "Occupy Wall Street Meets Tahrir Square." *New York Times*, October 25, 2011. http://cityroom.blogs.nytimes.com/2011/10/25/occupy-wall-street-meets-tahrir-square/.

Bearak, Max. "The World Reacts to the Mass Shooting in Orlando." *Washington Post*, June 12, 2016. https://www.washingtonpost.com/news/worldviews/wp/2016/06/12/the-world-reacts-to-the-mass-shooting-in-orlando/.

Beemyn, Genny, ed. *Creating a Place for Ourselves: Lesbian, Gay, and Bisexual Community Histories*. New York: Routledge, 1997.

——. "The Geography of Same-Sex Desire: Cruising Men in Washington, DC in the Late Nineteenth and Early Twentieth Centuries." *Left History* 9, no. 2 (Spring 2004): 141–59.

——. Interview with Deacon Maccubbin, Part 1, May 27, 1998. Genny Beemyn Queer Capital Oral History Collection, Rainbow History Project. https://archives.rainbowhistory.org/collections/browse.

——. Interview with Esther Smith, June 9, 1994. Genny Beemyn Queer Capital Oral History Collection, Rainbow History Project. https://archives.rainbowhistory.org/collections/browse.

——. Interview with Frank Kameny, March 20, 1994. Genny Beemyn Queer Capital Oral History Collection, Rainbow History Project. https://archives.rainbowhistory.org/collections/browse.

——. Interview with Haviland Ferris, May 16, 1994. Genny Beemyn Queer Capital Oral History Collection, Rainbow History Project. https://archives.rainbowhistory.org/collections/browse.

——. Interview with Pat Hamilton, January 13, 1995. Genny Beemyn Queer Capital Oral History Collection, Rainbow History Project. https://archives.rainbowhistory.org/collections/browse.

———. *A Queer Capital: A History of Gay Life in Washington, D.C.* New York: Routledge, 2015.

———. "A Queer Capital: Lesbian, Gay, and Bisexual Life in Washington, DC 1890–1955." PhD diss, University of Iowa, 1997.

———. "A Queer Capital: Race, Class, Gender and the Changing Social Landscape of Washington's Gay Communities, 1940–1955." In Beemyn, *Creating a Place for Ourselves,* 183–210.

Bennett, Michael, and Juan Battle. "We Can See Them, But We Can't Hear Them." In *Queer Families, Queer Politics,* ed. Mary Bernstein and Renate Remain. New York: Columbia University Press, 2001.

Bérubé, Allan. *Coming Out Under Fire: The History of Gay Men and Women in World War II.* New York: Free Press, 1990.

Bonilla, Yarimar, and Jonathan Rosa. "#Ferguson: Digital Protest, Hashtag Ethnography, and the Racial Politics of Social Media in the United States." *American Ethnologist* 42, no. 1 (2015): 4–17. https://doi.org/10.1111/amet.12112.

Borderstan (blog). "Part of 17th Street Named 'Frank Kameny Way' for Gay Rights Activist," June 10, 2010. https://www.borderstan.com/2010/06/10/part-of-17th -street-frank-kameny-way-for-gay-activist/#disqus_thread.

Boyd, Nan Alamilla. "San Francisco's Castro District: From Liberation to Tourist Destination." *Journal of Tourism and Cultural Change* 9, no. 3 (2011): 237–48.

Boykin, Keith. *Beyond the Down Low: Sex, Lies, and Denial in Black America.* New York: Carroll and Graf, 2006.

———. *One More River to Cross: Black and Gay in America.* New York: Doubleday, 1996.

Brammer, John. "Commentary: Pulse, and the Beautiful, Sad Joyful Tradition of Queer Grief." NBC News, June 12, 2017. https://www.nbcnews.com/feature/nbc-out /commentary-pulse-beautiful-sad-joyful-tradition-queer-grief-n770936.

Bray, Cindy. "Developing Identity: A Prelude to Activism." *OutHistory.* Accessed March 16, 2022. https://www.outhistory.org/exhibits/show/rainbow-richmond /developing-identity.

Brekhus, Wayne. *Peacocks, Chameleons, and Centaurs: Gay Suburbia and the Grammar of Social Identity.* Chicago: University of Chicago Press, 2003.

Brinkley, Sidney. "The Clubhouse Plans on 'Going Out in Style.'" *Washington Blade,* May 25, 1990.

Brodyn, Adriana, and Amin Ghaziani. "Performative Progressiveness: Accounting for New Forms of Inequality in the Gayborhood." *City & Community* 17, no. 2 (2018): 307–29.

Brown, Patricia Leigh. "Gay Enclaves Face Prospect of Being Passé." *New York Times*, October 30, 2007. http://www.nytimes.com/2007/10/30/us/30gay.html/.

Brown-Saracino, Japonica. "Aligning Our Maps: A Call to Reconcile Distinct Visions of Literatures on Sexualities, Space, and Place." *City & Community* 18, no. 1 (2019): 38.

——. "From Situated Space to Social Space: Dyke Bar Commemoration as Reparative Action." *Journal of Lesbian Studies* 24, no. 3 (2020): 311–325. https://doi.org/10.1080/10894160.2019.1684753.

——. *How Places Make Us: Novel LBQ Identities in Four Small Cities.* Chicago: University of Chicago Press, 2017.

——. *A Neighborhood That Never Changes: Gentrification, Social Preservation, and the Search for Authenticity.* Chicago: University of Chicago Press, 2009.

——. "Virtuous Marginality: Social Preservationists and the Selection of the Old-Timer." *Theory and Society* 36, no. 5 (2007): 437–68.

Bruce, Katherine McFarland. *Pride Parades: How a Parade Changed the World.* New York: New York University Press, 2016.

Buford May, Reuben. "Velvet Rope Racism, Racial Paranoia, and Cultural Scripts: Alleged Dress Code Discrimination in Urban Nightlife, 2000–2014." *City & Community* 17, no. 1 (2018): 44–64.

Cahill, Sean. "Op-Ed: The Slow Death of Gay Gathering Places May Be Aiding HIV." *The Advocate*, March 27, 2015. http://www.advocate.com/commentary/2015/03/27/op-ed-slow-death-gay-gathering-places-may-be-aiding-hiv.

Carter, David. *Stonewall: The Riots That Sparked the Gay Revolution.* New York: St. Martin's, 2004.

Castells, Manuel. *The City and the Grassroots.* Berkeley: University of California Press, 1983.

Castells, Manuel, and Karen Murphy. "Cultural Identity and Urban Structure: The Spatial Organization of San Francisco's 'Gay Community.'" In *Urbanism Under Capitalism*, ed. Norman Fainstein and Susan Fainstein, 237–59. Beverly Hills, CA: SAGE, 1982.

Castro, Melissa. "After Gay Migration, 17th Street Seeks a New Identity." *Washington Business Journal*, July 23, 2008. https://www.bizjournals.com/washington/stories/2008/07/28/story3.html.

Cavanaugh, Amy. "Gays Stage 'Hug-In' to Protest Couple's Eviction from Rite Aid." *Washington Blade*, November 2, 2007.

Centner, Ryan. "Places of Privileged Consumption Practices: Spatial Capital, the Dot-Com Habitus, and San Francisco's Internet Boom." *City & Community* 7, no. 3 (September 2008): 193–223.

Chandler, Michael Alison. "Street Fest Lets Gays Revel in Freedom." *Washington Post*, June 11, 2007.

Chauncey, George. *Gay New York: Gender, Urban Culture, and the Making of the Homosexual*. New York: Basic Books, 1994.

Chibbaro, Lou, Jr. "Annie Kaylor of Annie's Paramount Steakhouse Dies at 86." *Washington Blade*, July 25, 2013. https://www.washingtonblade.com/2013/07/25/annie -kaylor-of-annies-paramount-steakhouse-dies-at-86-washington-dc-gay-news/.

——. "Council Gives Final Approval to Marriage Bill." *Washington Blade*, December 18, 2009. http://www.washingtonblade.com/2009/12/18/council-gives-final -approval-to-marriage-bill/.

——. "D.C. to Install Rainbow Crosswalk Near Dupont Circle." *Washington Blade*, June 24, 2020. https://www.washingtonblade.com/2020/06/24/d-c-to-install-rainbow -crosswalk-near-dupont-circle/.

——. "End of an era, as Lambda Rising to Close." *Washington Blade*, December 11, 2009. https://www.washingtonblade.com/2009/12/11/end-of-an-era-as-lambda -rising-to-close/.

——. "Former Blade Employee Victim of Anti-Gay Attack." *Washington Blade*, November 15, 2010. http://www.washingtonblade.com/2010/11/15/former-blade -employee-victim-of-anti-gay-attack.

——. "Gay Waiter Killed After Leaving Annie's." *Washington Blade*, August 27, 2004.

——. "Gentrification: Gay Influx Has Its Ups and Downs." *Washington Blade*, September 14, 1984.

——. "'Kameny Way' Ceremony Highlights Capital Pride Events." *Washington Blade*, June 8, 2010. http://www.washingtonblade.com/2010/06/08/%E2%80%98kameny -way%E2%80%99-ceremony-highlights-capital-pride-events/.

——. "'Kameny Way' Street Signs Updated, Two Removed on 17th Street?" *Washington Blade*, March 24, 2021. https://www.washingtonblade.com/2021/03/24/kameny -way-street-signs-updated-two-removed-on-17th-street/.

——. "Petition Seeks Rainbow Crosswalks on 17th Street." *Washington Blade*, April 6, 2017. https://www.washingtonblade.com/2017/04/06/petition-seeks-rainbow -crosswalks-17th-street/.

Chingarande, Prince. "D.C. LGBTQ Community Reckons with Anti-Blackness, Gentrification After Nellie's Incident." *Washington Blade*, June 24, 2021. https:// www.washingtonblade.com/2021/06/24/d-c-lgbtq-community-reckons-with -anti-blackness-gentrification-after-nellies-incident/.

Clark, Terry Nichols, ed. *The City as an Entertainment Machine*. Amsterdam: Elsevier, 2004.

Clendinen, Dudley, and Adam Nagourney. *Out for Good: The Struggle to Build a Gay Rights Movement in America*. New York: Simon & Schuster, 1999.

The Club House—History: Origins and Location. Washington, DC: Small Wonder Media, 2021. https://www.youtube.com/watch?v=cXwkWwJ77FQ&list =PLHfRRW02LKFUomXaonMZzMyLX5w7aD4zG&index=1&ab_channel=.

Collins, Patricia Hill. "Learning from the Outsiders Within: The Sociological Significance of Black Feminist Thought." *Social Problems* 33, no. 6 (1986): S14–32.

Conquergood, Dwight. "Life in Big Red: Struggles and Accommodation in a Chicago Polyethnic Tenement." In *Structuring Diversity*, ed. Louise Lamphere. Chicago: University of Chicago Press, 1992.

Cooper, Mariah. "D.C. Has the Highest LGBTQ Population in the U.S." *Washington Blade*, March 6, 2019. https://www.washingtonblade.com/2019/03/06/d-c -has-highest-lgbtq-population-in-the-u-s/.

Crea, Joe. "Arrest Made in Killing of Annie's Waiter." *Washington Blade*, September 3, 2004.

Crouch, Angie, and Bill French. "'Flaunting It': Gay Bar Bans Straight Bachelorette Parties," *NBC News*, May 25, 2012. https://www.nbcnews.com/news/world /flaunting-it-gay-bar-bans-straight-bachelorette-parties-flna794647.

Davis, Tim. "The Diversity of Queer Politics and the Redefinition of Sexual Identity and Community in Urban Spaces." In *Mapping Desire: Geographies of Sexualities*, ed. David Bell and Gill Valentine, 284–303. London: Routledge, 1995.

DeForrest, Chris. "The Washington Post: A Response to 'Anything's Cool at the Discos.'" *Gay Blade*, November 1974.

Delgadillo, Natalie. "Community Mourns Zoe Spears, Second Trans Woman Killed on Eastern Avenue This Year." DCist, June 17, 2019. https://dcist.com/story /19/06/17/community-mourns-zoe-spears-second-trans-woman-killed-on-eastern -avenue-this-year/.

D'Emilio, John. *Sexual Politics, Sexual Communities: The Making of a Homosexual Minority in the United States 1940–1970*. Chicago: University of Chicago Press, 1983.

Dinh, Viet. "The Kids Are All Right—Youth Pride Day Brings Out Youths of All Ages." *Washington Blade*, April 25, 1997.

"District of Columbia: Census 2000 Profile." Washington, DC: U.S. Census Bureau, August 2002.

"District of Columbia Population 2019." World Population Review, June 5, 2019. Accessed January 21, 2020. http://worldpopulationreview.com/states/district-of -columbia/.

Douglas, Gordon C. C. *The Help-Yourself City*. Oxford: Oxford University Press, 2018.

Drexel, Allen. "Before Paris Burned: Race, Class, and Male Homosexuality on the Chicago South Side, 1935–1960." In Beemyn, *Creating a Place for Ourselves*, 119–44.

Duberman, Martin. *Stonewall*. New York: Penguin, 1993.

Durkheim, Emile. *Elementary Forms of Religious Life*, trans Karen Fields. New York: Free Press, 1912.

Edelman, Elijah Adiv. "'This Area Has Been Declared a Prostitution Free Zone': Discursive Formations of Space, the State and Trans 'Sex Worker' Bodies." *Journal of Homosexuality* 58 (2011): 848–64.

Edevane, Gillian. "LGBT Community in SF Shows Allegiance with Orlando Through 'Kiss-In.'" *NBC News Bay Area*, June 15, 2016. https://www.nbcbayarea .com/news/local/LGBT-Community-in-SF-Shows-Allegiance-with -Orlando-through-Kiss-In—383175001.html.

Engel, Stephen M., and Timothy S. Lyle. *Disrupting Dignity: Rethinking Power and Progress in LGBTQ Lives*. New York: New York University Press, 2021.

Escoffier, Jeffrey. *American Homo: Community and Perversity*. Berkeley: University of California Press, 1998.

Executive Office of the Mayor. "Mayor Muriel Bowser Signs Bill to Designate Go-Go Music as the Official Music of DC." News release, February 19, 2020. https://mayor.dc.gov/release/mayor-bowser-signs-bill-designate-go-go-music -official-music-dc.

Faderman, Lillian. *Odd Girls and Twilight Lovers: A History of Lesbian Life in Twentieth-Century America*. New York: Penguin, 1991.

Ferris, Haviland. "Has Gay Life Changed Much in Fifty Years?" *Washington Blade*, October 1, 1982.

Firey, Walter. "Sentiment and Symbolism as Ecological Variables." *American Sociological Review* 10, no. 2 (April 1945): 140–48.

Fitzgerald, Frances. *Cities on a Hill*. New York: Simon and Schuster, 1986.

Fitzpatrick, Sandra, and Mara Goodwin. *The Guide to Black Washington: Places and Events of Historical and Cultural Significance in the Nation's Capital*. New York: Hippocrine, 2001.

Florida, Richard. "Cities and the Creative Class." *City & Community* 2, no. 1 (2003): 3–19.

Forrester, Ladd. "D.C. Bars: From Parody to Poetry." *Washington Blade*, September 5, 1986.

——. "Rollerskating 'Round the '30s Grapevine in D.C." *Washington Blade*, September 26, 1986.

Forsyth, Ann. "Sexuality and Space: Nonconformist Populations and Planning Practice." *Journal of Planning Literature* 15, no. 3 (2001): 339–58.

Frizell, Sam. "Donald Trump Faces Backlash for Tweets About Orlando Shooting." *Time*, June 12, 2016. https://time.com/4365411/orlando-shooting-donald-trump-tweet-congrats/.

Gans, Herbert. "Urbanism and Suburbanism as Ways of Life: A Reevaluation of Definitions." In *Readings in Urban Sociology*, ed. R. E. Pahl, 95–118. Oxford: Pergamon, 1968.

Gawel, Anna. "Investigation Into Violent Night at Nellie's Sports Bar Goes to DC Attorney General's Office." WTOP News, June 30. 2021. https://wtop.com/dc/2021/06/investigation-into-brawl-at-nellies-sports-bar-goes-to-dc-attorney-generals-office/.

Ghaziani, Amin. "Cultural Archipelagos: New Directions in the Study of Sexuality and Space." *City & Community* 18, no. 1 (2019): 1–19.

——. "Culture and the Nighttime Economy: A Conversation with London's Night Czar and Culture-at-Risk Officer." Metropolitics, November 12, 2019. https://metropolitics.org/Culture-and-the-Nighttime-Economy-A-Conversation-with-London-s-Night-Czar-and.html.

——. *The Dividends of Dissent: How Conflict and Culture Work in Lesbian and Gay Marches on Washington*. Chicago: University of Chicago Press, 2008.

——. "Measuring Urban Sexual Cultures." *Theory and Society* 43, no. 3–4 (2014): 371–93.

——. "Post-gay Collective Identity Construction." *Social Problems* 58, no. 1 (2011): 99–125.

——. *There Goes the Gayborhood?* Princeton, NJ: Princeton University Press, 2014.

Giambrone, Andrew. "D.C. No Longer Has a Central Gay Neighborhood. Does It Matter?" *Washington City Paper*, June 2, 2016. http://www.washingtoncitypaper.com/news/article/20781582/dc-no-longer-has-a-central-gay-neighborhood-does-that-matter.

Gieryn, Thomas F. "A Space for Place in Sociology." *Annual Review of Sociology* 26 (2000): 463–96.

Gilbert, Ben W., and the Staff of the *Washington Post*. *Ten Blocks from the White House: Anatomy of the Washington Riots of 1968*. New York: Praeger, 1968.

Goodstein, Laurie. "Across Nation, Mosque Projects Meet Opposition." *New York Times*, August 8, 2010. http://www.nytimes.com/2010/08/08/us/08mosque.html.

Gotham, Kevin Fox, and Krista Brumley. "Using Space: Agency and Identity in a Public-Housing Development." *City & Community* 1, no. 3 (2002): 267–89.

Grablick, Colleen. "Demonstrators Formed a Human Chain to Stop Nellie's from Opening on Tuesday." DCist, July 14, 2021. https://dcist.com/story/21/07/14/nellies -shut-down-by-demonstators-months-after-assault/.

Granderson, LZ. "Commentary: Gay Is Not the New Black." CNN, July 16, 2009. http://www.cnn.com/2009/POLITICS/07/16/granderson.obama.gays/index .html.

Gray, Mary L. "From Websites to Wal-Mart: Youth, Identity Work, and the Queer- ing of Boundary Publics in Small Town, USA." In *LGBT Identity and Online New Media*, ed. Christopher Pullen and Margaret Cooper, 288–97. New York: Routledge, 2010.

Grazian, David. *On the Make: The Hustle of Urban Nightlife*. Chicago: University of Chicago Press, 2008.

Green, Adam Isaiah. "The Social Organization of Desire: The Sexual Fields Approach." *Sociological Theory* 26, no. 1 (2008): 25–50.

Greene, Theodore. "Aberrations of 'Home': Gay Neighborhoods and the Experiences of Community Among GBQ Men of Color." In *The Handbook of Research for Black Males: Quantitative, Qualitative, and Multidisciplinary*, ed. Theodore Ran- saw, Richard Majors, and Charles Gause, 189–209. East Lansing: Michigan State University Press, 2019.

——. "Gay Neighborhoods and the Rights of the Vicarious Citizen." *City & Com- munity* 13, no. 2 (2014): 99–118.

——. "Queer Cultural Archipelagos Are New to US." *City & Community* 18, no. 1 (2019): 23–29.

——. "Queer Street Families: Place-Making and Community Among LGBT Youth of Color in Iconic Gay Neighborhoods." In *Queer Families and Relation- ships After Marriage Equality*, ed. Michael Yarborough, Angela Jones, and Joseph Nicholas DeFilippis, 168–81. New York: Routledge, 2018.

——. "'You're Dancing on My Seat!': Queer Subcultures and the Production of Places in Contemporary Gay Bars." *Studies in Symbolic Interaction* 54 (2022): 137–65.

Hahn, Fritz. "The Halo Effect." *Washington Post*, September 23, 2004. http://www. washingtonpost.com/wp-dyn/articles/A44741-2004Sep23.html.

Han, C. Winter. *Racial Erotics: Gay Men of Color, Sexual Racism, and the Politics of Desire*. Seattle: University of Washington Press, 2021.

Hanhardt, Christina. *Safe Space: Gay Neighborhood History and the Politics of Violence*. Durham, NC: Duke University Press, 2013.

Hannerz, Ulf. *Soulside: Inquiries Into Ghetto Culture and Community*. Chicago: Uni- versity of Chicago Press, 1969.

Harlow, Summer. "Social Media and Social Movements: Facebook and an Online Guatemalan Justice Movement That Moved Offline." *New Media & Society* 14, no. 2 (2011): 225–43.

Harriet's Wildest Dreams. "Do Not Be Fooled. The Boycott Continues Until All Demands Are Met." Twitter, July 16, 2021. https://twitter.com/HarrietsDreams /status/1416135875189252102.

Heap, Chad. *Slumming: Sexual and Racial Encounters in American Nightlife, 1885–1940.* Chicago: University of Chicago Press, 2009.

Hennen, Peter. "Bear Bodies, Bear Masculinity: Recuperation, Resistance, or Retreat." *Gender and Society* 19, no. 1 (2005): 25–43.

Hess, Daniel Baldwin, and Alex Bitterman. "Who Are the People in Your Gayborhood? Understanding Population Change and Cultural Shifts in LGBTQ+ Neighborhoods." In *The Life and Afterlife of Gay Neighborhoods: Renaissance and Resurgence,* ed. Daniel Baldwin Hess and Alex Bitterman. New York: Springer, 2021. https://doi.org/10.1007/978-3-030-66073-4.

Hilton, Jasmine. "Protests to Boycott Nellie's Sports Bar Created Summer-Long 'Joy Space' for Black LGBTQ Community." *Washington Post,* August 31, 2021. https://www.washingtonpost.com/local/nellies-bar-dc-protest-block-party/2021 /08/30/d1e56f1c-0678-11ec-a654-900a78538242_story.html.

Holmes, Kwame. "Chocolate to Rainbow City: The Dialectics of Black and Gay Community Formation in Postwar Washington, D.C., 1946–1978." PhD diss., University of Illinois, 2011.

Hotchkiss, Sarah. "Don't Mute DC: How Go-Go Music Inspires the Beat Ya Feet Dance Movement." KQED, May 5, 2020. https://www.kqed.org/arts/13879679 /dont-mute-dc-how-go-go-music-inspires-the-beat-ya-feet-d%20ance-movement.

Hughes, Charles H. "Postscript to Paper on 'Erotopathia,'—an Organization of Colored Erotopaths." *Alienist and Neurologist* 14, no. 4 (October 1893): 731–32.

Hull, Anne. "Palace of Plenty: Food, Class and the Coming of Fresh Fields to Logan Circle." *Washington Post,* April 1, 2001.

Humphreys, Laud. *Tearoom Trade: Impersonal Sex in Public Places.* Hawthorne, NY: Aldine de Gruyter, 1975.

Hunter, Albert. "Persistence of Local Sentiments in Mass Society." In *Handbook of Contemporary Urban Life,* ed. David Street and Associates, 133–62. San Francisco: Jossey-Bass, 1978.

Hunter, Albert, and Gerald Suttles. "The Expanding Community of Limited Liability." In *The Social Construction of Communities,* ed. Gerard Suttles, 45–81. Chicago: University of Chicago Press, 1972.

Hunter, Marcus Anthony. "All the Gays Are White and All the Blacks Are Straight: Black Gay Men, Identity, and Community." *Sexuality Research and Social Policy* 7, no. 2 (2010): 81–92.

——. "The Nightly Round: Space, Social Capital, and Urban Black Nightlife." *City & Community* 9, no. 2 (2010): 165–86.

Hunter, Marcus Anthony, Mary Pattillo, Zandria F. Robinson, and Keeanga-Yamahtta Taylor. "Black Placemaking: Celebration, Play, and Poetry." *Theory, Culture, and Society* 33, no. 7–8 (2016): 31–56.

Hunter, Marcus Anthony, and Zandria F. Robinson. *Chocolate Cities: The Black Map of Urban Life*. Berkeley: University of California Press, 2018.

Hwang, Jackelyn. "The Social Construction of a Gentrifying Neighborhood." In "Reifying and Redefining Identity and Boundaries in Inequality," *Urban Affairs Review* 52, no. 1 (2016): 98–128.

Hyra, Derek. *Race, Class, and Politics in the Cappuccino City*. Chicago: University of Chicago Press, 2017.

Ingraham, Christopher. "In the Modern History of Mass Shootings in America, Orlando Is the Deadliest." *Washington Post*, June 12, 2016. https://www.washington post.com/news/wonk/wp/2016/06/12/in-the-modern-history-of-mass-shootings -in-america-orlando-is-the-absolute-worst/.

Isin, Engin, ed. *Democracy, Citizenship, and the Global City*. London: Routledge, 2000.

Janowitz, Morris. *The Community Press in an Urban Setting: The Social Elements of Urbanism*. Chicago: University of Chicago Press, 1952.

Johnson, David K. "The Kids of Fairytown: Gay Male Culture on Chicago's Near North Side in the 1930s." In Beemyn, *Creating a Place for Ourselves*, 97–118.

——. *The Lavender Scare: The Cold War Persecution of Gays and Lesbians in the Federal Government*. Chicago: University of Chicago Press, 2004.

Jones, William Henry. *The Housing of Negroes in Washington, D.C.: A Study in Human Ecology*. Washington, DC: Howard University Press, 1929.

Kahn, Richard, and Douglas Kellner. "New Media and Internet Activism: From the 'Battle of Seattle' to Blogging." *New Media & Society* 6, no. 1 (2004): 87–95.

Kameny, Franklin. Letter to the editor. "State ABC Board's Action Criticized." *Richmond Times-Dispatch*, April 26, 1969, A14.

Kanski, Alison. "LGBT, Gun-Control Groups Respond Quickly to Orlando Mass Shooting." *PR Week*, June 13, 2016. https://www.prweek.com/article/1398477/lgbt -gun-control-groups-respond-quickly-orlando-mass-shooting.

Kelly, Brian C., Richard M. Carpiano, Adam Easterbrook, and Jeffrey T. Parsons. "Exploring the Gay Community Question: Neighborhood and Network Influences on the Experiences of Community Among Urban Gay Men." *Sociological Quarterly* 55 (2014): 23–48.

Kennedy, Elizabeth Lapovsky, and Madeline D. Davis. "I Could Hardly Wait to Get Back to That Bar: Lesbian Bar Culture in Buffalo in the 1930s and 1940s." In Beemyn, *Creating a Place for Ourselves*, 27–72.

Kidder, Jeffrey L. *Parkour and the City: Risk, Masculinity, and Meaning in a Postmodern Sport*. New Brunswick. NJ: Rutgers University Press, 2017.

Kiviat, Steven. "The #DontMuteDC Go-Go Protests Aren't Done. They're Expanding." DC Line, May 27, 2019. https://thedcline.org/2019/05/27/the-dontmutedc-go-go-protests-arent-done-theyre-expanding/.

Knopp, Lawrence. "Gentrification and Gay Neighborhood Formation in New Orleans: A Case Study." In *Homo Economics: Capitalism, Community, and Lesbian and Gay Life*, ed. Amy Gluckman and Betsy Reed, 45–63. New York: Routledge, 1997.

——. "Some Theoretical Implications of Gay Involvement in an Urban Land Market." *Political Geography Quarterly* 9, no. 4 (1990): 337–52.

Kornicus, Jura. "Household Names." Washington Post, May 16, 2007. http://www.washingtonpost.com/wp-dyn/content/article/2007/05/16/AR2007051600342.html.

Krisberg, Kim. "Is Dupont Neighborhood Losing Its Gay-Mecca Status?" *Washington Blade*, January 25, 2001: 1, 6.

Kurzius, Rachel. "Go-Go Music Is Back at Shaw's Metro PCS Store." DCist, April 10, 2019. https://dcist.com/story/19/04/10/go-go-music-is-back-at-shaws-metro-pcs-store/.

——. "Shaw's Metro PCS Store Has Been Forced to Turn Off Its Go-Go Music, Owners Say." DCist, April 9, 2019. https://dcist.com/story/19/04/08/shaws-metro-pcs-store-has-been-forced-to-turn-off-its-go-go-music-owner-says/.

——. "'This Is the Sound of Florida and Georgia Avenue': Go-Go Fans Are Trying to Bring the Music Back to Metro PCS." DCist, April 9, 2019. https://dcist.com/story/19/04/09/this-is-the-sound-of-florida-and-georgia-avenue-go-go-fans-are-trying-to-bring-the-music-back-to-metro-pcs/.

Kyles, Kyra. "Boystown Shifting as More Families Move In." *RedEye*, December 10, 2007. http://articles.chicagotribune.com/2007-12-10/news/0712100253_1_gay-men-calendars-culture-clash.

Lait, Jack, and Lee Mortimer. *Washington Confidential*. New York: Crown, 1951.

Lang, Melissa. "D.C. Gay Nightclub Cobalt Closes with Little Warning." *Washington Post*, March 5, 2019. https://www.washingtonpost.com/local/dc-gay-nightclub-cobalt-closes-with-little-warning/2019/03/05/895b758c-3f85-11e9-922c-64d6b7840b82_story.html.

Lapadula, Phil. "Dupont Circle: A Totally Urban Experience." *Washington Blade—Supplement*, July 26, 1985.

Lauria, Mickey, and Lawrence Knopp. "Toward an Analysis of the Role of Gay Communities in the Urban Renaissance." *Urban Geography* 6, no. 2 (1985): 152–69.

Lautier, Louis. "The Capital Spotlight." *Washington Afro-American*, January 28, 1933.

Lefebvre, Henri. *The Production of Space*. Cambridge: Blackwell, 1991.

——. *Writings on Cities*. Cambridge: Blackwell, 1996.

Levin, Sue. *In the Pink: The Making of Successful Gay- and Lesbian-Owned Businesses*. Binghamton, NY: Harrington Park, 1999.

Levine, Martin P. "Gay Ghetto." *Journal of Homosexuality* 4, no. 4 (1979): 363–77.

——. "Gay Ghetto." In *Sociology of Homosexuality*, ed. Wayne Dynes and Stephen Donaldson, 196–218. New York: Garland, 1992.

Lew, Alan. "Tourism Planning and Place Making: Place-Making or Placemaking?" *Tourism Geographies* 19, no. 3 (2017): 448–66.

LGBT Demographic Data Interactive. Williams Institute, UCLA School of Law, January 2019. https://williamsinstitute.law.ucla.edu/visualization/lgbt-stats/?topic=LGBT&area=27#about-the-data.

Lipsky, Michael. "Protest as a Political Resource." *American Political Science Review* 62 (1968): 1144–58.

——. *Protest in City Politics: Rent Strikes, Housing and the Power of the Poor*. Chicago: Rand McNally, 1970.

Lloyd, Richard. *Neo-Bohemia: Art and Commerce in the Postindustrial City*. 2nd ed. New York: Routledge, 2006.

——. "Neo-Bohemia: Art and Neighborhood Redevelopment in Chicago." *Journal of Urban Affairs* 24, no. 5 (2002): 517–32.

Lockhart, Paul. *The Drillmaster of Valley Forge: The Baron de Steuben and the Making of the American Army*. New York: Harper Collins, 2008.

Lynsen, Joshua, and Lou Chibbaro Jr. "Be Bar Liquor License Fight Goes Before Board." *Washington Blade*, April 21, 2006: 10.

Martz, Steve. "Our Tenth Anniversary." *The Blade*, October 25, 1979: A-1, A-18.

Marzullo, Greg. "Church Leader Challenges D.C. Gay Bar: ANC Protests Be Bar License After Anti-Gay Pastor Complains." *Washington Blade*, March 24, 2006: 1, 14.

Mattson, Greggor. "Are Gay Bars Closing? Using Business Listings to Infer Rates of Gay Bar Closure in the United States, 1977–2019." *Socius* 5, no. 1–2 (2020). https://doi.org/10.177/2378023119894832.

——. "Shuttered by the Coronavirus, Many Gay Bars—Already Struggling—Are Now on Life Support." *Slate*, May 1, 2020. https://slate.com/human-interest/2020 /05/gay-bars-struggling-reopen-coronavirus.html.

——. "Style and the Fate of Gay Nightlife: Homonormative Placemaking in San Francisco." *Urban Studies* 52, no. 16 (2015): 3144–59.

Melder, Keith, and Melinda Young Stuart. *City of Magnificent Intentions: A History of Washington, District of Columbia.* Washington, DC: Intac, 1983.

Merchant, Canaan. "Dragons and Zodiac Symbols Will Decorate Chinatown's Streets." *Greater Greater Washington*, May 10, 2016. Accessed May 21, 2016. https://ggwash.org/.

Moeller, Gerard Martin, and Christopher Weeks. *AIA Guide to the Architecture of Washington, DC.* 4th ed. Baltimore: Johns Hopkins University Press, 2006.

Monroe, Irene. "The Garden of Homophobia." *The Advocate*, December 9, 1999.

Morello, Carol, and Tim Craig. "In Sign of Rebound, DC Population Set to Surpass 600,000." *Washington Post*, December 31, 2009. www.washingtonpost.com /wp-dyn/content/article/2009/12/31/AR2001231101310_pf.html.

Morello, Carol, and Dan Keating. "Number of Black DC Residents Plummets as Majority Status Slips Away." *Washington Post*, March 24, 2011. http://www. washingtonpost.com/local/black-dc-residents-plummet-barely-a-majority /2011/03/24/ABtlgJQB_print.html.

Murray, Stephen O. "Components of Gay Community in San Francisco." In *Gay Culture in America: Essays from the Field*, ed. Gilbert Herdt, 107–46. Boston: Beacon Press, 1992.

——. "The Institutional Elaboration of a Quasi-Ethnic Community." *International Review of Modern Sociology* 9 (July 1979): 165–77.

Muskal, Michael. "Occupy Wall Street Camps Are Today's Hoovervilles." *Los Angeles Times*, November 5, 2011. http://latimesblogs.latimes.com/nationnow/2011/11 /occupy-wall-street-hoovervilles.html.

Myrdahl, Tiffany Muller. "Ordinary (Small) Cities and LGBQ Lives." *ACME* 12, no. 9 (2013): 279–304.

Myrdal, Gunnar. *An American Dilemma: The Negro Problem and Modern Democracy.* New York: Harper and Row, 1944.

Naff, Kevin. "Blade Blog: Where Is the Outrage Over Black Pastor's Homophobia?" *Washington Blade*, 2006. http://washblade.com.

Najafi, Yusef. "Animus in the Aisles: Gay Couple Claims to Have Been Kicked Out of the U Street Rite Aid for 'Hugging.'" *Metro Weekly*, October 24, 2007. https:// www.metroweekly.com/2007/10/animus-in-the-aisles/.

———. "Fenty Signs D.C. Marriage Bill." *Metro Weekly*, December 18, 2009. http:// www.metroweekly.com/2009/12/fenty-signs-dc-marriage-bill/.

———. "Lambda Rising, DC's Only All-LGBT Bookstore, to Close After the Holiday Season." *Metro Weekly*, December 10, 2009. https://www.metroweekly .com/2009/12/book-ends/.

National Park Service. "Striver's Section: Historic District." National Register of Historic Places Travel Itinerary, 2010. Accessed September 21, 2010. http://www. nps.gov/nr/travel/WASH/dc49.htm.

Nelson, Laura J. "The Worst Mass Shooting? A Look Back at Massacres in U.S. History." *Los Angeles Times*, June 14, 2016. https://www.latimes.com/nation/la-na -mass-shooting-20160614-snap-story.html.

Nero, Charles I. "Why Are the Gay Ghettos White?" In *Black Queer Studies: A Critical Anthology*, ed. E. Patrick Johnson and Mae G. Henderson, 228–45. Durham. NC: Duke University Press, 2005.

Newton, Esther. "The 'Fun Gay Ladies': Lesbians in Cherry Grove, 1936–1960." In Beemyn, *Creating a Place for Ourselves*, 146–64.

O'Bryan, Will. "D.C. Community Mourns Annie Kaylor: Namesake of Annie's Paramount Steakhouse Dies at 85." *Metro Weekly*, July 25, 2013. https://www. metroweekly.com/2013/07/dc-community-mourns-annie-kayl/.

———. "Firmly Rooted: From Its Grassroots Beginnings to Its Current Magnificence, Pride Has Always Been a Day of Affirmation for the LGBT Community." *Metro Weekly*, June 8, 2005. https://www.metroweekly.com/2005/06/firmly-rooted/.

———. "Forever Annie's: The Steakhouse That Transformed 17th Street." *Metro Weekly*, March 1, 2006. https://www.metroweekly.com/2006/03/forever-annies/.

———. "Sweet 16: Youth Pride Day Returns to the Circle in 2012." *Metro Weekly*, April 19, 2012. http://www.metroweekly.com/2012/04/sweet-16-in-dupont/.

———. "Youth Pride 2012: Youthful Measures." *Metro Weekly*, April 26, 2012. https:// www.metroweekly.com/2012/04/youth-pride-2012-youthful-meas/.

O'Bryan, Will, and Chris Geidner. "Frank Kameny Dies at 86." *Metro Weekly*, October 11, 2011. https://www.metroweekly.com/2011/10/frank-kameny-dies-at-86/.

Olinger, John P. "The ClubHouse, a Remarkable LGBTQ Gathering Spot." DC History Center, April 12, 2021. http://dchistory.org/the-clubhouse/.

Orne, Jason. *Boystown: Sex and Community in Chicago*. Chicago: University of Chicago Press, 2017.

Owens, Cassie, and Mark Dent. "Straightwashing: Woody's and How Philly's Gay Bars Are Less Gay." *Billy Penn*, June 16, 2017. https://billypenn.com/2017/06/16 /straightwashing-woodys-and-how-phillys-gay-bars-are-less-gay/.

Paulsen, Krista E. "Making Character Concrete: Empirical Strategies for Studying Place Distinction." *City & Community* 3, no. 3 (2004): 243–62.

Pelaez Lopez, Alan. "It's Not Safe to Be a Queer Person of Color in America." *Splinter*, June 13, 2016. https://splinternews.com/its-not-safe-to-be-a-queer-person -of-color-in-america-1793857466.

Peralta, Eyder. "Putting 'Deadliest Mass Shooting in U.S. History' Into Some Historical Context." NPR, June 13, 2016. https://www.npr.org/sections/thetwo -way/2016/06/13/481884291/putting-deadliest-mass-shooting-in-u-s-history-into -some-historical-context.

Peters, Jeremy W. "The Gayest Place in America?" *New York Times*, November 15, 2013. https://www.nytimes.com/2013/11/17/fashion/Washington-DC-has-thriving -gay-lesbian-and-transgender-population.html.

Pew Research Center. *A Survey of LGBT Americans: Attitudes, Experiences and Values in Changing Times.* Washington, DC: Pew Research Center, June 13, 2013. http:// www.pewsocialtrends.org/2013/06/13/a-survey-of-lgbt-americans/.

Piven, Frances Fox, and Richard A. Cloward. *Regulating the Poor: The Functions of Public Welfare.* New York: Vintage, 1971.

Purcell, Mark. "Excavating Lefebvre: The Right to the City and Its Urban Politics of the Inhabitant." *GeoJournal* 58, no. 2–3 (2002): 99–108.

Quinn, Ben, and Nadia Khomani. "Orlando Shooting: World Pays Tribute to Victims with Vigils and Rainbow Flags." *The Guardian*, June 13, 2016. https://www. theguardian.com/us-news/2016/jun/13/orlando-nightclub-shooting-world-in -mourning-for-victims.

Rainbow History Project. "Community Pioneers: Deacon Maccubbin," 2012. Accessed May 25, 2019. https://archives.rainbowhistory.org/exhibits/show/pioneers/maccubbin.

——. "Places in Our History: The Community Building, 1724 20th St. NW," 2010. Accessed May 21, 2012. http://www.rainbowhistory.org/html/1724.html.

Raz, Guy. "DC Gay Bookstore Latest to Close." NPR, December 26, 2009. http:// www.npr.org/templates/story/story.php?storyid=121933065.

Reed, Christopher. "We're from Oz: Marking Ethnic and Sexual Identity in Chicago." *Environment and Planning D: Society and Space* 21 (2003): 425–40.

Reed, Dan. "Gay Neighborhoods Are Disappearing. How Do We Feel About That?" *Washingtonian*, October 6, 2017. https://www.washingtonian.com/2017/10/06/dcs -gayborhoods-disappearing-feel/.

Renninger, Bryce. "Grindr Killed the Gay Bar, and Other Attempts to Blame Social Technologies for Urban Development: A Democratic Approach to Popular

Technologies and Queer Sociality." *Journal of Homosexuality* 66, no. 12 (2018): 1736–55. https://doi.org/10.1080/00918369.2018.1514205.

Riggs, Marlon, dir. *Tongues Untied*. San Francisco: Frameline and California Newsreel, 1989.

Rios, Victor M. *Punished: Policing the Lives of Black and Latino Boys*. New York: New York University Press, 2011.

Robinson, Jennifer. *Ordinary Cities: Between Modernity and Development*. London: Routledge, 2006.

Romney, Lee, and Maria L. La Ganga. "Oakland Site Cleared, But Protest Lives." *Los Angeles Times*, November 15, 2011. http://www.latimes.com/local/la-me-occupy -oakland-20111115-story.html.

Rose, Nikolas. "Governing Cities, Governing Citizens." In Isin, *Democracy, Citizenship, and the Global City*, 95–109.

Rosse, Irving. "Sexual Hypochondriasis and the Perversion of the Genetic Instinct." *Journal of Nervous and Mental Diseases* 17, no. 11 (1892): 795–811.

Roundy, Bill. "Does Dupont Circle Remain the Center of DC?" *Washington Blade*, September 24, 1999, 12, 14.

Rousseau, Caryn (Associated Press). "Gay Bar Bans Brides to Be." Pantagraph.com, June 16, 2009, https://pantagraph.com/news/bride-ban-gay-bar-says-i-dont-to -bachelorettes/article_7c9e0847-a619-52e1-878f-946ccc2a18f2.htm.

Ruble, Blair. *Washington's U Street: A Biography*. Washington, DC: Woodrow Wilson Center Press, 2010.

Rule, Doug. "Upstairs Haven—17th Street's Landmark Steakhouse, Annie's Adds an Upscale Lounge Upstairs." *Metro Weekly*, August 6, 2008. https://www.metroweekly .com/2008/08/upstairs-haven/.

Rushbrook, Dereka. "Cities, Queer Space, and the Cosmopolitan Tourist." *GLQ: A Journal of Lesbian and Gay Studies* 8, no. 1–2 (2002): 183–206.

Russell, Ina, ed. *Jeb and Dash: A Diary of Gay Life, 1918–1945*. Boston: Faber and Faber, 1993.

Sampson, Robert. *Great American City: Chicago and the Enduring Neighborhood Effect*. Chicago: University of Chicago Press, 2012.

Sampson, Robert, Stephen W. Raudenbush, and Felto Earls. "Neighborhoods and Violent Crime: A Multilevel Study of Collective Efficacy." *Science* 22, no. 5328 (1997): 918–24.

Sassen, Saskia. "The Repositioning of Citizenship and Alienage: Emergent Subjects and Spaces for Politics." *Globalizations* 2, no. 1 (2005): 79–94.

———. "Whose City Is It? Globalization and the Formation of New Claims." In *Cities and Citizenship*, ed. James Holston, 177–94. Durham, NC: Duke University Press, 1999.

Savage, Rachel, Matthew Lavietes, and Enrique Anarte. "'We'll Die': Gay Bars Worldwide Scramble to Avert Coronavirus Collapse." Reuters, May 13, 2020. https://www.reuters.com/article/us-health-coronavirus-lgbt-nightlife-trf-idUSKBN22P1Z5.

Savin-Williams, Ritch. *The New Gay Teenager*. Cambridge, MA: Harvard University Press, 2005.

Schwartzman, Paul. "DC Gay Clubs' Vanishing Turf; City Earmarks Block of O Street SE for Stadium." *Washington Post*, June 8, 2005.

———. "End of the Story for Gay-Oriented Bookshop." *Washington Post*, December 7, 2009. http://www.washingtonpost.com/wp-dyn/content/article/2009/12/07/AR2009120702117_pf.html.

Scully, Robert. *A Pansy*, ed. Robert J. Corber. New York: Fordham University Press, 2016.

Seo, Jyunjin, J. Brian Houston, Leigh Anne Taylor Knight, Emily J. Kennedy, and Alexandra B. Inglish. "Teens' Social Media Use and Collective Action." *New Media & Society* 16, no. 6 (2013): 883–902.

Sernoffsky, Evan, Lizzie Johnson, and Nanette Asimov. "Vigil in SF's Castro Mourns Orlando Massacre Victims." *SFGate*, June 12, 2016. https://www.sfgate.com/news/article/SF-vigil-planned-for-Orlando-massacre-victims-8081843.php.

Shilts, Randy. *Conduct Unbecoming: Lesbians and Gays in the U.S. Military: Vietnam to the Persian Gulf*. New York: St. Martin's, 1993.

Shin, Annys. "From Georgetown to Adams Morgan, Liquor License Moratoriums Face Incremental Criticism." *Washington Post*, February 7, 2014. http://www.washingtonpost.com/local/from-georgetown-to-adams-morgan-liquor-license-moratoriums-face-increasing-criticism/2014/02/07/61fc0c74-7a21-11e3-8963-b4b654bcc9b2_story.html.

Sibalis, Michael. "Urban Space and Homosexuality: The Example of the Marais, Paris' 'Gay Ghetto.'" *Urban Studies* 41, no. 9 (August 2004): 1739–58.

Signorile, Michelangelo. "What My Partner and I Did When an Anti-Gay Bigot Called Us 'Disgusting.'" *The Blog, Huffington Post*, January 7, 2013, updated February 7, 2013. http://www.huffingtonpost.com/michelangelo-signorile-what-my-partner-and-i-did_b_2424253.html.

Silver, Hilary. "Editorial: Communities and Neighborhoods." *City & Community* 13, no. 2 (2014): 97–98.

Smith, Stacy Vanek. "Gay Bars Adjusting to a New Reality." Marketplace, April 25, 2008. http://www.marketplace.org/topics/life/gay-bars-adjusting-new-reality.

Snyder, Gregory J. *Skateboarding L.A.: Inside Professional Street Skateboarding*. New York: New York University Press, 2017.

Spruce, Emma. "LGBTQ Situated Memory, Place-Making and the Sexual Politics of Gentrification." *Environment and Planning D: Society and Space* 38, no. 5 (2020): 961–78. https://doi.org/10.1177/0263775820934819.

Stafford, Zach. "Even Under Donald Trump, Washington D.C. Is the Gayest Place in America." *The Advocate*, March 5, 2019. https://www.advocate.com/news/2019/3/05/even-under-donald-trump-washington-dc-gayest-place-america.

Steele, Jason. "Should Gay Bars Ban Bachelorette Parties?" *Chicago Tribune*, March 25, 2009. http://articles.chicagotribune.com/2009-03-25/news/0903250117_1_gay-bar-gay-marriage-gay-man.

Stein, Perry. "D.C.: The Gayest City in America." *Washington City Paper*, January 6, 2014. https://www.washingtoncitypaper.com/news/city-desk/blog/13068165/d-c-the-gayest-city-in-america.

Stewart, Jeffrey C. *The New Negro: The Life of Alain Locke*. Oxford: Oxford University Press, 2018.

Stillwagon, Ryan, and Amin Ghaziani. "Queer Pop-Ups: A Cultural Innovation of Urban Life." *City & Community* 18, no. 3 (2019): 874–95.

Stone, Amy L. "The Geography of Research on LGBTQ Life: Why Sociologists Should Study the South, Rural Queers, and Ordinary Cities." *Sociology Compass* 12, no. 11 (2018). https://doi.org/10.1111/soc4.12638.

Stone, Gregory P. "City Shoppers and Urban Identification: Observations on the Social Psychology of City Life." *American Journal of Sociology* 60, no. 1 (1954): 36–45.

Sullivan, Robert David. "Last Call—Why the Gay Bars of Boston Are Disappearing, and What It Says About the Future of City Life." *Boston Globe*, December 2, 2007.

Summers, Brandi Thompson. *Black in Place: The Spatial Aesthetics of Race in a Postchocolate City*. Chapel Hill: University of North Carolina Press, 2019.

Suttles, Gerald. "The Cumulative Texture of Local Urban Culture." *American Journal of Sociology* 90, no. 2 (1984): 283–304.

Swisher, Bob. "Anger Surfaced Here Months Before Stonewall." *Richmond Pride*, June 1, 1989, 13.

Taylor, Don. "DC Store Blasting Go-Go Music Sparks Neighborhood Controversy." *Patch*, April 10, 2019. https://patch.com/district-columbia/washingtondc/dc-store-blasting-go-go-music-sparks-neighborhood-controversy.

Taylor, Verta. "Social Movement Continuity: The Women's Movement in Abeyance." *American Sociological Review* 54 (1989): 761–66.

Taylor, Verta, and Alison Dahl Crossley. "Abeyance." In *The Wiley-Blackwell Encyclopedia of Social and Political Movements*, ed. David A. Snow, Donatella della Porta, Bert Klandermans, and Doug McAdam. Malden, MA: Blackwell, 2013. https://doi.org/10.1002/9780470674871.wbespm001.

Teal, Donn. *The Gay Militants.* New York: Stein and Day, 1971.

Thomas, June. *The Gay Bar: Its Riotous Past and Uncertain Future.* Washington, DC: Slate Magazine, 2014.

Thompson, Brock. "There Goes the Gayborhood?" *Blot Magazine*, August 3, 2015. https://www.theblot.com/there-goes-the-gayborhood-7748649.

——. "Time to Make 17th Street Our Official Gay Street." *Washington Blade*, October 20, 2016. https://www.washingtonblade.com/2016/10/20/time-make-17th-street-official-gay-street/.

Trice, Dawn Turner. "Gay Rights Battle Puts Strain on Parties." *Chicago Tribune*, March 23, 2009, 15.

Truscott, Lucian, IV. "Gay Power Comes to Sheridan Square." *Village Voice*, July 3, 1969.

Vargas, Jose Antonio. "In Shaw, Pews vs. Stools." *Washington Post*, April 20, 2006.

Venkatesh, Sudhir. *American Project: The Rise and Fall of a Modern Ghetto.* Cambridge, MA: Harvard University Press, 2000.

——. *Off the Books: The Underground Economy and the Urban Poor.* Cambridge, MA: Harvard University Press, 2006.

Villareal, Daniel. "What the F*ck Is Killing Our Gay Bars, and Is It Our Own Fault?" Hornet, January 3, 2020. https://hornet.com/stories/gay-bar-decline-apps/.

Washington Post. "Lambda Rising Bookstore Moves to Connecticut Ave.; First Satellite Store Also Opens in Baltimore." December 10, 1984.

Washington Post. "A Negro Dive Raided: Thirteen Black Men Dressed as Women Surprised." April 13, 1888.

Webber, Esther. "Why Are London's Gay Bars Disappearing?" BBC, August 29, 2015. https://www.bbc.com/news/uk-england-london-33608000.

Webber, Melvin. "Order in Diversity: Community Without Propinquity." In *Cities and Space: The Future Use of Urban Land*, ed. Lowdon Wingo Jr., 23–56. Baltimore: Johns Hopkins University Press, 1963.

Wheeler, Linda. "Dupont Circle." In *Washington at Home: An Illustrated History of Neighborhoods in the Nation's Capital*, ed. Kathryn Schneider Smith, 179–95. Baltimore: Johns Hopkins University Press, 2010.

———. "Transformation of a Drug-Ridden Street." *Washington Post*, November 26, 1983.

Whelan, Catherine. "Nellie's Sports Bar Fires Contracted Security Company After Bouncer Dragged a Black Woman Down a Flight of Stairs." DCist, June 14, 2021. https://dcist.com/story/21/06/14/dc-protesters-nellies-sports-bar-security-dragged-woman-stairs-keisha-young/.

White, Edmund. *States of Desire: Travels in Gay America*. New York: Dutton, 1980.

Williams, Elliott. "Why Last Night's #Moechella Protest Was a Big Deal for DC." *Washingtonian*, May 8, 2019. https://www.washingtonian.com/2019/05/08/why-last-nights-moechella-protest-was-a-big-deal-for-dc/.

Winchester, Ashley. "Exploring the 'Occupy' Protest." *New York Times*, March 20, 2015. http://intransit.blogs.nytimes.com/2015/03/20/exploring-the-occupy-protest/.

Wynn, Jonathan R. *Music/City: American Festivals and Placemaking in Austin, Nashville, and Newport*. Chicago: University of Chicago Press, 2015.

Zabus, Chantal. *Out in Africa: Same-Sex Desire in Sub-Saharan Literatures and Cultures*. Suffolk, UK: James Currey, 2013.

Zafar, Aylin. "L.A. Bar Bans Bachelorette Parties Until Gay Marriage Is Legal." *Time*, May 26, 2012. http://newsfeed.time.com/2012/05/26/l-a-gay-bar-bans-bachelorette-parties-until-gay-marriage-is-legal/.

Zito, Tom. "Anything's Cool at the Discos." *Washington Post*, October 17, 1974.

Zorbaugh, Harvey W. *The Gold Coast and the Slum*. Chicago: University of Chicago Press, 1929.

Zukin, Sharon. *The Culture of Cities*. Malden, MA: Blackwell, 1995.

———. *Naked City: The Death and Life of Authentic Urban Places*. Oxford: Oxford University Press, 2010.

INDEX

GPSR Authorized Representative: Easy Access System Europe, Mustamäe tee
50, 10621 Tallinn, Estonia, gpsr.requests@easproject.com